The AfterGrief

THE
AfterGrief

FINDING YOUR WAY ALONG
THE LONG ARC OF LOSS

Hope Edelman

Ballantine Books

NEW YORK

Copyright © 2020 by Words Etcetera, Inc.

Published in the United States by Ballantine Books, an imprint of Random House, a division of Penguin Random House LLC, New York.

BALLANTINE and the HOUSE colophon are registered trademarks of Penguin Random House LLC.

Hardback ISBN 9780399179785
Ebook ISBN 9780399179792

Printed in the United States of America on acid-free paper

randomhousebooks.com

2 4 6 8 9 7 5 3 1

First Edition

Figures by Mapping Specialists, Ltd., Fitchburg, WI
Book design by Fritz Metsch

For Liz Perle
1956-2015
Forever missed

The loss happens in time, in fact in a moment,
but its aftermath lasts a lifetime.

—ELISABETH KÜBLER-ROSS

Contents

Getting Over Getting Over It

A MEDIUM ONCE told my sister that our mother was living in a corner of her kitchen. Being our mother's daughters, we took this news in stride. She'd raised us to be open-minded and humble. Who were we to believe we knew better than anyone else? Also, our mother in a kitchen made good sense. Hers had been the nucleus of our childhood home, the place where she'd spent much of her time: standing at the kitchen island, prepping chicken cacciatore in her Crock-Pot, drinking Maxwell House coffee at the speckled Formica table with neighborhood friends, sitting at the corner desk and winding the avocado-green phone cord around and around her index finger as she settled into a leisurely call. With three children and a husband for whom tidiness was forever an abstraction, she was always struggling to keep the space clean. My mother would have loved my sister's kitchen. Mine surrendered to chronic disorder long ago, but my sister's kitchen is always shiny and pristine. I'd choose to hang out there, too.

My sister and I live across the country from our family's burial plots and rarely get to visit the graves. So she placed a framed black-and-white photograph of our mother in the corner of her kitchen between a neat row of mason jars and the countertop range. When I dog-sit for her boxers I give them treats from a jar and we say hello to my mom. I might let her know that her children and grandchildren are doing fine. If I'm facing a big decision, I'll brush my fingertips across the glass and silently ask her for advice.

I have to imagine how she'd answer. We had only seventeen years together, and I was pretty much tuning her out for the final two. I've long since forgotten the sound of her voice and the timbre of her laugh. She died in 1981, and we never made tapes of her talking. In my dreams she speaks in an unfamiliar pitch, her words sometimes garbled, sometimes clear. I haven't heard her real voice in almost thirty-nine years.

Thirty-nine years. I know. That's a long time. Says pretty much everyone, ever.

Thirty-nine years and you're not over it yet?

Anyone with major loss in the past knows this question well. We've spent years fielding versions of it, explicit and implied, from parents, siblings, spouses, partners, relatives, colleagues, acquaintances, and friends. We recognize the subtle cues—the slight eyebrow lift, the soft, startled "Oh! That *long* ago?"—from those who wonder how an event so distant can still occupy such precious mental and emotional real estate. Why certain, specific nodes are still so tender when poked.

How many of us have wondered the same?

You're still *not over it yet?* As if the death of a loved one were a hurdle in a track meet that could be cleared and left behind.

I wish there were a foolproof method for "getting over" the death of someone we love. So much, I do. Except everything I've experienced, learned, and observed over the past thirty-eight years has taught me otherwise. Since the publication of my first book, *Motherless Daughters*, in 1994, I've collected stories from thousands of women in the United States, Canada, Australia, New Zealand, the United Kingdom, Europe, India, and the Middle East whose mothers died when they were young. I've spoken to, emailed, and met with their brothers, husbands, fathers, daughters, and sons. Five file cabinets in my office are filled to capacity with research into how the human body, intellect, and spirit respond to major loss. In nonfiction writing classrooms for the past twenty years, I've helped graduate students and aspiring writers identify, question, and articulate their stories of trauma and loss. And for this book, I conducted in-depth interviews with eighty-one men and women who had experienced the deaths of significant loved ones in the past—most of whom were children, adolescents, or young adults at the time, and whose bereavement needs were frequently mismanaged or misunderstood.*

Taken together, that adds up to a staggering number of losses. Which is how I can report with assurance that the death of a loved one, especially for someone at a tender age, isn't something most of us get over, get past, put down, or move beyond. That's a myth of diminishment. Instead, a major loss gets folded into our developing identities, where it informs our thoughts, hopes, expectations, behaviors, and fears. We carry it forward into all that follows.

"It's phenomenal, how it never really goes away," says author and therapist Claire Bidwell Smith. "It changes shape and form all the time and comes back in different ways, even when you think it's gone. I'm twenty-four years out from the death of my mother and seventeen years from the death of my father and those losses have been with me, in some fashion, every day since they died."

When psychologist Leeat Granek and author Meghan O'Rourke surveyed nearly eight thousand adults who'd lost a close loved one for *Slate* magazine in 2011, they observed—in their words—that "the alterations of loss are subtly stitched throughout one's ongoing life." Nearly one-third of their survey participants had experienced the death of a close loved one eight or more years earlier. Instead of feeling "over it," they wanted to keep talking about how grief had shaped their present-day experiences and how it might continue to affect their imagined futures.

"This process is a longer one than most people realize," explains psychologist Robert Neimeyer, a professor of constructivist psychology at the University of Memphis and the founder of the Portland

---

*Because my focus is on living with long-ago loss, with an emphasis on early loss, the majority of my interviewees experienced the death of a parent, sibling, romantic interest, or close friend during childhood, adolescence, and early adulthood. I touch on adult loss of a spouse, partner, or child only briefly throughout, since these are treated as separate and distinct categories in the bereavement literature and a number of excellent books exist to address their long-term effects.

Institute for Loss and Transition, "unfolding over years rather than months, and involving periodic 'grief spikes' years or even decades later." The *Slate* survey found the same. One-quarter of the respondents said they'd felt normal only one to two years after the loss. More than one-quarter said they'd never gone back to feeling like themselves afterward.

Nonetheless, when random cross sections of Americans have been asked how long grief should last after a significant loss, their answers range from several days up to a year. The majority of respondents in one study placed the outer limit at two weeks. *Two weeks*. In some cultures that's barely enough time to hold a funeral, let alone put emotional pain into any perspective and start making sense of the loss.

A terrible disconnect exists between what the average person thinks grief should look and feel like—typically, a series of progressive, time-limited stages that end in a state of "closure"—and how grief, that artful dodger, actually behaves. This means a whole lot of people getting stuck in the gap between what they've been told to expect after someone dies and what they actually encounter when it happens.

An estimated 10 to 15 percent of bereaved individuals will experience what's known as "complicated grief," a state in which a mourner's emotional pain becomes so intense and so persistent that they can't resume daily functioning on their own. It's a bit like the mind getting stuck on the Grief channel. Recent research suggests that the majority of these mourners may suffer from preexisting depression or anxiety, or possess traits that contribute to what's known as a "grief-prone personality." Much of the past seventy years' worth of bereavement research has focused on psychiatric patients who suffer from complicated grief, a group that has historically tended to skew female. As a result, much less is known about the other 85 percent, the population of "normative mourners," both female and male, most of whom manage to adapt to their changed circumstances on their own.

What comes next for them? What can they reasonably expect to face ten years later? Twenty years? Forty? What kind of adjustments do they make over time? Which have been most helpful? How do their losses continue to show up throughout their lives?

Well, those aren't easy questions to answer. For one thing, grief is a very, very individual process. Any single outcome depends on a long list of variables and the subtle interactions between them. These include the following:

- one's age at the time of loss
- the cause of death
- the relationship with the deceased
- the amount and type of social support available
- gender
- temperament
- personal worldview
- a family's communication style
- religion, culture, race, and ethnicity
- socioeconomic status
- historical period
- other stressors at the time and afterward
- the management of prior losses
- the amount of short- and long-term change that occurs in a family system

Those are a lot of variables, with a nearly unlimited number of possible outcomes.

In addition, very few studies have tracked bereaved individuals over long periods of time to see how they're coping much further down the road. Most of the existing research follows mourners for six or seven years at most. We don't have much empirical data to tell us how people continue to adjust and make meaning over the long arc of loss.

Yet many of us know from experience that while the facts of a loss remain static, our relationship to those facts can change quite a bit over time. For example, my mother died of breast cancer in July 1981, when she was forty-two and I was seventeen. Those details are fixed. I can't do anything to alter them. But what these facts have *meant* to me at different moments in my life—that part is constantly evolving. The same details looked one way when I encountered them as a fiery, self-righteous seventeen-year-old searching for someone to blame; a different way when I became a mother at thirty-three and experienced firsthand a mother's love for a child; and different still as I approached and passed forty-two myself. That's when I understood, really understood, how foreshortened my mother's life had been and what she'd missed out on by dying so young. I couldn't have understood that at thirty-three, or even at forty-one. Definitely not at seventeen. I'm now more than a decade older than my mother got to be and I'm telling you, some days it's just plain weird to be this much older than your mom.

The men and women interviewed for this book spoke of similar shifts in perspective as they matured. But their accounts were all in retrospect and memory has a crafty habit of conflating and distorting events. I couldn't find any studies that tracked, in real time, how people's relationships to their losses might change over decades. Then I remembered the boxes in my garage that held the tapes and transcripts from the ninety-two women I interviewed for *Motherless Daughters* in the early 1990s. Each of those interviews had captured a woman's story of mother loss, as she understood it, at a specific moment in time, sticking a pin into the steady flow of their human experience. I wondered how those women might interpret the same details nearly three decades later, from the vantage point of middle age and beyond. Relying on Google, LinkedIn, Facebook, and Whitepages.com, I was able to locate eighteen of the original ninety-two women and reinterview them in 2018 and 2019. Reconnecting with these women, comparing their present-day points of view with their younger perspectives, and discussing how their perceptions had (and hadn't) changed over nearly three decades was one of the most extraordinary and rewarding parts of writing this book.

These women, along with the sixty-three other men and women interviewed, revealed how long-term bereavement is qualitatively different from the shock, numbness, confusion, disbelief, exhaustion, anxiety, disorganization, reorganization, and adaptations that take place immediately after a death. "Grief" is a fine descriptor for the liminal, surreal, exquisitely painful zone of adjustment between what existed in the past and what comes next. What comes next, however, is broader and more far-reaching. For 85 percent of us, the volume knob of distress eventually turns down low enough to allow laughter and joy to return but is liable to amp up at key moments, and often without warning.

What comes next is the part where we adjust to a long list of events that now do and don't, can and cannot happen, both celebratory and sad. The texts and calls that stop coming; a relationship started; a relationship ended; a solo walk down the aisle; a child born; questions that can't be answered; goals achieved without witness; holiday traditions perpetuated or abandoned; a deep, deep appreciation for every day; the frustration when mere language cannot express what is so truly known and felt.

We move on, yes, but most of us do not leave our departed loved ones behind. We carry them forward as models, as advisors, as cautionary tales. We journey with them into a new plane where our relationship shape shifts over time, potentially becoming even more multi-dimensional, more nuanced, and more emotionally complex than it was before.

This thing we call "grief" is just the beginning of a much longer engagement with the thing we call "loss." This next part is what I call the Aftergrief.

The Aftergrief—until now, underappreciated, underreported and largely misunderstood—is where the questions "What now?" and "What next?" begin to be answered. It's where we continuously recalibrate our perceptions of past events, refresh our inner relationships with the deceased, and reconsider the meanings we attach to the loss. The Aftergrief is where we learn to live with a central paradox of bereavement: that a loss can recede in time yet remain so exquisitely present.

"The Aftergrief came after I'd gotten used to the death," explains my friend Nancy, whose nineteen-year-old son died by suicide twenty-one years ago. "And by 'getting used to the death' I mean my bones and my muscles had gotten used to carrying it, and I'd built up enough strength to pick up other things, too."

The Aftergrief begins as the most acute elements of grief start to subside. And then it keeps on going. And going. Which is to say, the Aftergrief spans the whole rest of your life.

IN 1981, the year my mother died, few resources existed for bereaved families in our town. Religious communities offered pockets of assistance, but local hospices and children's bereavement services were still at least a decade away. The Parents Without Partners group my father sought out was made up mainly of divorced women who passed him their phone numbers at the end of his first meeting, which was also his last. In 1981, for the most part, a family walked out of a hospital or away from the scene of an accident and returned home to figure out their next steps alone.

By the time my father died in 2005, the landscape had changed considerably. By then, hospice programs, nonprofit bereavement centers, support groups, grief programs, and weekend bereavement camps existed throughout the United States. These resources have been, and continue to be, enormously beneficial to individuals who have access, especially in validating and normalizing the wide array of responses to loss.

Nonetheless, with only a few exceptions, these services are designed for the recently bereaved. If an adult who's lost a parent, sibling, child, spouse, or close friend more than a few years in the past experiences a resurgence of grief and contacts a bereavement organization for support, their inquiry is likely to stall with the question "When did the death occur?" Answering "twelve years ago," "twenty years ago," or "thirty years back" frequently results in a heartfelt expression of regret that no services exist for losses of such vintage.

And this is downright puzzling, since millions of Americans are living with historical grief. According to a 2009 study conducted by the New York Life Foundation, one out of seven American adults surveyed—that's 14 percent—had lost a parent or sibling before turning twenty. Applied to the adult population as a whole, that means *more than thirty million people* in the United States have experienced the death of an immediate family member during childhood or adolescence. That's an astonishing statistic, and one that climbs higher when we include those who lost a boyfriend, girlfriend, or close friend to death by that age, and higher still when we account for those who were in their twenties or thirties when a parent, sibling, friend, young spouse, or young child died.

Those who faced their losses during the pre-grief-support eras of the 1960s, 1970s, and 1980s—as well as many in the years that followed—did so in a culture with some very wonky messages about how and how not to grieve. *Life goes on. Everything happens for a reason. What doesn't kill you makes you stronger. Don't upset your mother/father/grandmother/anyone with your tears. Don't wallow. Stop living in the past. Don't think about it and you won't be sad.*

About half of early-loss survivors surveyed report they never adequately grieved their losses, often because they were discouraged or prohibited from expressing distress. And this is an enormous problem, since an extensive body of literature has linked unexpressed grief in children to disruptions in development, juvenile delinquency, difficulty concentrating in school, substance use and abuse, depression and anxiety, and delayed and distorted grieving patterns later. Among adults—men, especially—who were taught to equate emotions with weakness, the impulse to paper over grief with more socially acceptable behaviors may be strong. And those overwhelmed by the demands of work, childcare, or basic survival needs after someone close to them dies may need to deliberately or unconsciously suppress their distress—a state that's been associated with later substance use and abuse, depression, anger, violence, difficulties with intimacy, and increased risk for certain physical and mental illnesses.

Imagine tens of millions of adults carrying stories of major loss, many of them unspoken and suppressed. Now look around at the faces in every crowd. Some people will have left their "in-public masks" at home and their pain will be glaringly apparent. But the larger number will be normaling up in public and quietly struggling at home. Unexpressed grief from the past may be one of the most overlooked public health crises of our time.

If this many people have encountered significant loss in the past, why don't we have a better cultural understanding of long-term bereavement? Why do we have such an extensive vocabulary for pathologies and diagnoses, yet such limited language to discuss the ordinary, enduring adjustments and readjustments that people make on their own?

These questions lie at the heart of this book. They're the ones that inspired me, thirty-five years after my mother's death and twelve years after my father's, to start searching for an interdisciplinary model of long-term bereavement. It's been hard to find.

Although you'll see published research sprinkled throughout this book, I'm more interested in how bereaved individuals perceive their own experiences than in data collected from psychiatric patients or analyzed from questionnaires. To this end, the eighty-one individuals interviewed for this book, most of whom survived early loss during childhood or their teens, graciously shared their stories with me during hours of discussion, both in person and over Skype. These interviewees ranged in age from twenty-two to seventy-three, with an average age of forty-nine. Their losses occurred between two and sixty-six years ago, with an average time since loss of thirty-four years, and their loved ones died of varied causes—about two-thirds from long-term illnesses and one-third from forms of sudden loss.

From these individuals, I learned how the Aftergrief delivers a more fluid, multidimensional, and extended arc than most of us are led to expect or believe. But anyone who lives with historical loss already intuitively knows this. We've just been waiting a long time for the rest of society to catch up.

Existing, widely accepted ideas about grief are rarely questioned by those who are invested in the promised outcomes. So it's been with the concept of stage theory, which appeared to offer a series of uni-directional steps to follow to achieve acceptance and resolution. Many of us do achieve those states, but they're not the end of our stories. Not by any means.

To change existing cultural perceptions about grief, we'll need to overcome several long-standing obstacles:

First, we'll need to stop thinking of grief as a predominantly emotional and psychological experience and adopt a more holistic view—one that includes cognitive, behavioral, physical, philosophical, spiritual, historical, and cultural components. We'll need to allow mourners the dignity of their own individual responses without expecting their behaviors to conform to ill-fitting, outdated models.

We'll also need to start viewing grief support as a social responsibility. Eventually, everyone loses someone important, some of us sooner rather than later. The 2020 viral pandemic of Covid-19 made this painfully obvious to us all. Mourners who are discouraged or blocked from expressing their distress today go on to interact with countless others, raise the next generation, create policy, and shape history tomorrow. Supporting children and adults both at the time of loss and also over the long arc is a worthwhile investment in the collective good.

Most crucially, we'll need to redirect some of the attention that goes to alleviating short-term painful symptoms toward a longer-range view of mourning. We have to get over the idea of getting *over* it to embrace the prospect of moving on *with* it, and all this involves. Research in the field of post-traumatic growth reveals that within only a few years, a majority of trauma survivors can identify at least one positive outcome of their struggles. These include an increased sense of empathy, a deeper appreciation for life, a radical restructuring of priorities, and a feeling of inner fortitude. Mourners who are able to make meaning of their experiences also exhibit lower levels of complicated grief and better mental and physical health later on. In fact, meaning making after trauma is the most powerful predictor of good long-term outcome among adults.

This is not to say that a loved one's death should be rebranded as a wholly positive experience. Not at all. The parts that are awful are legitimately awful. But a society that focuses principally on reducing the short-term pain of distress risks losing sight of the long-term value of sorrow.

"I think you either let it destroy you completely or you find a way to fold it into your life and keep going," says Sadie, forty-six, who was twelve when her best friend died. "It sounds really weird saying it out loud, but I think I was lucky to figure that out at such an early age."

As Claire Bidwell Smith, who lost both of her parents by age twenty-five, explains, "I can go to a place of deep sorrow very quickly, like a root system that leads back to loss all the time. But it's had a really positive impact on me, too. It's made me such a deep-feeling person. I'm so appreciative of life all the time. I have such wonder and gratitude that we get to be here at all. It took me a while to get to that place, though. There was kind of a midway point over the last twenty years, and once I tipped over into that area I just wept all the time at the beauty of everything. Like, I look at my kids and maybe it's just a Tuesday morning and they're in their pajamas and my daughter's hair is sticking up and something's funny, but it's such magic to me that it's happening at all."

Many of the participants who took part in Granek and O'Rourke's grief survey for *Slate* also described reaching a state where hardship and gratitude intertwined. "They wrote about how they had been expanded by their grief, and about how they both gained and lost parts of themselves from it," Granek observed. "They had suffered terribly and had learned valuable life lessons. They were still in the grips of their pain even 10 years later *and* had become better people through the experiences of their mourning. They wanted their suffering to end *and* they wouldn't change a single thing about their grieving process."

The Aftergrief asks us to hold such competing truths side by side, not as contradictions but as companions. Over time, the gravity of sorrow can exist alongside an appreciation for the insights that arise from that suffering. Available language fails me: I can't find a word in English to express this idea. The closest I can come is the Portuguese *saudade*, a feeling of longing for a person, place, or object that's been loved and lost, with equal measures of joy for having had the love and sadness for having lost it. *Saudade*, also known as "the love that remains," stationed at the midpoint along the spectrum between gratitude and sorrow.

EVERY WEEK I place fresh daylilies in the crystal vase my parents received as a wedding gift in 1960, and whenever I walk from my living room into the kitchen I pass their framed photos on the wall. They're both long gone by now, but it's no exaggeration to say I think of them every day. In many ways, they're still here. I've taught my daughters how to cook my father's signature breakfast, and we use my mother's *Better Homes and Gardens* cookbook to bake her apple pie. My spontaneous, frequent, and often embarrassing crying jags are a legacy from my father, and my commitment to social justice is my mother writ large. Both of my parents are so vivid in my external and inner worlds that sometimes I feel closer to them now than I remember feeling when they were alive.

Still?

"Yes, *still*," says Maggie, whose father died more than fifty years ago. "Still and always."

The residual affection, the comfort, the longing, the love, the sadness, the compassion, the anger, and the precocious knowledge that develops from the struggle to adapt: Do I carry all this separate from myself, or has it become inscribed onto my personality, my history, my identity? It's part of me by now, I think.

"I think of my dad's death not as something that happened to me, but as a characteristic about me," says the poet Gabriel Ojeda-Sagué, now twenty-nine, who was eleven when his father died. "One of the things that made me *me* is that my dad died. It's something that fundamentally makes me a different person than I was at age ten. So can I call that living without, if I feel that it's fundamentally shifted my values, my perception, my conscience? That's a hinge for me. It *is* like adapting. It *is* like learning to live without him. But it's also like living anew, in a different frame."

Sometimes I wonder what "getting over" the deaths of my parents would look like. Would it mean that I'd stop thinking about them so often? Stop being who I became as a result of their deaths? Would it mean not feeling a brief pang of sadness and identification when I pull out my slow cooker and remember my mother's mustard-yellow version simmering on her kitchen island? Would it mean building a wall between myself and my past so I don't feel my father sitting beside me in the TV room every time I hear the *thwack* of a bat hitting a baseball, followed by the cheer of a stadium crowd? Because people who build those kinds of walls are the people I worry about, not the ones who tear up for a moment when they encounter a kitchen appliance.

"If someone said to me, 'Terrie, to be a healthy mourner you have to forget the people you've loved and lost,' I would say, 'Show me to the line with the unhealthy mourners,'" says Therese Rando, a psychologist and bereavement specialist in Warwick, Rhode Island, who lost both of her parents by age nineteen. "Because I've already lost them in the physical world. I'm not going to lose them in my heart and in my mind."

Every bereaved person embarks on a path along which sadness and longing can be alchemized into meaning and purpose. Sometimes this happens on its own. Sometimes it requires help from others. Sometimes it involves the focused, sustained effort of stitching a fractured past back together. I think of how many truly tragic stories I heard while writing this book, and how many were also tales of transcendence and hope, from thirty-two-year-old Chelsea who lost her mother, her father, and then her boyfriend all by the age of seventeen and is now a devoted mother of three; to forty-six-year-old Sadie, who wrote a novel based on the death of her childhood friend; to Julian, a fifty-three-year-old business owner whose parents' deaths in his twenties helped him recognize the "broken-ness" in his employees who'd suffered adversities in the past and inspired him to create a workplace where everyone can feel like they belong.

Adjusting to loss is a lifelong process, but it doesn't have to be a lifelong struggle. "All sorrows can be borne if you put them in a story or tell a story about them," the author Isak Dinesen said. The best approach I've found to softening the sharp points is to recalibrate our perceptions about what grieving is, isn't, or should be; strengthen our inner relationships with the deceased; and give ourselves the permission and the opportunity to revisit and revise our stories of loss and the meanings we attach to them. This is how our stories become ones of growth as well as hardship.

A story of loss is a dynamic, expansive organism with a remarkable capacity for change. This book, hopefully, will become part of yours. Let's begin.

Hope Edelman
Los Angeles, California

The AfterGrief

CHAPTER ONE

* * *

The Story of Grief

I'M DRIVING south on Pacific Coast Highway, heading for the supermarket, when a string of familiar guitar chords comes rippling across the airwaves. It's the opening riff to "The Weight" by The Band, and Levon Helm's raspy Southern baritone follows close behind.

I pulled into Nazareth, was feeling 'bout half past dead. Two lanes of traffic stream steadily ahead of me as I sing along. On my left, steep cliffs angle toward the sky. To my right, the Pacific Ocean surges and swells. *He just grinned and shook my hand. No was all he said.*

Then nine fast piano chords go tumbling straight into the chorus. Those piano chords.

My mother was a classically trained pianist who could play pop songs by ear. I see her so clearly now, sitting at the upright piano in our living room, her perfectly manicured red nails rippling up and down the keyboard as she played both Chopin etudes and Barry Manilow songs. This must be what Hamlet meant by "the mind's eye." It's not that memory obscures my view of the road, or that I'm dissociating from the car, but that all of these images, present and past, *are equally accessible at the same time.* Then comes that familiar tweak of longing beneath my ribs. The feeling of nostalgia. The feeling of *home.* A white Toyota abruptly changes lanes ahead of me, nearly cutting me off. I press gently on the brakes. *She said, I gotta go, but my friend can stick around.* "My friends say I have piano hands," my younger daughter told me the other day. "Like mine," I said. "We get them from my mom." We pressed our palms together to compare the length of our fingers, just as my mother and I once did on her piano bench. The pressure under my ribs expands and spreads like an ink-blot, filling my stomach and chest.

This is how the Aftergrief tends to show up for me now. A random sight or sound or smell pushes a memory up to the surface, and time does its funky little twitch. The future pulls back and the distant past rushes up close, both compressing into the present. Then is now and now is then, and later ceases to exist. The images are dazzling in their clarity. If I'd known they were coming today, I might have planned better. Like, maybe, not been in sole control of a four-thousand-pound moving vehicle on a crowded scenic highway when they arrived.

The song ends as I pull into the supermarket parking lot and turn off the ignition. I inhale slowly and do a quick check-in. Am I okay? Do I need to wait it out in the car? Nah. I'm good.

As I walk into the market, comfort and sadness and yearning cling to me like sweet campfire smoke. These feelings will work their way through me soon enough. I know that by now. By the time I've pulled a plastic bag from the roll in the vegetable aisle, they're mostly gone.

I didn't always understand this was possible. For many years, I thought if I allowed myself to feel the full impact of my mother's early death, the sorrow might never end. And then what? How would I function? Who would piece me back together if I fell apart? And wasn't falling apart mostly for children and the emotionally weak?

At my mother's funeral, in 1981, the messages I received from the adults around me—all well-meaning, no doubt—were about being strong and moving on, about getting back to life, and about how my mother wouldn't have wanted me to be sad. The implication there being that I shouldn't feel that way, and if I did, I shouldn't let anyone know. The overriding climate in our family and community was one of grim stoicism, of fortitude in the face of hardship. *Buck up, brave soldier!* Like that.

Emotionally I still may have been a teenager, but practically, I'd just been propelled onto the turf of adult responsibility. My father was going to need help with my younger siblings and with running the house. Someone was going to have to make sure the refrigerator was stocked, doctor's appointments made, pets fed. So it was time for me to start acting like an adult. And to be an adult meant to persevere, impervious to tragedy. Those were the messages I heard, observed, absorbed, and eventually started telling myself.

The past is in the past. You have your whole future ahead of you. Life goes on.

To my genuine amazement, life *did* go on. My siblings went back to summer camp a week after the funeral. My father took about a month of bereavement leave, made possible because he worked for the family business, before resuming his daily commute into Manhattan. I returned to bussing tables at a local seafood restaurant during the week and taking tickets at a drive-in on Friday and Saturday nights. When school started in early September, I showed up on weekday mornings and handed assignments in on time. I set the table for dinner every evening as if four place settings had always been the norm. Haircuts happened. Weekly laundry was sorted, washed, folded, and put away. To others, I imagine, we looked like a family that was recovering, and then like a family that had recovered. But really, we were blindly stumbling forward as if sheer momentum could propel us into a new state of equilibrium. And we did it all in a fog of silence.

Within weeks of the funeral, we'd stopped talking about my mother at all. A cataclysmic act of subtraction had just occurred, yet we were working overtime to pretend nothing had changed. *What was* that *about?* I wonder now. I could, and still can, understand not wanting to dwell on the dying part, the images of end-stage cancer still so horrible and so raw. But to stop speaking about her entirely? She'd lived for forty-two years before she died, yet now it was as if she were being erased from family history. Except—there she was above the yellow Parsons table in the living room, smiling down upon us from the family portraits on the wall. Her meticulously labeled spice jars were still lined up in the yellow spice rack in the kitchen. To make phone calls we relied on her address book, where the names and numbers of all our friends and relatives were recorded in her careful, angular script.

To say this was bewildering doesn't fully capture the sentiment, but it comes close.

I didn't know it at the time, but my family embodied the 1970s and '80s American ethos of grief so perfectly we could have been a commercial for Reagan-era bereavement. The dominant ideology of that time was all about breaking ties and "letting go" after a loved one died, and we marched in time to that cultural drumbeat. Silence and pretense weren't ideal coping strategies, but they were strategies, sort of, and as a family without other tools we became very skilled at both.

That first year was when I discovered how easily silence and pretense are mistaken for dignity, and how dignity inspires praise. *You're so grown up. Your mother would be so proud.* To be honest, I craved the approval. Sought it out, even. In the midst of so much wrongness, positive feedback made me feel as if I were doing something—anything—right. Whatever grieving I allowed myself occurred in private, behind my closed bedroom door.

"Fine," I said when people asked how I was doing. "I'm doing fine." Then they'd tell me, "You're so strong," even when everything was inverted and confusing and nothing felt solid or reliable anymore, nothing at all.

"Grief can make a liar out of you," Maria Shriver has observed. "You say you're doing fine, when really your heart is shattered into a thousand tiny pieces. But everyone wants you to say you're okay, so you do."

The truth? For the first five years after my mother died, even the most bland, innocuous questions like "Are both your parents coming tonight?" or "What was your mother's maiden name?" could make my heart rate spike and my limbs go cold and numb. I couldn't even say "my mother" without starting to cry. Neither could I remember the sound of her laugh or how she'd trilled "Good morning, Sunshines!" through the door of our shared bedroom to wake me and my sister for school. For years the only memory of her I could summon was how she'd looked in the hospital at the very end, jaundiced and panicked. Sometimes that mental image would puncture a day without warning, jolting me with a physical charge in the middle of a Comp Lit seminar or while swimming laps in an indoor pool.

Only much later did I recognize these episodes as symptoms of unaddressed trauma. At the time, my most reliable coping skill—my only coping skill, really—was to avoid any agent of distress. So, no looking at family photos. No manicures. Definitely no hospitals. I would even take an alternate route to avoid passing the hospital where she died. Because in my seventeen-, and eighteen-, and nineteen-year-old mind, I had to be an adult. And for adults, life goes on. And because I should have gotten over it a long time ago.

Right?

Well, no. None of it was anywhere close to that simple. Grief rarely is, even when it's packaged and marketed that way. Even after I'd exerted savage violence on dozens of innocent pillows, spent a hundred hours in therapy, and could finally talk about my mother again without breaking down, little hot spots flared up from time to time. If I saw an adult daughter shopping with her mother or heard a Muzak version of "Mandy" piped into a dentist's office, my esophagus would involuntarily start to constrict. Then I'd berate myself for the lack of control. *What's wrong with you? Why aren't you over it yet?* When my lived experience didn't mirror the path I'd been told normal grieving should take, I assumed the failure was mine. I never considered that the definition of normal might be flawed.

Here's what I've learned since then: "Normal" is both a construct and a moving target. It's a collectively sanctioned idea of what's acceptable at a particular place and time—a practical point of reference for assessing human behavior. Variations from its standards are considered outliers (at best) and deviant or abnormal (at worst). These distinctions then filter down into public consciousness, where ordinary people rely on them for guidelines on how to behave.

If I'd been grieving the death of a family member a hundred years earlier, "acceptable" mourning behavior would have looked very different. A thousand years earlier, and the practices would have been unrecognizable to Americans today. For most of Western human history, rituals around death and bereavement were tightly woven into the religion, traditions, and customs of the larger society. Funerals in ancient Greece and Rome, for example, were raucous public spectacles that included extravagant feasts and funerary games. During the Middle Ages in Europe, when death was an accepted, commonplace, and shared event, dying with an audience was considered the ideal way to depart the mortal world. Family, friends, and neighbors of all ages would crowd around a deathbed to witness the final moment of transition. Until well into the nineteenth century, ritualized communal gatherings to express sorrow were common, and townspeople often came together to mourn the death of an individual as the loss of one of their own. A nuclear family left to grieve alone would have been anomalous and odd.

When her beloved Prince Albert died in 1861, Queen Victoria's extended mourning period set the tone for four subsequent decades of elaborate bereavement rituals in Britain, the wider British Empire, and, to a lesser extent, the United States. Funerals of the Victorian era tended toward the lavish and expensive. Burial monuments were large and ornate. Anyone walking down a crowded city street during the period of Victorian high mourning (roughly 1850–1890) could immediately tell which households had suffered a loss by the special wreath hanging on the front door and knew which women were in "high" or "low" mourning from the color and style of clothing they wore.

Middle- and upper-class women in particular were expected to follow strict rules around social interactions and dress, whether a death had occurred among their relatives or their husband's. Victorian housewives kept bound copies of *The Queen* or *Cassell's* reference manuals in their homes to consult about the complicated rules and regulations that applied to mourning different family members. The length of a mourning period ranged from a full two years of mourning for widows, to twelve months if you had lost either a parent or child, to six months after the death of a sibling, all the way down to four weeks after a first cousin died.

Mourners of the nineteenth century were granted special status in society. Today, mourners rush to return to status quo. When societal norms shifted away from supporting the experience of grief in favor of constricting it, silence, suppression, and stoicism took over as the dominant features of Western mourning. This movement found its icon in the quiet reserve of Jacqueline Kennedy at her husband's funeral in 1963. So quick to admire and praise her countenance as an admirable example of courage, a large swath of American citizens never stopped to consider that such stoicism may have been a psychological defense against the trauma of witnessing her husband's assassination at close range only three days earlier, or a mask she wore for public consumption. Instead, social suppression of grief became a culturally sanctioned ideal.

The eulogy for the dead in the modern funeral is one of the few rituals left to follow in Protestant-influenced Western society. Shaping a story of the relationship, delivering it to an audience, and listening to others' accounts is a collective act that helps make meaning of the deceased's time here. We have yet to see what kind of effect the truncated and virtual funerals of the Covid-19 era will have on mourning behavior. A widespread emphasis on what author Meghan O'Rourke calls "muscle-through-it grief" to navigate losses on a pandemic scale and adapt to new restrictions on mourning our dead is not likely to lead to wholly positive outcomes. Not if history offers any clues.

I can't count the number of adults I've worked with who lost a parent or sibling during childhood and were sent to school the day after a funeral or even the morning after a death, either because the adults in charge had been told to preserve the family's normal routines or because nobody knew what else to do. Or the number of bereaved families that numbly adopted postures of emotional strength that barely concealed a disarming fragility, simply because they believed that's how they were supposed to behave. Or all the school and workplace environments where adults barely paused to acknowledge a student or colleague's sudden, traumatic loss because they'd never received training about how to discuss grief or extend compassionate support.

When Maggie's father died of a sudden heart attack in the 1960s, "you just sucked it up because you had to," she recalls. "Back then, the teachers treated me as though something was inherently wrong with me because my father had died. Nobody else's parents had died. The other parents started treating me like if their kids were around me, death would get into their house, too."

Maggie's peer group, even less versed in coping with loss, took cues from the adults. "A couple weeks after my dad died," she remembers, "my closest friends came up to me on the quad in the middle of a morning break and said, 'We can't be friends with you anymore, because you're too depressed,' and they walked away and just left me standing there. All I could figure out was that I must have been really bad to be punished in this way."

I wish I could say that cultural messages about grief have done an about-face since then. In the academic and therapeutic worlds, they have. In the public domain, not as much. Just two weeks after the 2018 shooting that took seventeen students' and teachers' lives at Marjory Stoneman Douglas High School in Florida, a surviving student who was unable to focus on her writing was told by a teacher to put her grief "in a box" so she could finish the paper and focus on schoolwork again. *Two weeks.*

The most disheartening part of this story is that the teacher, most probably, was trying to be helpful. Only 7 percent of American teachers in a 2012 national survey said they'd received training to support grieving students, even though 92 percent said childhood grief was a serious problem that deserved more attention, and 69 percent had at least one grieving child in their classrooms.

How did a society travel so far from the elaborate mourning rituals of the past to arrive at the muted, abbreviated protocols so many feel compelled to follow today? We have to look back a full hundred years to find the answer. Only then can we consciously decide, individually and collectively, what we'd like to reclaim. Because modern Western culture is no longer serving its mourners well. I'm not convinced it ever did.

Death, Dying, and the Echo That Spanned a Century

THE ROMANTIC era of the eighteenth and nineteenth centuries has been called the "broken heart" period of grief, and for good reason. Romantics were a passionate and emotional crowd, with deep reverence for the hidden, mysterious forces of the human spirit. Every attachment was viewed as unique and irreplaceable, and to "move on" hastily after a loved one died was considered a show of disrespect to the bond that had existed. In fact, those who appeared to rebound quickly were considered to lack emotional depth.

This line of thinking continued, more or less, until the late nineteenth century. That's when history took several dramatic turns.

First, the British middle class started to reject the excesses and regulations of Victorian mourning culture in favor of more private displays of grief. This movement was led by women, who bore most of the family's responsibility for following the socially required rituals. The female emancipation movement in the United Kingdom and the United States earned women both the right to vote and freedom from the strict obligations of etiquette, including that of public mourning.

Second, when World War I broke out in 1914, the public was introduced to technology capable of creating carnage on an unprecedented scale. In just under four and a half years, an estimated 10 million civilians and 8.5 million military personnel died worldwide, including about 116,000 servicemen in the United States, more than 900,000 in the United Kingdom, nearly 1.4 million in France, 1.7 million in Russia, and close to 1.8 million in Germany. Servicemen who died in action were often buried on the front, leaving their loved ones back home with neither bodies to bury nor graves they could easily visit. Families were unable to practice the familiar, comforting rituals they'd relied on for centuries to mourn their dead. They were left to either follow fractured traditions or adjust to a vacuum that remained unfilled.

And then—as if the trauma of war weren't crisis enough—the worldwide Spanish flu pandemic of 1918 unleashed a strain of influenza so contagious and so virulent it could kill an entire family within hours. U.S. population growth was negative in 1918 for the only time in the entire twentieth century. By the time the flu pandemic ended in 1919, after three waves of contagion, up to 50 million people had died worldwide, an estimated 675,000 in the United States alone. The world would not see such a devastating, rapid spread of lethal disease again until the HIV/AIDS crisis of the 1980s and the Covid-19 pandemic of 2020.

The death toll from Spanish flu rose so quickly that some cities had to revert to mass burials. Funerals that did occur were, by necessity, smaller and more private than in the past. Just as in 2020, groups were not allowed to congregate in public, which meant Catholic wakes, Jewish shivas, and social visits to surviving family members to pay respects were canceled or curtailed. Mourning periods contracted. If not, some families would never have experienced a break.

It's hard to overestimate the effects that the dual crises of war and pandemic had on twentieth-century mourning practices in the West. Either would have been devastating in its own right. Together, they created a tsunami of loss so swift and so large it wiped out a culture's ability to perform its own rituals. The remaining rites of the Victorian era became impossible to maintain either emotionally, practically, or financially. On top of this add secularization (which led to fewer religious rituals), urbanization (which increased dependence on the nuclear family instead of an extended family network), and rapid medical advances (which transferred death and dying from the home to the hospital), and you had all the elements of a perfect mourning storm. By the time World War II claimed another sixty million lives worldwide, grief had gone underground and families had learned to suffer silently and alone.

History sometimes generates long echoes. The dominant attitudes toward death, dying, and bereavement that surround us today have more in common with the attitudes of 1920 than the attitudes of 1920 had with those that existed in 1910. Western society is still feeling the effects of hundred-year-old events so dramatic they fundamentally changed how people responded to death and—with assistance from an Austrian neurologist named Sigmund Freud—how survivors were expected to behave.

What We Think about When We Think about Grief

DID OUR great-great-grandparents ask themselves if they were grieving correctly after a loved one died? Probably not. Probably, like others of their time, they were more focused on caring for the souls of the departed than on analyzing their own distress. Would they have compared their grief to a checklist to make sure they were staying on track? Most definitely they would not have. The perception of grief as an individual, interior, time-limited sprint with "normal" and "abnormal" lanes is exclusively a twentieth-century invention. And this may not have been for the better.

"The question, 'Is there something wrong with me because I'm not grieving properly?' puts a lot of extra weight and shame and guilt and despair on the mourner," explains Leeat Granek. "The grieving process is difficult enough. On top of this, we don't need a constant critical voice that's judging, 'Am I doing this right?' That's something that's constructed. It's new. It's not innate."

Granek, an associate professor of health psychology at York University in Toronto, has been researching and writing about the history of grief for the past decade. A three-hour Skype session with her is a deep dive into the effects of two world wars, the growth of psychology as a science, and the relentless twentieth-century effort to quantify and categorize patterns of human behavior. Granek's breadth and depth of knowledge is pure gold to a history nerd like me.

For her, the subject is also deeply personal. She was twenty-five and working toward her doctorate in psychology when her mother died of breast cancer, an event she describes as "a profound, life-changing, life-altering loss."

"I was extremely, extremely close to my mom," Granek explains. "So it made sense to me that it would take me a long time to grieve this loss, and that I was kind of going into a dark hole. And that was okay. I really trusted the process. But I started to notice immediately that the people around me, the people in my program, my family, my friends, were all very eager for me to move on with things. It was really puzzling to me. I was sort of marinating in the grief, and at the same time I was looking at the culture and wondering, *Why do we feel the way we feel? Why do we think the way we think?*"

These questions so intrigued her that she devoted her dissertation to answering them. "I wanted to understand how we moved from understanding grief as a normal and natural part of life that was dealt with in communities and in families and through relationships, to seeing it as a private psychological experience that you deal with in a therapist's office," she says. "How did we move between those very radical poles?"

Her research led her back to writings of the seventeenth and eighteenth centuries, when grief was considered a potential source of madness and even a cause of death. (A list of diseases and casualties that killed Londoners in 1632 indicated that eleven people that year had died of "Grief.") But it would be the turn of the twentieth century before scientific attention was directed toward the subject, when Freud and other psychoanalysts in Vienna became interested in how the human psyche handles loss and trauma.

Mourning as "Work"

FREUD WROTE about mourning in 1895, 1909, and 1915, but the watershed moment for serious writing about grief came in 1917 when he published a brief paper titled "Mourning and Melancholia." He originally set out to explore the difference between grief and melancholia, or what we'd now call depression. While the two states looked similar on the surface, Freud saw them as distinctly separate conditions.

Mourning, he proposed, was a basic human reaction to the loss of a loved person, object, or closely held ideal and did not, he emphasized, require outside intervention. In fact, Freud said, to interfere with someone's grief was often useless and sometimes even harmful.

He saw depression, on the other hand, as the result of grief gone awry. According to Freud, depression resulted when grief turned inward and led to self-recrimination and guilt. While depression rarely resolved spontaneously, he had observed, grief in most cases would achieve a "successful" completion when left to its own mysterious devices.

Applying the term "successful" to mourning was a decidedly new perspective. "Successful mourning," according to Freud, was achieved only after an individual fully relinquished all emotional and psychic attachments to the lost object and reinvested that energy in a new relationship. He called this process of detachment and reattachment (also known as decathexis and cathexis) the Work of Mourning, or *Trauerarbeit* in the original German. It would later become more popularly known as the "grief work hypothesis" or the Breaking Bonds model of grief.

Freud published "Mourning and Melancholia" in the midst of World War I, as Romanticism was being replaced by the progressive, efficient, individualistic ideas of modernism. The Work of Mourning functioned as a perfect bridge between both movements. Freud's model had one foot grounded in the Romantic's dream of a mysterious inner world and the other firmly planted in the modern thinker's machine view of human functioning. (First the psyche does *this*, then it does *that*, and with enough effort, ultimately it winds up *here*.) His theory was also a good fit for an industrial, capitalistic economy, as it promised to guide workers out of grief and back to their labors quickly and with minimal disruption to productivity. No wonder Freud's model found quick traction.

Success in anything, of course, implies the potential for failure. So, too, did this new theory of mourning. Although sadness and longing had always been considered natural human reactions to a death, new sets of criteria were developed to determine just how much sadness and longing was appropriate and how long these states should last. Too much grief? That was a problem. Not enough grief? Problem of a different kind.

Mourning behaviors that had previously fit along a broad continuum of acceptable responses now acquired labels such as "pathological," "excessive," "chronic," "delayed," "suppressed," "suspended," "inhibited," "maladaptive," "abnormal," "unhealthy," and "unresolved." This marked the birth of a lopsided Goldilocks and the Three Bears mentality of bereavement, in which people could grieve too much or too little, too noisily or too quietly, yet with little agreement on how much was just right.

Any theory is the product of a singular mind, situated within a particular culture and grounded in a specific moment in historical time. A thinker can only build upon whatever resources, personal and professional, are available there and then. Freud's view of mourning grew out of common Western assumptions about grief at the time, which still included the visible, prolonged, and arguably extreme practices of Victorian England. He also based his Work of Mourning on twenty years of psychoanalytic work with clients in Vienna and his evolving ideas about ego development and narcissism, as cultural values were shifting from a focus on community to an obsession with individualism.

The Work of Mourning was, in effect, the result of observations

Freud had made and conclusions he'd drawn, up to and including the events of 1917.

It would be three more years before Freud's personal experience with mourning factored into this equation. In January 1920, twenty-six-year-old Sophie Halberstadt-Freud, the doctor's fifth child, succumbed to complications of the Spanish flu. She left behind a husband, two young sons, and a father who, in his own words, slid into a state of "blunt necessity, mute submission." Three years later, the death of Sophie's younger son Heinele from tuberculosis dealt his grandfather a devastating second blow, from which he never fully recovered. Little Heinele's death was the only occasion upon which Freud had been known to cry.

In 1929, on what would have been Sophie's thirty-sixth birthday, Freud composed a letter of condolence to a friend who was grieving the death of his own young son. "Although we know that after such a loss the acute state of mourning will subside, we also know we shall remain inconsolable, and will never find a substitute," Freud wrote. "No matter what may fill the gap, even if it be filled completely, it nevertheless remains something else. And actually this is how it should be. It is the only way of perpetuating that love which we do not want to relinquish."

Only after two significant losses of his own did Freud understand how persistent and enduring our emotional ties to close loved ones can remain. He never revised his original theory, though it might not have mattered if he had. By 1929 the ideas he put forth in "Mourning and Melancholia" had taken on vibrant psychoanalytic and academic lives of their own. The Work of Mourning would never be empirically proven or even scientifically tested, yet more than a half century's worth of doctors, academics, and clinicians would adopt Freud's description of mourning as an effortful, internal, linear process culminating in a discrete endpoint as the dominant model of grief. It would serve as inspiration for some of the most influential twentieth-century thinkers in the field, including psychiatrists Erich Lindemann, who became known as the father of grief pathology; John Bowlby, who developed attachment theory; and Elisabeth Kübler-Ross, whose seminal work with the dying shape shifted into what became popularly known as the five stages of grief.

It would take sixty years for the profession to circle back to the knowledge Freud had acquired in 1929. In the meantime, several generations of mourners, including my family, were along for a wild ride.

We Were Going through a Stage

THE DAY before my mother died, a social worker at Good Samaritan Hospital appeared from I don't know where and backed me into a corner of a carpeted fourth-floor hallway. I mean literally, with her hands pressed against the opposing walls.

"Your mother is dying, Hope," she said.

I must have looked like someone resisting the obvious—and to an extent, I suppose I was—because she repeated it, this time with emphasis. *"Hope, your mother is dying."* Then she pressed a four-color glossy brochure into my hand.

I looked down at the cover. *The Five Stages of Grief*, it read.

This social worker meant to be helpful, I'm sure. She was sharing the resources available to her at the time. Remember, this was 1981. There were no hospices or bereavement centers in our community. We didn't have grief groups for children or adults. But we did have the five stages of grief. Everyone did, by then. They'd been introduced by Dr. Elisabeth Kübler-Ross in her groundbreaking book *On Death and Dying* in 1969, and by the early 1980s the stage theory of grief was on everyone's mind.

I opened the pamphlet. *Denial, Anger, Bargaining, Depression, Acceptance.* That linear, sequential quintet. Lined up in formation, the five stages looked like a blessedly fast speedway out of this mess. And there were only five of them. How hard could they be?

I can do this, I thought. And, overachiever that I was at seventeen, I thought, *I can do this faster than anyone else.*

As it turned out, mastering the Five Stages was easy. When I revisited the pamphlet after the funeral, I saw I'd already completed four of them.

Denial? I knew my mother was dead. I mean, *duh*. We'd buried her that afternoon. Trying to deny that would be delusional. *Check.*

Anger? Well, that hadn't seemed very useful. Anger would only have gotten in the way of action when action had been necessary. And now? Anger wasn't going to bring her back. I was already past the point of giving any mind space to anger. *Check.*

Bargaining? I'd done that when she was in the hospital and it hadn't made a difference. So, *check.*

Depression? No. I was sad, powerfully sad, but I wouldn't call it depression. Also, I'd never thought of myself as a person who got depressed. Not capital *D* depressed, anyway. So, *check* on depression, too, because I'd obviously leapfrogged over that one.

Which brought me to the fifth stage—acceptance—which was where I figured I must have landed. *Done.*

(I know. I know.)

Eleven months later, I was managing . . . pretty well, I thought. By then, the visceral shock of separation had passed. I'd stopped listening for my mother's footsteps on the floor above my room at night, and in the spring, thick white envelopes starting arriving in the mail from colleges, each one pregnant with a new and different promise for the future. I was doing *just fine*. That is, until the day of my high school graduation arrived.

As I stood in the bathroom that morning in my gold gown, holding a gold cap in one hand and a green graduation tassel in the other, it seemed impossible to be taking this step without my mother there. I stared at my reflection in the mirror, and the force of missing her came crashing down on me with nearly as much strength as it had on the morning she'd died. My next thought arrived with a brutal punch.

If a daughter graduates from high school and a mother isn't there to see it, does it really happen?

And then—*What the hell is* this? Because I'd already sailed through those five stages of grief a year ago. Hadn't I?

I placed my palms on the countertop and stared hard into my eyes. Stared until they filled with tears. I hadn't sailed through the stages in that pamphlet, I understood then. Not even close. Which was how the morning of my high school graduation marked the birth of a shameful secret I carried for the next dozen years: that I must have gotten grieving wrong.

The real secret, I would learn only much later, was that those five stages had never been meant for me. Initially, they'd never been meant for anyone grieving the death of a loved one. They were the stages that Dr. Kübler-Ross had observed among terminally ill patients at Billings Hospital in Chicago as they approached the endpoints of their own lives. Before Kübler-Ross sat at their bedsides to ask about their experiences, dying patients in America had been treated more like objects to be saved than human beings in the midst of a dense and complicated experience. Kübler-Ross changed all that through her fierce commitment to help dying individuals share their stories, in their own words. By inviting the public to bear witness to the cognitive, emotional, social, and philosophical aspects of dying, Kübler-Ross cut straight through decades of death taboo. Terminal illness would never be viewed, or experienced, quite the same way again.

By giving voice to those who were dying, Kübler-Ross had hoped to jumpstart a broader dialogue about death. Initially, she never intended for the Five Stages of Dying to be applied to the mourners left behind. But just as with Freud's Work of Mourning, Kübler-Ross's five-stage model developed a cultural momentum she soon became powerless to stop. Like the Work of Mourning model, hers would never be empirically proven. No matter. It made logical and emotional sense to the general public and created accessible talking points for the media. And so the Five Stages of Dying became rebranded as the Five Stages of Grief, and public fixation on the latter took off.

To watch television clips of Kübler-Ross from the 1970s is to chart her growing exasperation as interviewer after interviewer presses her for sound bites about the stages of grief, even after she labels them as "old news" and encourages viewers to push them aside.

"So the person should actually allow themselves to go through the stages?" a young Oprah Winfrey asks Kübler-Ross on the 1974 daytime show *People Are Talking*.

"Just be you!" Kübler-Ross replies. "If you feel like screaming, you scream! If you feel like crying, you cry! Don't try to follow a textbook or have somebody else tell you what to do. Trust yourself, your own natural emotions."

Because grief is so individual and unique, some people may, in fact, go through what look and feel like these five stages. For the majority of us, however, lived experience resists being distilled down to narrow categories or defined by single terms. Emotions don't occur in silos. The human heart and brain are amazingly complex organs. They're capable of handling more than one emotion at a time.

Bereavement specialists now roundly agree that the Five Stages of Grief are a reductive and insufficient model for grieving. "Just last week I was in South Carolina doing some work and somebody said something about Kübler-Ross's stages," Terrie Rando recalls. "And I said, 'Let me tell you this. That really has not been empirically validated, and everyone in this field who has any ounce of credibility will tell you that's not how it works.'"

Nonetheless, the Five Stages have remained remarkably pervasive and persistent in the culture at large for the past fifty years. The degree to which they've shaped public discourse about grief is nothing short of impressive. How often do we hear someone say they're stuck in the anger stage after a divorce, or can't get past denial after losing a job?

It's not hard to understand how this happened. Imposing a tidy framework on a long and haphazard process offers a tantalizing illusion of order over chaos. And a discrete series of stages promises structure, guidance, and agency instead of leaving mourners to feel like passive victims of strong emotions they can't control. In a culture where mourning rituals have been scaled back or compressed into a handful of days, a five-step prescription functions as a ritual of its own. Mourners use the stages as mile markers to gauge their progress on a journey they never wanted to take and hope will quickly end.

The Five Stages also plug into a seductive and familiar narrative. The classic hero or heroine's journey thrusts a protagonist out of his or her comfort zone to encounter hardships that can be overcome only with personal struggle, persistence, and courage. Think of the protagonists of our most enduring Bible stories, myths, and fairy tales: Joseph and Moses, Odysseus and Atalanta, Peter Pan, Snow White, Hansel and Gretel. Ordinary prophets, adventurers, castoffs, and orphans, they head out into the forest (or desert, or sea) and face off against adversarial forces to return much later, victorious and forever changed. The drought has ended! The witch is vanquished! Salvation arrives in a kiss! Who wouldn't, after calamitous pain, find such a narrative appealing?

"In some ways, stage theory became grief's monomyth," explains Robert Neimeyer. "It offers a similar kind of narrative that begins with a sense of disbelief, disillusionment, denial, and then moves through shocking and difficult encounters with anger and bargaining, trying to undo the circumstance, then lapsing into the inner work of depression and ultimately, when circumstances are favorable, arriving at a place of acceptance."

From this perspective, the Five Stages of Grief empowers mourners to become the tragic heroes and heroines of their own stories. Except for one not so small problem. Grief rarely adheres to such a clearly defined narrative. Grief doesn't hop agilely from stepping-stone to stepping-stone along a tidy path to acceptance, except, perhaps, in textbooks. Real-life grief is a jumbled, unpredictable fiasco.

It refuses to take orders or follow rules. If grief were an art form, it would be abstract expressionism. If it were a type of music, it would have to be improvisational jazz.

Stage theory helped initiate the broader cultural dialogue about death and dying that Kübler-Ross had hoped to inspire. Then it became an ill-fitting model for grief. Intentional or not, instead of allowing people's stories to unfold naturally, stage theory told people how their stories ought to be organized, and created expectations for experience to follow a singular plot. It didn't leave room for complicated truths, long digressions, and cyclical returns, especially over the long arc.

Perhaps most damaging, stage theory strongly implied how the final sentence of a story of loss should read: *And then she/he arrived in the land of Acceptance.* Yet as anyone who's experienced major loss knows, "Acceptance" is a way station, not a final destination. It's a place we arrive at and depart from, and return to and depart from, again and again.

"With any traumatic event, resiliency isn't as easy as getting to the other side and saying, 'Hooray! Huzzah! Done!'" says Jessica Koblenz, a psychologist in New York City who specializes in early bereavement. "It's a constant, back-and-forth struggle of being attached to what was turned upside down and making sense of its absence."

Koblenz's interviews with nineteen adults who'd lost one or both parents before age eighteen revealed how these sons and daughters kept returning to and renegotiating the loss at different points in their development. Their adaptation, she points out, had been slow and gradual and for some had spanned many years.

These back-and-forth cycles of return were more than just a common thread between stories, Koblenz found. They seemed essential to each participant's long-term process of integrating, accommodating, and living with their memories of the loss. "It was in that constant struggle that meaning continued to be unpacked and unfolded," Koblenz explains. "The participants who did the best [over time] were the ones who could tolerate the idea that this is something that would continue to get trudged up—that this is an existence, not something that's one and done." Growth in mourners, she found, appears to happen *because* of struggle, not in spite of it.

I wish I'd known that when I sat on my bed after my mother's funeral, checking off stages in a pamphlet. It would have been dispiriting to hear at the time, no doubt. If someone had told me, at seventeen, to suit up for a lifelong, open-ended quest to make meaning of her death, I probably would have said, "*No thanks. Not for me.*" But I'd like to think I would have remembered their words, and that at some later point I would have been grateful to have heard them, to have been in the presence of someone who encouraged me to imagine, even if just for a moment, that grief could be a long and awkward process of surrender instead of something that had to be quickly soldiered through.

* * *

CHAPTER TWO

Getting It Together

THE GRASS that lines Cornwall Street glistens with a sheen of morning dew as I head to a corner café in the Kitsilano neighborhood of Vancouver, British Columbia. Strangers greet me cheerfully as we pass. One even tips his hat in my direction. Granted, it's Canada. But still. It's barely 9 A.M. on a Saturday and the street is already pulsing with life.

So it feels a bit out of sync to be meeting up with Stephen Madigan this morning to talk about death. Madigan, a Canadian psychotherapist, is the director of the Vancouver School for Narrative Therapy, which is based on a form of counseling developed in the early 1980s by the late Australian social worker Michael White and the New Zealand therapist David Epston. Madigan trained with Michael White and White is one of my therapy heroes, so I'm eager to hear Michael White stories. But we're not going there yet, because we're here to discuss Western concepts of death and the cultural context of bereavement, and it's an important conversation to have.

For the past twenty-five years I've focused mainly on the emotions, thoughts, and behaviors that different groups of mourners have in common, to help minimize isolation and build community around shared experiences. Today, however, Madigan is challenging me to locate those shared experiences within a limited cultural context.

Ideas around death, dying, and bereavement that are currently taken for granted in modern Western culture, Madigan explains, are just that: ideas. "They're not universally accepted," he says. "They're not truths and they're not facts. They're constructs developed within a context that struggles with what death is and what grief is, and this is what we've been left with."

It's a good thing we're meeting in a coffee shop, because my mind is starting to spin. I take another big sip from my mug.

As Madigan emphasizes, a century of research that's been conducted mainly on Western subjects, with studies that were designed mostly by Western social scientists, hardly provides the definitive word on what grief should look like in all places and at all times. He's right. Expecting the grief experience to follow a preferred set of guidelines is more than unrealistic. It's actually pretty myopic. I'm thinking of my Japanese American friends who set up altars in their homes to communicate with their ancestors, and my Mexican American and Filipino friends whose families celebrate the Day of the Dead every autumn. They'd be justified in raising quizzical eyebrows at the Breaking Bonds theory of grief. Or shrugging it off entirely.

As Madigan and I talk, it occurs to me that "Western" is hardly a homogeneous term itself when immigration and expatriation have produced a substantial number of people living in hybrid cultures. Although Madigan and I would both be classified as "Westerners," between us we represent multiple subcategories—Canadian, American, Irish, Eastern European, native Torontonian, native New Yorker—each with its own subtle messaging about death and its own prohibitions and expectations regarding how to grieve.

The Social Rules of Bereavement

SORROW, ANGER, and fear appear to be universal reactions, existing in every known culture, after a loved one dies. However, outward displays of grief—meaning the when, where, how, and how long these emotions are publicly expressed—can vary widely from culture to culture. Rules and prohibitions may exist around

- the length and content of mourning periods;
- gender roles and responsibilities;

- the type and amount of social support offered;
- ideas about coping with trauma;
- ongoing relationships with the deceased; and
- acceptable pathways to recovery.

The mourning practices of any culture tend to be an outgrowth of that culture's belief system. For example, in traditional Navajo, or *Dineh*, culture, mourners grieve openly for four days after a death while the body is ritually prepared for burial. On the fourth day, family members cleanse themselves as if washing off their grief. Afterward, they can mention the deceased but must avoid saying his or her name out loud. That's because the *Dineh* believe that the soul takes a journey to the afterlife and saying the person's name out loud after death can impede its passage.

Traditional Balinese culture, on the other hand, teaches that negative emotions like sorrow and fear are harmful to one's health, while positive emotions strengthen the soul. When families lose a loved one in Bali, relatives will often conceal their sadness with laughter, even when recounting details of a tragic death. Balinese mourners may feel deep, private distress when a loved one dies, but in public they're discouraged from showing it.

Non-Western collectivist cultures are more likely to view a single death as a rupture in a community's social fabric. Social rituals are designed to heal that break. Certain Hindu castes, for example, observe twelve days of mourning between the day of the death and the day of cremation. If the deceased was a male head of household, the men in the family will direct their grief into the practical tasks of arranging the funeral. Women are expected to be more emotionally expressive. Female neighbors and relatives will arrive every afternoon to sit with the widow and her daughters in a room designated specifically for women's mourning. An experienced female elder leads the group through ritual sessions that encourage the women to cry, wail, shriek and otherwise externalize their grief. The hope is that after twelve days, the women will have released enough emotional pain to be able to speak freely about the deceased and start adjusting to life without him. Still, feelings of grief are common and expected long after the socially observed portion of a family's mourning has come to a close.

In modern, individualistic, Protestant-influenced societies like the United States and the United Kingdom, the social component of bereavement rarely extends beyond funeral and burial services. Social media tributes offer mourners collective space online, but with limited interaction. I often think of a scene in *The Namesake*, the 2006 film based on the book by the same name. The protagonist, Gogol, is a young Indian American man finding his way into adulthood who moves to New York after college and becomes involved with an American woman, Max. After his father dies suddenly, Gogol brings Max back to Michigan. As a second-generation immigrant, Gogol has lived as a Westerner his whole life. Nonetheless, he finds comfort and shared identity in performing the traditional Hindu rituals of shaving his head and dressing in a white dhoti and kurta after his father dies. His familiarity with these customs in a house filled with Indian food, language, and friends, stand in such marked contrast to the scaled-down rituals Max's upper-middle-class Protestant family would follow, the couple finds themselves forced to acknowledge the cultural divide they've been willing to overlook until then.

My family followed the customary funerary and bereavement rituals of Judaism after my mother died, though my father had never been observant. We went through the motions mechanically, mostly out of respect to my mother's family. During the seven-day mourning period called shiva, family and friends paid condolences at our home. Tradition dictated that we cover all the mirrors to discourage vanity and keep the focus on the deceased, and sit on low boxes to symbolize being humbled by the death. I'd just turned seventeen. It all seemed wholly archaic and unnecessarily complicated to me.

The seven-day buffer zone after the funeral was a public acknowledgment of the loss, and useful for that reason, I suppose. Social support after a loss is important enough that mourners who don't receive it wind up at higher risk for both short- and long-term mental and physical distress. Still, seven days was a long time for a teenager to sit still. One could only eat so much baked chicken and sit knee to knee with a squad of grim great-aunts for so long. I spent most of the time in my bedroom with friends whose parents had dropped them off, the boys sitting stiffly in a line on the bed, the girls sprawled cross-legged on the floor. No one else had lost a parent, so no one knew what to do or say, but their presence alone was a comfort. Mostly, we talked about our summer jobs and the ongoing major league baseball strike. The days wore on.

On the morning of the eighth day, we rose and resumed business as usual so abruptly that exiting the transitional period was nearly as unnerving as entering it had been. I returned to the same part-time jobs, where only my bosses knew why I'd been gone. Bizarrely (to me), my friends continued going to the same parties and listening to the same music as we all had before. I'd spent seven days in a suspended, liminal state, but I had little to show for that liminality other than seven days of lost wages. Nothing—and everything—had changed while I was gone.

Somewhere in that week had been rituals designed to help me, I understand now. I wish I'd been able to access them. Instead, the week functioned mainly as a holding pen that delayed my return to the outer world. Judaism offers integration rituals, mainly in the form of prayer, throughout the first year of mourning, but my family didn't practice them. We were surrounded by people yet still felt terribly alone. So maybe this is why, of all the cultural beliefs and rituals around mourning I've researched and encountered, I keep coming back to the traditions of the Dagara tribe of Burkina Faso.

Dagara teachings emphasize letting go of what no longer serves a person and fully grieving its departure. Unexpressed grief is believed to be a root cause of blame, shame, guilt, depression, spiritual drought, and physical illness. Periodically surrendering to sorrow and releasing grief, the Dagara believe, is essential for good mental, physical, and spiritual hygiene.

"Hanging on to old pain just makes it grow until it smothers our creativity, our joy, and our ability to connect with others," writes the late Dagara spiritual teacher Sobonfu Somé. "It may even kill us."

At the same time, as a collective culture the Dagara see individual pain as something that must be borne and released by the group. Frequent grief rituals are held across the Dagara's tribal lands in West Africa, in which members are encouraged to unburden themselves after a loss of any kind—the death of a loved one, the end of a marriage, a sudden rift between close friends, the loss of a job, or a natural disaster. A mourner's grief is meant to be released openly and publicly until all the emotions have been fully expressed. Instead of asking, "Aren't you over it yet?" the Dagara would be more likely to ask of one another, "Have you grieved enough?"

Imagine growing up within such a belief system, and how it might shape a perception of how, when, and where to grieve. A very different mindset would develop than the type in Glasgow or Cleveland.

"I thought this [the Dagara] perspective on grief was natural for everyone until I came to the U.S.," recalls Somé, who left Africa to study in America as an adult. "I was with a friend who was having a conflict with her family and I knew the situation was not easy for her. But one day I heard her alone in the bathroom crying! I said, through the door, 'Are you OK?' She said, 'Yes, I'm fine!' I said to myself, *Oh my god, something is not right here.* The people who were supposed to support her were not there."

Each time I read this passage I'm struck by what, being born and raised in the West, my mind perceives as Somé's generosity of spirit, only to remember that what looks generous to me is standard practice in many other parts of the world. And then I close my computer and return to California in 2020 where crying alone in the bathroom is still an unfortunate twenty-first-century norm.

That's why any generalizations about "normal" mourning have to consider the norms of a specific culture. What's normal to the Dineh might be considered harmful to the Dagara, whose practices might seem bizarre and even spiritually dangerous to a native of Bali. And few of these rituals would be embraced in a Western culture where grief is treated as something to be concealed from view and internally resolved.

"The message in our society is that grieving is a weakness," says fifty-year-old Sasha, who was twelve when her father died of a heart attack, and who lost her mother to breast cancer five months later. "As if there's a weakness to not pulling yourself up by your bootstraps, or pulling out your checkbook and going shopping. It's like, 'Okay, this is terrible. This is awful. Now let's move on.' If you're not ready to do that, there's almost a shaming that goes along with it."

It's true: Individuals who stray from social norms are often shamed by their social groups, explains Darcy Harris, an associate professor of psychology at King's University College in Ontario, Canada, who writes about grief in Western society. That sense of shame may then be internalized by the bereaved individual, who becomes frustrated by his or her inability to perform according to cultural expectations. Pressure to conform to the social rules of grieving then may win, Harris explains, even if following those rules prolongs or increases suffering.

Quite a conundrum develops, doesn't it, when the rules you're told to follow to "get past" a loss are themselves a source of distress? This was a problem during the Breaking Bonds era, when mourners were told that healing depended on ending attachments to the deceased, yet intuitively understood that staying close to their loved ones was crucial to their well-being, their identity, and their connection to the love that was shared.

"You can see the double bind there," Stephen Madigan says. "In order to say goodbye and let go, to put the loss and the experience of that person behind you, you would have to breach your own ethics. That's where a lot of the pain comes from."

Forty-one-year-old Dana found herself in that position in 1991 after her single mother died of breast cancer. As an only child she'd been "very, very close" with her mother, Dana explains. After the death she moved three hundred miles away to live with her father, stepmother, and stepbrothers and finish high school. Removed from everything familiar, Dana felt even further out of sync in a family that wasn't grieving and didn't know how to accommodate a new member who was. Her sadness, as she remembers, was treated like a disruption to the family's prior equilibrium.

"The dominant message at home was that you don't share," Dana says, "and if you need to, we'll pay a therapist so you can go somewhere else to talk about the life you had for fifteen years, and then don't talk about it anymore when you get home. I want to convey that, in my heart and in my gut, I just knew that wasn't enough for me."

The family prohibition against expressing grief meant that Dana had no one with whom to talk about her mother. Her vivid memories of their time together started to fade. As the close connection that had once sustained her also began to loosen, Dana swore she'd find a way to preserve it on her own.

When she was old enough to move out of her father's home, Dana slowly and deliberately created a network of friends with whom she could speak freely about her past. Their conversations helped her realize that messages aren't mandates, and that she could choose which ones to carry forward and which to leave behind.

The message about moving on quickly? That was the first to go.

"I mean, my mother is someone I think about on a regular basis. Like, *every day*," says Dana, who now has two young daughters of her own. "I feel she's very present in my life from a spiritual standpoint. I knew what I needed to do to carry her memory forward, and I've continued to do that."

Dana held her younger daughter's Communion on her mother's birthday so the date would have double significance moving forward. On the twenty-fifth anniversary of her mother's death, she ran in a race near the town where they'd lived. Afterward she organized a dinner for some of her mother's friends and former colleagues and encouraged everyone to share anecdotes about her mom.

"I can remember certain things about her and special moments that we had together," Dana explains, "but I'm trying to understand, through my eyes today, what kind of person she had been as an adult."

Dana didn't know it in 1991, but by resisting the message about letting go and moving on she had joined a burgeoning movement in the bereavement world. By the late 1980s and '90s, a growing number of academics and mental health practitioners were questioning whether the Breaking Bonds model was helping their patients or potentially harming them instead. These inquiries led to the next big shift in the bereavement world: the emergence of a relational theory of grief and the concept of Continuing Bonds.

Saying Hullo Again

IN THE early 1980s, social worker Michael White began noticing a curious pattern among new clients in his practice in Adelaide, Australia. After being diagnosed elsewhere with delayed grief and pathological mourning, they would arrive at his office in states of desperation and distress. These clients, White observed, were all well versed in the popular model of grief work. They understood they needed to detach from their loved ones in order to get on with their lives. So they'd tried. And they'd tried again. And again. Their repeated attempts and failures had only left them feeling inept. They'd become self-critical. They talked about feeling empty, worthless, and depressed.

To White, these clients seemed to have lost not only the people they'd loved but also crucial parts of themselves. He couldn't see how continuing to push them to separate from the deceased would bring them empowerment or relief. On the contrary, he thought, maybe the pain they were feeling came from having already said goodbye too completely and too well.

Maybe, he thought, what they needed were some chances to say "hullo."

White understood, of course, that certain assumptions and expectations for the future must inevitably change when someone dies. At the same time, he believed his clients needed opportunities to develop new relationships with their deceased loved ones. He began by asking gentle questions of these clients to help them transform their past relationships with the deceased into new relationships in the present. Questions like *If you were seeing yourself through your loved one's eyes right now, what would he be appreciating about you?*

How did she know these things about you?

What difference would it make to how you feel right now if you could appreciate those things about yourself?

Once the clients were satisfied with their answers, White helped them move their new self-knowledge into action through a second series of questions. *What difference will knowing what you now know about yourself make to your next step? In taking this next step, what else do you think you might find out about yourself that could be important for you to know?*

"Mike would look at how that [deceased] person might think about this living person going forward, discuss memories they shared together and what they've cherished and what that might mean for the future, and learn how the living person holds the loved one in daily conversation," Stephen Madigan explains.

"What he was getting at is the relational experience that we have with memory," he continues. "And so, memory is not a memory of suffering. Memory is actually something we can bring forward, and then we're bringing the person forward. We're not saying goodbye, we're saying hello again in the context of a different kind of experience."

When bereavement was reframed as "saying goodbye and then saying hullo again," White's clients experienced immediate relief. They discovered the kind of continuity, meaning, and purpose that had evaded them before. They also began acting kinder and more compassionately toward themselves. Whether a death had occurred recently or long ago, the results appeared to be the same.

By integrating their lost relationships into their current lives, White's clients, in effect, were authoring new stories for themselves moving forward. Instead of leaving their loved ones behind, they'd begun writing new narratives in which their loved ones could still play a part.

The Children Who Led the Way

AT THE same time that Michael White was helping his clients say hullo again in Australia, two American psychologists were studying the effects of early parent loss beyond the crucial first year. Six thousand miles away, near Boston, Phyllis Silverman and J. William Worden were interviewing 125 children between the ages of six and seventeen and their surviving caregivers. About three-quarters of the families had experienced the death of a father. The rest had lost a mother. The parents had died from a mix of both long-term illnesses and sudden causes. The data collected over this two-year period became the landmark 1996 Harvard Child Bereavement Study, still considered the gold standard for research into children's grief.

In the course of their study, Silverman and Worden interviewed the children and their surviving parents three times: four months after the death and again at one- and two-year intervals. They asked the children not only about their mourning behaviors but also about their thoughts about the death, and about the parent who'd died. Silverman conducted a similar, parallel study with children in Israel for cross-cultural comparisons.

When the investigators sat down to review the interview transcripts, they noticed a curious pattern. Children in both countries were talking about parents who'd died as if they were still in a living relationship. Fifty-seven percent of the kids said they still spoke to their mother or father. More than half reported seeing the parent alive in their dreams, and 77 percent had kept a personal item that had once belonged to the parent. Eighty-one percent felt the parent was watching them, although most were worried the parents wouldn't approve of their actions.

The children weren't fantasizing that their parents were still alive or thinking a dead person could return—nothing like that. Instead, the children had, on their own, developed sets of memories, feelings, and behaviors to help them to continue feeling close to their deceased parents. Silverman and Worden called this phenomenon "constructing" the deceased. As one twelve-year-old girl who'd lost her father shared,

> I keep my room nice and tidy now, that's the way he had everything. Before, I would just throw stuff down. Now every morning I pick everything up. I know it would please him. He'd understand if I screwed up in school. Mom would get real mad. So now when I get a bad grade I "talk" to him about it.

Turning a parent's absence into a new type of presence seemed to give the kids a sense of comfort. It also functioned as a helpful strategy for coping with the pain of separation. The study found that children who lost a parent of the same gender were more likely to stay connected to that parent, and kids tended to stay more connected to mothers than to fathers. Girls developed stronger connections to their deceased parents than boys did, and the least connected children were the teenage boys.

Interviews with the surviving parents revealed that they, too, had constructed similar relationships with their late spouses. Silverman and Worden also noticed how the children's relationships with their dead parents shifted and changed as they matured and came to know themselves and others differently.

A commitment to maintaining relationships with the deceased has always existed in cultures where the veil between life and death is believed to be permeable and thin. That wasn't the case in the America of the early 1990s, however. The traditional, psychoanalytic "grief

process" model of mourning still dominated medical and psychological curriculums. But its paradigm, based on separation between
people, wasn't applying to the children and adults in the Harvard
study. Instead of relinquishing their emotional ties to the deceased,
children and surviving spouses had been looking for and finding
ways to stay connected. That the responses were consistent between
the United States and Israel made Silverman and Worden's discovery
even more notable.

The psychologists shared their findings with other colleagues in
the field, including Dennis Klass, who was working with bereaved
parents in Missouri. Klass had noticed how his clients adjusted to the
loss of a child by creating new inner representations of their children
to carry forward. In Israel, psychologist Simon Shimson Rubin had
been observing the same phenomenon for more than a decade, starting with his doctoral study of mothers who had lost children to sudden infant death syndrome (SIDS). And in Brookline, Massachusetts,
psychiatrist Steven Nickman had noticed similar inner constructions
in his work with adoptees.

All this raised an obvious question: What, exactly, was going on?

Had people suddenly started grieving differently in the latter part
of the twentieth century? That was doubtful, given that mourners of
prior centuries and in countless other cultures also found ways to
stay connected to their dead.

Were therapists now asking new questions, and soliciting new information from their clients in response? This was possible, though
it wasn't happening as a coordinated effort. The therapists just
seemed to be noticing this pattern at the same time.

Had cultural restrictions on grief started to relax, giving mourners the freedom to reveal inner thoughts and feelings they'd previously been reluctant to share? I'd put my money on this one.

Maintaining inner relationships with lost loved ones wasn't a new
development. Mourners had been doing it all along. They'd just been
doing it quietly and privately, to avoid being told they were grieving
wrong.

In 1996 Silverman, Klass, and Nickman published *Continuing Bonds: New Understandings of Grief.* Psychologists, professors, nurses, sociologists, and social workers wrote about their experiences with clients who'd found ways to stay connected to parents, spouses, children, and siblings who had died. Their book marked another paradigm shift in bereavement theory.

Since then, the concept of continuing bonds has been steadily adopted and implemented into clinical practice. It's even been folded into other bereavement theories, most notably J. William Worden's Four Tasks of Mourning, developed in 1991 and revised in 2009. Worden developed these four tasks as a set of objectives that mourners face in the aftermath of a loss:

1. Accept the reality of the loss;
2. Work through the pain of grief;
3. Adjust to an environment in which the deceased is missing;
4. Find an enduring connection with the deceased while embarking on a new life.

Worden's step four is key to moving forward with attachment rather than detachment. "That's the ever-shifting beauty of the fluidity of the relational experience," Stephen Madigan explains. "The idea of leaving people behind, cutting them off, and becoming more isolated is not only absurd, but it marginalizes people and marginalizes their experience. In some ways, it's earmarked for more suffering."

Pain is inevitable, as the ancient Buddhist saying goes, but suffering is optional.

Continuing the bonds and re-membering the deceased into our stories extends the relationship instead. I think about this often with regard to a message so many of us receive after a loved one dies, the gentle pressure to be happy because our father/mother/sister/brother/spouse/child wouldn't have wanted us to be sad. It can come across as a request to suppress sadness, often to alleviate the speaker's discomfort with witnessing strong emotion. But it may contain an inadvertent altruistic impulse as well.

My coaching client Ruby and I were talking about this the other day. The twenty-first anniversary of her mother's death had recently passed and she'd spent part of the day at the cemetery. Afterward, she received a text from her maternal aunt that read, "We love you. I'm sorry you've been hurting for so long. Your mother wouldn't have wanted that for you. She would just want you to be happy and re-member the special times you had together."

Ruby's aunt may have been encouraging her to live in ways her mother could no longer live, as a tribute to her and to their enduring bond. To Ruby, an only child who was thirty when her mother died, feeling sadness on the annual anniversary of her mom's death *is* a reminder of the love they once shared. But her aunt is not entirely wrong about the benefit of remembering happy times. Sadness re-surfaces on this cyclical, annual event when Ruby is reminded of what was lost. The rest of the year, remembering the happy times they shared and living in tribute helps her maintain a strong inner connection with her mother that she has carried forward.

Remembering isn't a zero-sum game: We don't have to decide between sad and happy memories when constructing a relationship with the deceased. We can choose both/and.

Re-Membering the Departed

WHEN WE lose a loved one, we're tasked with finding meaningful ways to *stay connected* after a death. But if a loss occurred in the past and the inner relationship was disrupted, blocked, or became frozen in time, our task today may be to find meaningful ways to *reconnect*. These are the mourners I encounter most frequently, those whose inner connection to a loved one was disrupted and who've never stopped feeling the absence. They know something important is missing, but they're not sure how to regain it. They don't know how to find or where to put the love that was once shared. Their grief feels congested, and they don't know how to fix that.

I've witnessed visible relief appear on women's faces when they learn that not only do they not have to let go of their mothers but it's possible (and even preferable) for them to maintain an ongoing relationship. At one Motherless Daughters Retreat, the group got into a lively discussion about Michael White's work on saying "hullo," and the importance of continuing bonds. On our final morning, Brianna, whose mother had died nine years earlier, told us about her plan to embark on a "saying hullo road show" in which she'd drive around the East Coast visiting her mother's friends and collecting stories to help her connect with her mother as a woman, rather than just as a mom.

As Brianna was soon to discover, inner relationships with deceased loved ones can be activated and developed no matter how long ago the loss occurred. Displaying photos, telling stories, collecting new information, writing letters to them, and talking to them out loud are all ways to engage in what the philosopher Thomas Attig has termed "loving in absence."

The story of a shared life, after all, is much richer and more elaborate than the story of how a life ended. My mother wasn't just a woman who died, she was also a woman who lived for forty-two years, seventeen of which were spent with me. Surely, her forty-two years of lived experience are more significant than the sixteen months between her diagnosis and her death.

That's the emphasis of the opening session in narrative therapist Lorraine Hedtke's "Re-membering" bereavement group, when participants are invited to introduce themselves by introducing the person who died. It's a very deliberate request. A bereaved person's natural impulse is typically to start with the story of the death, but that tends to reify a single event, says Hedtke, a professor of social work at California State University in San Bernardino. "It entrenches us in saying that what was often a very small moment was the most important moment of their lives, when in fact there are thousands of other moments to draw upon," she explains. "If the death was tragic or sudden, like a suicide or murder, that story is immediately going to come up along with 'Introduce me to . . . ' But I'm still going to farm for the stories of a life."

This may seem counterintuitive for a group that purports to help the bereaved. Because wouldn't remembering happy times with that person only awaken deeper pain? As it turns out, no. Acknowledging the bond that was shared, Hedtke explains, leads to a feeling of connection, and that feeling of connection helps to relieve the pain around what's missing. Blocked access to memories of those bonds is what keeps us in a state of perpetual mourning.

Whether a client's loss occurred recently or in the distant past, Hedtke starts from the same place: "Where can we bridge the divide between the living and the dead so your loved one can keep walking with you?" Small, ordinary moments often offer the best opportunities. Hedtke remembers a group member who shared that she thought about her father every time she prepared a pan with cooking spray, because she remembered him doing the same.

By using the subjunctive "would," Hedtke helps her clients enter spaces of virtual reality with their departed loved ones. Together they construct statements like "My father probably *would have* told me to do it this way." "She *would have* done this for me if she were here." "I imagine that *would have* made him happy."

Then those statements are coaxed into actualized reality as Hedtke encourages talk about the differences this knowledge might make in a client's life and how, as a result, they might continue to respond or act moving forward.

Hedtke's method can be adjusted slightly for mourners who were too young to have retained conscious memories of time spent with the deceased. That person can still hold a storied identity in some form, Hedtke explains, through photos, letters, songs, family stories, recipes, jewelry, or possessions. "Our job is then to say, 'Let's craft those places into a story that walks with you,'" she explains. Building upon facts that are known, what can be learned from others, and what can be assumed to be true, Hedtke then asks questions like "Knowing her the way you've come to know her through photos or stories or other relatives, how would you introduce her to others? What kind of things would you say about what he liked and what he was proud of about you?"

"In these moments we're saying, 'My love for you is still present, and I can feel your love for me,'" Hedtke says. "And that stands, personally and politically, against the discourse that says, 'You need to get over it.'"

That voice inside of me when I was seventeen, the one that told me to push the pain down, to insist everything was fine, and to soldier on—it wasn't mine. It was the voice of a specific time and place (namely suburban, white, middle-class America in the early 1980s), amplified by adults who didn't realize this wasn't their voice, either. All of us were echoing ideas that had developed in the fertile minds of psychoanalysts and psychiatrists at the turn of the century and were then adopted and repeated by the public until they became accepted as fact.

And that secret I carried for so many years, the one that told me I'd gotten grieving wrong? As Stephen Madigan helped me understand on that Vancouver morning, exactly the opposite was true. I'd done everything right. That was the problem. I, and so many others like me, had done precisely what our time periods, our families, and the culture we'd lived in had expected of us. That we wound up feeling isolated and shamed nonetheless didn't mean we'd failed as a griever. It meant the rules we were trying to conform to were failing us instead.

CHAPTER THREE

* * *

Something New

THE YEAR was 1993. The place, New York University's Bobst Library. Outside: a frigid February morning, sleet angling forty-five degrees toward the ground. I can still see myself so clearly, even after all these years, sitting at a long table in a sixth-floor reading room with a view of Washington Square Park. Head down, winter boots crossed at the ankles, focused, always so focused, as I paged through a bound volume of *OMEGA—Journal of Death and Dying* to find an article about early bereavement while researching my first book.

Up on East Sixty-fourth Street, the living room in my subleased apartment was a chaotic tinderbox of books and papers and transcripts that I hoped could explain how a loss I'd experienced at seventeen still had such a hold on me. If I could only arrange the research in the proper configuration, I believed, the answer would emerge with a resounding *click* and—success!—I'd be fixed.

It was a nice idea, for a while.

I was flipping through that volume of *OMEGA* when the title of a different article flashed by. I thumbed back a few pages to make sure I'd read it properly: "Old Pain or New Pain: A Social Psychological Approach to Recurrent Grief."

"Old Pain or New Pain." That's the part that caught my attention.

Lucky stumbling, I call it, when I'm looking for a piece of information and trip over a different, even more relevant item purely by chance.

"Old Pain or New Pain" had been published a few years earlier by Sarah Brabant, a sociology professor at the University of Southwestern Louisiana. At the time, most articles about grief were being written by psychiatrists and psychologists trained in the "grief work" model of psychoanalysis. Their writings offered little agreement, however, about how long this work of grief might last. Some said a couple of weeks. Others gave it a matter of months. A few allowed for a year or more.

A similar lack of consensus existed around "anniversary reactions," the catchall term for flare-ups of grief that can recur years or even decades after a death. These reactions typically surface at times of annual significance to a mourner such as birthdays, holidays, and the anniversary of a death. They can also show up around one-time transitions like graduations, marriage, parenthood, and reaching a certain age. Sometimes an anniversary reaction expresses as a physical symptom that mimics how a loved one died, such as chest pains when the cause of death was a heart attack or headaches if a brain tumor had been the culprit.

Although anniversary reactions are and have been common—one psychiatrist estimated they affected about a third of his patients—they were consistently viewed as abnormal responses to grief and were believed to be evidence of unresolved or incomplete mourning. Freudian analysts viewed anniversary reactions as repeated unconscious attempts to master unresolved emotions from the past, a phenomenon that Freud called "repetition compulsion." Other doctors described them as a "puzzling human behavior" and "a time-related illness." One even labeled them a disease. In the 1960s and '70s, patients who experienced anniversary flare-ups were commonly misdiagnosed with a cyclical form of manic depression.

Psychiatrists of the mid-twentieth century devoted large amounts of time and paper to trying to understand and treat anniversary reactions in their patients. Case studies from those decades are filled with stories of dramatic, inexplicable, and sometimes alarming mental and physical ailments that appeared as an anniversary date approached. Depression, heart problems, rheumatoid arthritis, skin rashes, migraines, back pain, ulcerative colitis, phobic fears, and even suicide attempts and psychotic reactions were cited. In many cases, the patient was unaware of a time correlation to a past event. When the psychiatrist pointed out the specific day, season, or time of year and helped the patient make a conscious connection, the symptoms often spontaneously resolved. It was almost as if, the doctors observed, the patients' bodies were acting out what their minds had suppressed.

I find the term "unresolved grief," when used to describe any form of sadness or distress that persists beyond an arbitrary point, to be reductive and, frankly, not very useful. Most bereaved individuals never achieve full resolution of their grief, if such a thing is even possible. Yet the degree to which anniversary reactions were pathologized in the past left little room to view them as predictable and normative responses to major loss.

Sarah Brabant's article injected a fresh perspective into the conversation. She proposed that a grief episode that occurred years after a death might not be linked to incomplete mourning at all. She believed some of these episodes were reactions to an entirely *new* type of loss. In such a circumstance, emotional pain could be viewed as a time-appropriate response instead of a delayed reaction.

To illustrate the point, Dr. Brabant told the story of an adult college student who'd lost her mother at the age of three. The student had "apparently recovered" (Brabant's words) from her early loss and recently had married. Soon after her wedding, however, she began experiencing sleeplessness, lack of appetite, and a strong desire to spend time at her mother's grave. On the surface, Brabant wrote, these behaviors looked very much like an episode of fresh, acute grief.

Could this daughter have been regressing to a state of incomplete mourning from early childhood? Brabant didn't think so. To her, the woman's reaction didn't resemble the anguish of a toddler. It looked more like the sadness and anger of an adult daughter longing for a mother's advice and support at a time of transition. Instead of grieving for the actual mother who'd died when she was three, Brabant proposed, the daughter was grieving for the *imagined* mother she'd projected into the future, the one who would have helped her plan and celebrate a wedding if she had lived.

The student, in other words, had encountered her old loss in a new way.

I pushed the bound volume back a few inches on the library table and stared out the wall of windows. Across the street, the bare upper branches of sycamore and ginkgo trees in a corner of Washington Square Park shivered and swayed in the cold wind. Just a few months earlier, I'd walked under those trees and gazed up at their full canopies of rust and yellow leaves.

Same trees, different season, different perspective.

Yes, I thought. *It's like that.*

For the first few awful months after my mother died, the pain of separation and the horror of its permanence had been overwhelmingly immediate and present tense. I went through my daily motions in a fog of disbelief, numbness, sleeplessness, weight loss, helplessness, anxiety, pretense, and fear. How could *my mother* have just . . . *died*? Where had she *gone*? Even after all this time, those months are still white space in my memory. My friends from high school tell stories of things I did that autumn, but really, they could be talking about anyone. I don't remember being there, even when presented with photographic evidence that proves I was. All of my mental energy must have been diverted into adjustment and survival. Or maybe trauma affected my memory-storage process for a while. I don't know.

The brain fog and the hollow ache between my ribs eventually dissipated—five months, six months, somewhere in that range, as I recall—but the longing for my mother's presence never went away. That part accompanied me right into adulthood, where it kept bubbling up at times both expected and not. As Mother's Day approached each year. Every July 12—the anniversary of her death. When I walked into a restaurant and saw a mother and daughter eating lunch at a table set for two. When I spied a mother and her pregnant adult daughter shopping for baby clothes. When I witnessed a friend treating her mother poorly. And, for a long time afterward, every time a romantic relationship ended or someone else I was close to died.

Sometimes these grief episodes came and went quickly. Other times they'd linger for days, leaving me shredded and blinking in their wake. "*It feels like losing her all over again,*" I would say, for lack of better language. But it wasn't that. Not really. In 1981, I'd been mourning the physical loss of *my* mother, the one with the wide smile and graceful hands who'd packed ham sandwiches smeared with Gulden's brown mustard into my lunch bag every morning and shouted, "Have a good day!" as I darted out the front door. These later episodes felt more like painful, generalized reminders that I didn't have *a* mother anymore, and that I would continue not having one in the yawning expanse ahead.

The women I'd been interviewing talked of having similar pangs of grief-but-not-exactly-grief long after their mothers died. They, too, described their episodes as brief, typically lasting anywhere from a few minutes to a few days. Their flare-ups didn't feel like emotions that had been repressed from childhood, they said. There is such a thing, but this was rarely that. Most of these women had mourned their losses to some degree over the years. The surges, as they described them, felt more like offspring of the original loss showing up in new and different ways.

"Loss is loss is loss," I often hear people say. What they mean, I think, is that no matter who died, no matter how they died, and no matter what a mourner's age was at the time, all loss is painful and all pain is legitimate pain. In the words of the inimitable Elisabeth Kübler-Ross, "There is no competition in suffering."

There is, however, plenty of variety. As I began to understand in the NYU library that winter afternoon, this thing we call grief starts to branch out and diversify over time. Like a water spill that finds different channels to follow, so does long-term bereavement find different pathways for expression. Some are so common among so many different types of mourners that we might think of them, if not strictly as "normal," then at least as forms of normative behavior.

Three expressions of grief in the short and long term appear so often I've come to think of them together as "the grief trinity," and separately as New Grief, Old Grief, and New Old Grief. Together they offer a descriptive means for thinking and talking about long-term bereavement without the framework—or the labeling—of diagnosis.

New Grief: Here and Now

NEW GRIEF is exactly what its name implies: a grief that didn't exist before. Fresh, raw, and immediate, New Grief rushes in to fill the vacuum when a specific loved one dies.

Disbelief, shock, numbness, panic, sorrow, rage, crying spells, helplessness, hopelessness, fear, ruminations, avoidance, heart palpitations, skin rashes, sleeplessness, weight loss, brain fog, restlessness, disorganization, loss of motivation, anxiety, fatigue, guilt, relief, release: New Grief is a full-body experience.

"Time has stopped. Nothing feels real," writes therapist and author Megan Devine, whose fiancé Matt died eleven years before she wrote her first book, *It's OK That You're Not OK.* "Your mind cannot stop replaying the events, hoping for a different outcome. The ordinary, everyday world that others still inhabit feels coarse and cruel. You can't eat (or you eat everything). You can't sleep (or you sleep all the time). Every object in your life becomes an artifact, a symbol of the life that used to be and might have been. There is no place this loss has not touched."

On a pain scale of 1–10, New Grief is a 14.

"I remember thinking, 'How do I go on? I don't understand. I don't know how to do anything anymore. I don't understand,'" recalls fifty-one-year-old Sandra, who was fifteen when her mother died in bed, at home, from sudden heart failure. "It was a total existential crisis of not knowing how to live or function if I wasn't in connection or relationship to my mom, and just feeling like my guts had been ripped out. For the first couple of years, my constant feeling at rest was like all of my nerves were on the outside of my body and everything hurt."

In the first systematic study of grief, conducted in the 1940s, psychiatrist Erich Lindemann observed an acute grief phase punctuated by episodes of "somatic distress" among his subjects. Most of them were survivors and relatives of victims who'd died in Boston's Cocoanut Grove fire of 1942, which remains the deadliest nightclub fire in U.S. history. Their episodes of distress included breathlessness, weakness, restlessness, and painful mental disruptions, or what we might now call intrusive thoughts. All together they formed a state of "crisis grief," which is particularly—though not exclusively—a feature of sudden, unexpected loss.

Phoebe, now forty-two, remembers the intense phase of New Grief she plunged into after a private plane crash took both of her parents' lives sixteen years ago. "It was like grief became an extra lobe in my brain that took over everything I had prided myself in before," she recalls. "My ability to be logical and reasonable and rational were all affected. Grief became like a virus that infiltrated every aspect of my life, from work to my ability to help the attorneys to the way I dealt with family members."

New Grief is piercing and acute, narrow and deep. Especially when a death involves trauma or violence, the volume of shock, panic, and confusion may feel like more than a single body or mind can bear. That's when New Grief becomes a memory thief, hijacking our capacity to properly store memories of the aftermath and therefore leaving us unable to retrieve them later.

"My father called to tell me what happened," says Charlene, whose younger brother died by suicide eight years ago at the age of forty-two, "but there are a lot of blank spots in my memory from there. People have told me that they spoke with me that day, and I just plain old don't remember. I know I got to my brother's house somehow. I think my husband came home from a business trip, urgently, and drove me up there? Something."

In New Grief, the aperture of time shrinks so we can focus just on getting from day to day. Yet even within these diminished borders, small tasks may nonetheless feel too overwhelming to perform. Nothing feels safe anymore. Potential tragedy waits around every corner, crouched and eager to pounce.

Such a level of intensity can't be borne 24/7. It would be like staring straight into the sun: blinding, overwhelming, and unsustainable.

I don't know how I'm going to survive this, you might think. *I can't do it.*

Except . . . you can. And you do. Because you have a natural, built-in coping mechanism that helps you.

Some call this inner safeguard "denial." Others call it "avoidance." Dutch psychologists Margaret Stroebe and Henk Schut call it "dosing," which they credit with keeping us from tumbling into bottomless pits of sorrow.

In a series of studies with widowed spouses at Utrecht University in the Netherlands, Stroebe and Schut noticed that instead of steadily advancing from one state to the next, as the grief-work hypothesis predicts, bereaved individuals seemed to alternate between two different states. They would move back and forth between periods of acute emotional distress and periods where they focused on practical, restorative tasks. Stroebe and Schut called these two oppositional states "loss-oriented" and "restoration-oriented" coping.

When the widows engaged in loss-oriented activities they would cry; feel guilt, regret, or despair; look at old photos; tell stories about the loved one; long for a reunion; and think about their fate and changed identity. After a while—and the amount of time varied from person to person, and episode to episode—the mourners shifted into restoration-oriented tasks that helped them adjust and continue to exist in the larger world. These included handling financial matters, keeping up at work, taking care of dependent children, and spending time with friends to combat loneliness. The restorative side of the pendulum could also include some denial and avoidance, which seemed to function as shock absorbers to soften the impact of pain on the other side.

The widows, as Stroebe and Schut observed, oscillated back and forth between the poles of loss and restoration unevenly until, gradually, loss-focused activities began to include more happy memories than sad ones, and task-oriented periods became pleasurable in their own right instead of serving as refuge from the pain of grief. This "dosage of grieving" resembled an organic pattern of self-regulation. They called this natural oscillation the Dual-Process Model of Coping with Bereavement.

A Model for Everyone

UNLIKE THE grief-work hypothesis, the Dual-Process model can accommodate the grieving patterns of different cultures, temperaments, and genders. Some cultures, for example, sanction long and loud periods of loss-oriented activities, while others urge mourners back into restoration tasks very quickly. In addition, a traditionally "feminine" approach to grieving emphasizes inner processing, emotional expression, and open discussion of feelings, all of which can be found on the loss-oriented side of the pendulum. A classic "masculine" grieving response, which had previously been missing in grief-work models, tends to look more like the restoration side.

According to Tom Golden, a therapist in Gaithersburg, Maryland, who writes and speaks extensively about men's bereavement, after a major loss about 80 percent of men gravitate toward restoration-oriented tasks that prioritize action, problem solving, and emotional restraint, while about 80 percent of women find their comfort in loss-oriented activities that prioritize emotional expression. In addition, popular perceptions of what grief looks like involve images of dependency, Golden says, which creates problems for men in Western culture.

"Dependency is forbidden in our culture for men," he explains. "It's literally forbidden. If you show yourself being dependent, you're considered less than a man. And that creates a double bind, because if men admit they're dependent, they are shamed. But if they don't admit they're dependent, then they don't get help."

Journalist Neil Chethik received a comprehensive lesson in male bereavement patterns when he conducted in-depth interviews with seventy men for his 2001 book *Fatherloss: How Sons of All Ages Come to Terms with the Deaths of Their Dads.* "I would sometimes ask the men, 'Did you grieve the death of your father?' and they would interpret that to mean, Did they cry?" he recalls. "They would say 'No, I've never grieved.' Then I'd say, 'Well, what did you do?' Then they'd tell me long stories about 'I took all his records home and played them every night,' and 'Oh, I went out and started a foundation for him and raised half a million dollars.' And I'd be like, 'That's grieving.' What is that if it's not grieving? It's doing what it takes to feel better and release the tension between what you want and what isn't the case. You're doing things that speak to that pain."

I'm reminded of a story my friend Cecile, who taught high school journalism for twenty-four years, told me. During her long tenure as a teacher, a number of students at her school died from sudden and unexpected causes, often in auto accidents. As a survivor of two sudden losses herself, Cecile could intimately understand her students' shock and disorientation. She'd lost her first child just after birth, and three years after that her younger brother had died in an accident. Although the high school where she taught offered on-campus support after a classmate's death, word got around campus that Cecile was a teacher who could talk about loss. Students often made their way to her newspaper room after a friend died.

One year, as Cecile recalls, a female student at the school died in a car accident in which her boyfriend was the driver. At the school's memorial assembly a few days later the boyfriend, who'd survived the accident, broke down in Cecile's arms. For the next few days he avoided going to class, withdrew from his friends, and stayed away from the room on campus that had been designated for students to talk with counselors and one another. His friends and teachers became concerned that he might be avoiding the reality of the loss. During that time, however, he sequestered himself in Cecile's newspaper room, where he quietly and diligently worked on a photo montage of his girlfriend for the school paper's next edition.

This student was processing an enormous load of New Grief. He was just doing it differently than the people around him expected it to look.

Are male and female patterns of grief the result of biology or of social conditioning? Probably both, Golden says. While links between biology and behavior are notoriously hard to prove, social prohibitions against male emotional displays are well documented worldwide.

Is one pattern more helpful than the other? Not necessarily. It appears we benefit from some balance of both. When Stroebe and Schut encouraged a mixed group of widows and widowers to adopt the other gender's coping skills, both groups reported lower levels of distress. Widowers who were helped to be more emotion-oriented and widows who were taught to be more task-oriented were the ones who seemed to fare best.

Proportions of time spent in loss-oriented versus restoration-oriented activity also varies quite a bit among individuals. That's because differences in temperament, age, and other stressors all factor in. After my mother died, my father allowed himself to cry only when driving to and from work, because as a newly single father of three, those were the only hours he had to himself. The thought of my father weeping alone in his car twice a day without anyone to comfort him gutted me when I found out about it. To be honest, it still does. But now I understand that he was dosing his grief, and I'm grateful that he could.

Because mourners whose dosing becomes impaired—meaning those who focus exclusively on the pain of loss, or those who quickly and completely immerse themselves in tasks like work or dating—

typically have a harder time adjusting to a loss. That's what happened to Patrick, now thirty-five, after his mother died from complications that developed during a routine surgery thirteen years ago.

Patrick had been living at home with his single mother and her aging parents, working and attending school part-time, when his mother was admitted to the hospital for minor surgery on her spine. She never regained consciousness after the operation, and she died three days later.

In the span of just a few days, Patrick went from being a carefree twenty-two-year-old to a bereaved son and head of a household that included two elderly grandparents with multiple physical needs. His period of New Grief quickly became engulfed with practical tasks. He had a lot to figure out, and quickly. But his body struggled with the stress of keeping loss-oriented activities at bay.

"In July I broke out in a rash that started on my foot, and then it was on my leg and then it was all over," he recalls. "I was covered in it. I thought that I was really sick, but I went to the dermatologist and it turns out it wasn't any sort of outward infection. It was just my body's stress reaction. So I didn't really deal with the grief all that well."

Thirty-four-year-old Simone also describes a protracted period before she was able to feel any grief after her second parent died. Simone was twelve when she lost her father to a five-year struggle with cardiomyopathy, a progressive heart condition, and twenty when her mother died from kidney cancer. An only child, she quickly turned her attention to her program of study; her serious boyfriend, who's now her husband; and building a family with him. She relished the absence of the restrictions that years of family illness had imposed on everyone.

"From the age of twenty until, probably, recently, I was totally one hundred percent forward-focusing," Simone recalls. "I felt quite free. It was liberating, almost. That's how I genuinely felt, but I realize I just hadn't grieved at all at that point. I'm a very, very delayed griever.

I don't think I started grieving until my eldest child was born, so I'm probably in year three now."

Shifting back and forth between loss- and restoration-oriented activities, and the friction that develops between those two poles, appear to be what helps mourners struggle their way back to mental and emotional stability. Without this short-term struggle, enduring long-term adjustment may be harder to achieve.

What More Is New Grief?

IT'S RELATIONALLY SPECIFIC. New Grief occurs when *a particular person or persons* die. A clear line can be drawn between source and outcome, cause and effect. The death of a specific loved one is the cause. New Grief is the effect.

I don't know what I'll do without her. I'm going to miss him so much. Why did God have to take them? These are the kinds of statements that characterize New Grief.

Veronica, now thirty-four, was seventeen when her older and only brother, James, died. James, born two years before Veronica, was a joyous free spirit who loved English class and music and played football and lacrosse. "I *idolized* him," Veronica recalls. "I literally followed him everywhere. I hung out with him, hung out with his friends, and dated his friends, much to his dismay. He was my big brother. I thought he hung the moon."

One night, the summer that Veronica turned seventeen, James went out with a friend. On their drive back, the car flipped and James was killed instantly.

"To me, the entire world just crashed," Veronica says. "I wanted my brother back. If I couldn't have that, I wanted nothing else but to die with him that day, the next week, the next few months. I could never go through with something like that, but I totally shut my family out. I went into my own bubble and only wanted to be with his friends. I was just so sad all of the time. I didn't know how to get this brick of sadness off my chest. I would start crying randomly in the middle of Spanish class. Something would make me cry and I couldn't stop sobbing.

"I'd lost grandparents before, but this was something completely different," she continues. "My dad was really angry. My mom was really broken. My sister was like the quiet afterthought, because she's the youngest one. I attribute where all of us are today to my mom holding us together. I didn't feel connected to my family at all. I took some college trips with my dad but I don't remember much about them. I think we were just sort of going through the motions of getting there. My parents were of course very understanding about all my needs, but it was a wild few months before anybody in the house laughed again. That came after about three months. It just got to the point where grieving had become exhausting."

IT'S REPETITIVE. New Grief isn't something we go through once and then we're done. We'll experience it again, and again, each time someone close to us dies. Most of us will have several encounters with New Grief in a lifetime. Some of us, unfortunately, will have many.

We all know people who seem unfairly tasked with carrying a heavier grief load than others are asked to bear. These Sherpas of Sorrow may come from families that suffer from inheritable fatal diseases, or live in environments plagued by violence or addiction, or seem destined to face tragedy after tragedy without much respite in between.

"It almost started feeling like the norm," remembers thirty-six-year-old Ann Marie, who attended fifteen funerals for relatives and friends by the time she turned twenty-one. "Losing people became familiar, but not easier. It was hard every time for different reasons."

IT'S CUMULATIVE. When episodes of New Grief occur in quick succession or when several deaths occur at once, such as in a combat situation or in accidents that take multiple lives, a state known as "bereavement overload" can develop. Gay men in the 1980s and 1990s, for example, suffered terribly from this during the AIDS crisis when so many friends and lovers died in a relatively short period of time. The Covid-19 pandemic has caused similar tragedy within specific families and communities where multiple losses, sequential or simultaneous, have occurred. These need not all be losses by death; a pileup of losses may also include breakups, divorces, job losses, and the loss of one's own good health.

When it rains it pours, my mother used to lament, and in such a deluge one loss can barely be accommodated before a new one occurs. Just as we feel we're gaining some traction, or even experiencing some growth, another one comes along. As fifty-five-year-old Oscar, who suffered three major losses by age fifteen, describes his adolescence, "I was grieving three different ways, and they were all tributaries of grief into one big fucking lake."

When losses pile up like this, grieving each individual loss separately becomes impossible. A loss-oriented focus may take over, rendering even the simplest practical tasks unachievable or to be consciously or unconsciously pushed aside as a matter of emotional survival. A person struggles to exercise some movement, any movement, when momentum feels painful and nearly impossible to attain. Just getting from one day to the next may be all the adjustment that can be managed, and that has to be enough. Sometimes, the magnitude of pain and trauma really *is* more than one person can bear.

That's what Phoebe experienced when both of her parents died in a private plane crash sixteen years ago. They'd taken off one morning for a weekend getaway, just the two of them in her father's small airplane. A few hours later Phoebe and her three younger siblings learned the plane had gone down en route. There were no survivors.

Within weeks Phoebe arranged for a cross-country job transfer and moved back into the family home. As the oldest child, and a newly minted attorney, she assumed the responsibility for settling her parents' estate. Her days soon filled up with phone calls from attorneys and accountants and government investigators, each with urgent questions to be answered or paperwork to be read and signed or gruesome new details of her parents' deaths to be shared.

Juggling these tasks and the demands of her new workplace left Phoebe with little time to process her emotions. So she made a conscious choice to focus just on the practical matters at hand. Nighttime was the only time she let her guard down. Her sleep became interrupted with violent dreams about her parents' deaths. Fire and crash sites figured prominently. In one recurring dream she would crawl desperately through harvested cornfields to find her parents. In another, she'd be standing in a hot sandstorm screaming at her mother to turn around and notice her. Then she'd wake up exhausted, and start a new day.

"I felt like a rag doll that had been crudely stitched together, with stitches that became more strained with each passing month," Phoebe remembers. "I was trying very hard to keep it all inside, because crying and being sad, at the time, was a luxury I couldn't afford to indulge in. But death demands a reckoning. You either have to deal with it or it will sneak up on you, and that's what happened to me."

Five months after her parents' accident, Phoebe sank into a deep depression. On the recommendation of a therapist, she took a medical leave from work to attend to her grief. First, she worked with the therapist to stabilize the trauma of losing her parents in such a sudden, violent manner. Then, slowly and deliberately, the therapist helped Phoebe dose in and out loss-oriented activities—crying, raging, longing. Only when she began achieving some balance did Phoebe's nightmares begin to recede.

IT'S UNIQUE TO EACH EPISODE. Each iteration of New Grief is particular to the relationship that was lost. The characteristics of any episode will be driven by, among other factors, who died, how they died, the nature of the relationship, the amount of support available, and what was happening in your life at the time.

For example, the New Grief I felt after my mother died was very different from the New Grief I felt when my father died, for several reasons. These included the types of relationships we'd had (with my mother, close; with my father, more emotionally distant); the circumstances of their final days (my mother's in a sterile, impersonal hospital setting; my father's at home, in hospice, surrounded by family); my intellectual and emotional maturity (seventeen years old versus forty); what was required of me as a child versus as an adult (as a child, not much; as an adult, a lot); the stressors I faced at seventeen versus those I faced at forty (school, friends, normal teenage development, and the expectation that I'd help around the house and with my siblings versus full-time work, financial obligations, and two young children); as well as the resources available to me before, during, and after each death (in 1981, almost none; in 2004, much more).

Kat, now forty-four, lost three close family members over a ten-year period. Each experience could hardly be more different, she says. She was twelve and the youngest of three children when her father died from kidney and heart failure. Her dad had been a quiet and introverted man, and though he was always physically present, "I didn't really know him," Kat admits. The period after he died was a time of sadness and shared grief, she recalls. "He had been sick for a while, so I kind of had a sense things might go either way," she says. "I was devastated, but I had my mom and other family members and friends [to comfort me]. There was a huge support system there for me at that point."

Two years later, when Kat's mother died of a heart attack, that support network was no longer accessible. Her mother had been at its center. "Total opposite experience," Kat recalls. "It still makes me very emotional to talk about. I moved in with my sister, who lived only a mile away. She tried her best, but she was thirty-three, with two children and a husband who really wasn't there for her emotionally or physically, and she was trying to preserve her marriage and take care of her kids. For about a month afterward she would ask me, 'How are you doing?' After that it was 'Okay. Enough. This is your life now. Time to move on.' And we hardly talked about my mother again. My mom had a brother, and he and his wife basically said, 'Get over it. It's done. You can't get back that time, and showing your feelings is a weakness.' So there was a lot of shaming there, and I thought there was something wrong with me to still have all this grief."

Kat also felt confused about how her future might unfold without either parent. She developed a sense of fatalism, with thoughts like *I'm not going to make it through this*, she recalls. "And I was really upset with my brother, because I felt that he'd aggravated my mother's heart condition with his drinking," she says. "So at fourteen I put the blame on him for contributing to her death, and I didn't talk to him for five years. I was very angry at the time anyway, and I made him the scapegoat."

Kat's relationship with her brother David, who was fifteen years older, had been marked by highs and lows throughout her childhood. When he was sober, he had been thoughtful and loving and shared his favorite music and television shows with her. When he drank, he turned into someone different—antagonistic and mean. "He was a mixture of a mentor and a bully," Kat remembers.

Still, their family was small now, and the two siblings became committed to healing their rift. By the time Kat was in her early twenties, she and David were communicating from time to time. She was working full-time and living in the family home, and he lived in a house nearby. One day, about a year after they'd last seen each other, David left Kat a voice message about coming over to help with yard work. Kat figured she'd return the call the next day to make plans. But before she had a chance to call, her sister showed up on her doorstep crying, bearing news that David had died a few hours earlier in his sleep. The cause of death was unknown. He was thirty-seven years old.

Unlike in the aftermath of her father's death, when Kat had felt sad but supported, or the long stretch after her mother's death when she'd felt isolated and angry, this time Kat's dominant responses were remorse and guilt. Thoughts of "What if?" and "If only . . ." tormented her. *I wish I'd had more time with him. I wish I could have seen him before he died. What if I'd called him back right away?* She'd already been struggling with depression, and David's death only amplified her distress. A blanket of sadness weighed her down.

Although Kat had support from her boyfriend, his family, and some close friends, the messages she received from her family were the same as before. This time, however, she knew to resist them. "As a kid, you tend to think, 'Okay, they're right. They must know what they're talking about,'" she says. "You're not able to say, 'Well, I disagree. I challenge that. I think you're wrong.'" This time Kat had the agency, and the resources to seek counseling, that she didn't have as a child. Today, she credits therapy, her work with disadvantaged children, and prayer with helping her achieve a state of self-compassion that had eluded her before.

IT'S OFTEN TRANSFORMATIVE. After the most painful months subside, Elisabeth Kübler-Ross has written, "what is left is a new you, a different you, one who will never be the same again or see the world as you once did. A terrible loss of innocence has occurred, only to be replaced with vulnerability, sadness and a new reality where something like this can happen to you and has happened." The world of prior assumptions has been shattered. A worldview undergoes revision. So can an identity, which is to say, our very sense of self.

"A lot of the way I look at this is that this is the me before February 15, 2000, and this is who I was after," explains thirty-two-year-old Lora, who was fourteen when her best friend/first boyfriend died by suicide. "I'm different now than I think I would have been had it not happened. I process things differently. I look at the world differently. I don't know that I was ever a happy-go-lucky, naïve person, but after it happened I had a more jaded perspective. I have a little bit more appreciation for life, but also I don't allow myself to get that close to other people or let them in too far. Maybe, had it not happened, I wouldn't have such a guard up."

Western culture prizes a narrative that frames hard times as occasions for growth, and one's impulse after a loss may be to quickly nudge events in that direction. Yet as Megan Devine reminds us, transformation must be kept in perspective. It's one of many possible outcomes, not an expectation or a demand. Grievers don't need to be told they're getting it wrong if they don't experience grief as a metamorphic affair.

"No one needs life-changing loss to become who they're 'meant to be,'" she explains. "Life is call and response. The path forward is integration, not betterment."

IT'S ALSO SELF-CONTAINED. In its purest form, New Grief is a grief with clear margins. It's not complicated by residual pain from prior losses, and it doesn't require that a mourner revisit or re-grieve a death from the past. If someone close to you dies and you think, *I remember feeling exhausted like this when my sister died*, you're probably comparing a fresh episode of New Grief to a prior one. But if you find yourself thinking, *This feels like losing my sister all over again*, something more than New Grief is probably going on.

I discovered this firsthand about two years ago when my very dear friend Sky died. She'd been diagnosed with a glioblastoma sixteen years earlier—which, if you know anything about glioblastomas, is a remarkable sentence to be able to type. When the tumor was discovered, Sky was told she wouldn't live to see her newborn daughter walk. She lived to see her learn to drive. Over those sixteen years, Sky survived two recurrences of brain cancer, two more surgeries, and more chemotherapy and radiation than anybody should have to bear. She was doing more than just beating the odds: She was beating them into submission. Her doctors and her friends all viewed her as a medical miracle. For sixteen years, she was. Until the third recurrence, which offered little hope of a cure.

Toward the end of her life Sky and I would talk about her sorrow over leaving her daughter, and how grateful she was to have outlived her prognosis by so many years. On good days, we discussed the possibility of an afterlife. Sky believed in one; I was optimistic, but still holding out for proof. On bad days, I'd climb into bed next to her and we'd yell *"FUCK!"* at the ceiling as loud as we could.

On one of my last visits, Sky could no longer speak, but when she saw me a tear rolled down her cheek. I touched my finger to it and put it in my mouth. "Your DNA is inside me now, which means I'll carry a piece of you with me always," I told her. I promised to never pee her out, and she laughed, because it wasn't something I'd normally say, but Sky was sassy and irreverent that way. When she gripped my hand tightly and pressed it to her lips our eyes locked. We both knew. It was the last conscious moment we'd share. I wept so fiercely on the drive home I had to pull over until I could see the road again.

Both of my parents died from end-stage cancer, and during my visits with Sky, memories from their final days would occasionally flutter to the surface. *You remember this part,* they would whisper. *This is how it goes.* Then the thoughts would float away, without emotional charge. Sky's illness and death didn't reactivate old traumas from my past or ask me to reprocess sorrow or anger about what went down when I was seventeen. My sadness was scrupulously attached to *her* suffering, to her family's imminent loss and, after she died, to the absence of her vibrantly cheerful and witty self. God, how I missed her.
Her.

That's how I knew I was experiencing New Grief.

Now, might I find myself missing Sky in one, or five, or ten years and having a resurgent grief response then? Definitely. I fully expect it to happen when her daughter graduates from high school, knowing as I do how much Sky wanted to be there. What I feel on that day will be painful and messy and real. But it won't be New Grief anymore.

The Childhood Exception, Part One: Staggered Grief

BEFORE PSYCHIATRIST John Bowlby's seminal work on separation and loss during childhood, popular opinion held that children couldn't mourn like adults. A child's grief was short-lived, it was believed, if mourning even occurred at all. Bowlby's research taught us that the opposite was true. As one of the first child psychiatrists to directly observe children's behavior, Bowlby studied how even very young children responded when they were separated from their mothers. Their reactions, he concluded, were "substantially the same" as those exhibited by older children and adults when a loved one died.

Relying on his own lab experiments as well as Anna Freud's work with Jewish war orphans during World War II, and research on children in hospitals and residential nurseries, Bowlby observed that even infants as young as six months passed through a series of mourning phases. First they entered a state of protest, marked by crying and frantic attempts to find their mothers. They eagerly awaited her return. This phase could last for as long as a week or more. When the mother could not be located, the child would transition into a state of longing, followed by despair as hope of a reunion faded. If the separation persisted, the child often became hostile, avoidant, and detached, which Bowlby interpreted as a natural defense against emotional pain. When the mother finally returned, the child often rejected her at first, then clung to her as if trying to prevent her from leaving again.

And if she never returned? Fortunately, controlled lab experiments didn't allow these separations to persist. Bowlby could only speculate about where a child's protest, despair, and avoidance might lead if the separation became permanent. He estimated that a child's yearning and searching for a lost loved one could last for months to years.

Without a sense of history, or enough experience to know that life can go on after an essential loved one dies, children can't imagine how anything can continue in the midst of such sorrow. Discovering that life will go on, but without this person, happens bit by bit rather than in a single action or moment of awareness. Only by waking up every morning and going through each day, day after day, does a child learn how to adjust.

Even in familiar surroundings, children can't tolerate the pain of New Grief for long without support and comfort from an adult. That's why children tend to dip into loss-oriented tasks and then step out very quickly. Their oscillation occurs in short, abrupt bursts. This is especially true for younger children, who may act despondent for a brief period and then quickly run off to play for hours, only to burst into tears without any obvious provocation later in the day. An adult who sees a child playing outside after a father's funeral service or notices a teenager goofing around with friends at a sibling's wake and thinks, *Children bounce back so quickly. Children are so resilient!* or wonders, *Doesn't that kid care?* might instead be seeing a child who can't handle the pain of grief in more than small doses, if at all, or who's working through their emotions through play.

Dosing during childhood requires two key components. The first is the assurance that someone will help the child contain their emotions. Young children are amazingly resourceful this way: They'll avoid letting go until they know an emotionally available adult is there to support them. This is why some kids hold off on grieving the loss of a parent or sibling for a year or more, until they notice their surviving parent or parents starting to cope better.

Gender and age also play a role here, with boys typically receiving messages to suppress their emotions and "be the man of the house" and teens often wanting to hide any distress that might invite unwanted attention or make them feel different from their peers. In general, boys are more affected by the death of a parent, and girls by the death of a sibling. According to J. William Worden, a co-principal investigator of the Harvard Child Bereavement Study, one year after the major loss of either a sibling or parent, about 25 percent of children of both genders are at risk for serious emotional or behavioral disturbances, while three-quarters are either adjusting without major incident or "making do."

Second, kids—especially teens—need to be able to move in and out of states of emotional distress. This type of self-regulation is a learned behavior, and children need adults to model this behavior and teach them how it's done. If adult caretakers are incapacitated by their own grief or are suppressing or dismissing their distress, a child might not witness self-regulation in the home. Children in this situation fare better when a different adult can take over this role. Any trusted adult can do this for a child. Sometimes a person outside the family circle who isn't mourning the same loss—a teacher, mentor, family friend, or coach—is better equipped to offer consistent and objective support.

"My father shut down and didn't know how to support me in the immediate aftermath," remembers Darcy Krause, forty-one, the executive director of the Uplift Center for Grieving Children in Philadelphia, who was fifteen when her mother died. "My mother's parents, with whom I was very close, were supportive, but they lived far away, and I think they were somewhat traumatized because this was their second child to die. What I will say, and I don't see this very often in my grief-experience world, is that my school did a great job. The counselor sort of took care of me. There was a teacher who stepped in like a surrogate and became a mentor and life-long friend. These things do not always happen, but they were distinguishing factors about my experience and how I was able to handle it."

For fifty-two-year-old Alisa, that person outside of the family was a neighbor named Lucy. Alisa was six years old and the youngest of four children when her father died after a long struggle with colon cancer. The family was plunged into immediate "crisis mode," Alisa explains. Her mother sank into a deep and persistent depression that lasted for much of Alisa's childhood. Losing her father felt like also losing a part of her mother, she says.

When the death of one parent results in the functional impairment or emotional withdrawal of the other, a form of double parent loss occurs, explains New York City therapist George Hagman. The de facto departure of a surviving parent due to depression, addiction, or a previous lack of availability is especially difficult for kids, he says, because it creates an ongoing secondary loss—a "double jeopardy"—for them on top of the primary one. And this creates a terrible situation, given that consistent parenting is known to be the most important factor in a child's long-term adjustment.

"As a consequence, not only does the mourning process often cease," Hagman explains, "but there may also be a skewing of normal development, as emergency adaptations are initiated to cope with possible, or actual, family collapse." A child's coping strategies, developed as workarounds for a lack of parental attention or support, may persist long after that child leaves the family home.

When the surviving parent is unable to parent effectively for a long period of time, the child's distress is compounded. In the short term, dysfunction of the surviving parent has been associated with children's withdrawal, anxiety, depression, health problems, sleep disturbances, social problems, helplessness, and difficulty remaining connected to the dead parent. Years later, growing up in such an environment has been linked to decreased levels of self-worth and self-esteem among adults.

Alisa recalls the fear and frustration she felt when she was unable to engage her mother's attention in meaningful ways. "As a kid, I felt like, 'Mom, I'm still here!' " she says. " 'I know you're so sad that Dad has died, and I know this is a terrible thing, but I want to be a kid and you still have a family. Can't you just enjoy us?' It was like his death created a void inside her that no one else could fill, and even though other people tried, we could never be enough for her, because her happy was gone. She could only focus on the loss of my dad. At least that's how it felt to me."

When Alisa was fourteen, she took a job babysitting for a local family. Lucy, the mother in that family, encouraged Alisa to express her feelings, especially around her father's death, which was never discussed at home.

"She would ask me questions like 'How did that feel?' " Alisa recalls. "Having someone ask that question and listen to my answers helped me realize: Actually, this was kind of big. At my house it was always 'Don't cry,' but Lucy gave me the opportunity to cry, and she did it without expressing pity. I can't overstate the importance of having somebody say, 'This is okay. This is normal' when I responded that way."

In my coaching practice, I often work with people who say they never grieved the loss of a parent or sibling who died when they were young. As adults, they're hesitant about opening the grief box now. "I'm afraid that if I start crying, I'll never stop," they say.

I know this fear. I once had it myself. The possibility of losing control of my emotions, without knowing how to regain it, was too unsettling to consider.

This fear defies both logic and science, I know. Emotional states are, by their very definition, transitory. The average crying episode for a man lasts only two to three minutes; for women, six minutes is the average. Only in extreme instances do tears continue, nonstop, for more than an hour. In fact, it's *physiologically impossible* to start crying and never stop. Even people with neurological conditions that cause uncontrollable outbursts of weeping can't sustain those episodes for very long.

But that's not really what these people are talking about, is it?

The fear of uncontrollable crying is a fear of faulty self-regulation, of feeling distress without the presence of a compassionate, stable other to help us contain and process it. That's the fear of a vulnerable child. It's not an inevitable outcome for an adult.

In the past it may have been the case that someone *wasn't* there to comfort you when you cried. You may not have had the maturity or the agency or the inner fortitude when you were young to cope with extreme distress on your own. Even brief ventures into New Grief may have felt threatening. Keeping a safe distance from those emotions, for as long as you could, may have been a necessary form of self-protection.

Fortunately, dosing that didn't occur in the past can be activated or reactivated in adulthood. At every retreat I lead there are motherless daughters in middle age and beyond who were never encouraged or permitted to speak about their mothers' lives or deaths. On our first morning together, we start with a lengthy session of "Story Witnessing," an activity that therapist Claire Bidwell Smith and I developed in 2016. Every woman in the circle—typically twenty-six in total—has five uninterrupted minutes to speak about anything she wants. We encourage starting with "I've been waiting a long time to talk about . . ."

Five minutes is a lot of time to fill when you're the only one talking. For some women, it's the first opportunity to have their stories received with curiosity and compassion instead of pity or impatience. For some, it's the first time they've had permission to speak freely about this past event. And a new identity starts to take shape almost in real time. These women are no longer daughters who have to keep their story of loss secret and undercover. They're now women who've shared it with a room of compassionate others. It's also the first time most of the women have heard so many other stories that resemble their own. As we make our way around the circle, one by one, the room becomes so quiet with all the listening you can hear a tissue crumple.

I'd led twelve retreats before I realized Story Witnessing was a forum to practice dosing. Group members can see that when they dip into grief with the support of the larger circle, they don't start crying and then find themselves unable to stop. That does not ever happen. When the iPhone timer chimes after five minutes, the women very much *do* have the ability to tuck their emotions back in. They'll "fall apart" for their five minutes in the morning session and by lunchtime they'll be laughing and talking about their jobs or their kids or the book they're reading this month. They're perfectly capable of regulating their emotions. They just needed a safe, contained environment for testing this out, the social support of compassionate others, and the self-confidence that can only come from trying, and discovering it works.

CHAPTER FOUR

Old Grief: Recurrent and Resurgent

Caught in the throes of New Grief, you may worry that the pain will never end, that you'll never find a pathway out of its intensity. This is unlikely to happen. Only in very rare cases does grief continue uninterrupted. It might, however, never completely disappear. Grief likes to go dormant for long stretches, offering extended periods of normalcy that are punctuated by occasional and often unanticipated spikes of sadness or longing.

The spikes? Those are episodes of Old Grief.

New Grief is a present-day reaction to a recent loss. Old Grief is something very different. Old Grief is a *response in the present to a loss from the past.* It's recurrent and often unpredictable, capable of bubbling up years or even decades after the original loss event.

What's going on? we might wonder.

Why now, after all this time?

I thought I was over this already.

Or maybe just *Here we go again.*

Old Grief can be a trickster: Sometimes you recognize it, sometimes you don't. You might understand exactly what's happening while it's happening, and why. That's called a "reality type" of reaction. Or you might not recognize what's going on until someone helps you make the connection. That's called an "unconscious sense of time."

In both instances, you may find yourself sucked into what feels like an earlier physical, cognitive, emotional, or behavioral state and—after months or even years of quiet, steady adjustment—there you are, missing that person or grieving the loss of the relationship all over again. You'd found purchase on solid ground and now you find yourself trying to gain traction on a floor covered with marbles.

Such Old Grief reactions are also known as Sudden Temporary Upsurges of Grief, or STUGs. STUG reactions, a term coined by Therese Rando, are brief periods of acute grief attached to the loss of a loved one. They occur when a trigger in the present reactivates thoughts, emotions, physical symptoms or social behaviors associated with the loss. You might feel confused or even ashamed of what feels like an inability to control regressive impulses. You might feel restless, angry, anxious, or afraid. Sadness and longing come rushing back in.

Old Grief frequently recurs around annual dates of remembrance, such as Father's Day or Mother's Day, and on dates that hold personal meaning, like a birthday or the anniversary of a death. "Holiday Syndrome," also a form of Old Grief, is common between Thanksgiving and New Year's Day, when expectations of cheerful family gatherings can lead to feelings of isolation, helplessness, irritability, depression, nostalgia, or bitterness about holidays past, and regressive behavior in those whose families have lost their cohesion.

Old Grief can also hitch a ride on New Grief, when a new loss sends us back in time to revisit and reevaluate pieces of a prior loss that weren't addressed in the past. And sometimes Old Grief shows up spontaneously and unannounced, and smacks us sideways in the middle of an otherwise ordinary day.

Fortunately, Old Grief is a short-term visitor. It's like the Airbnb of bereavement: No matter how bad a stay is, you know it's eventually going to end. Flare-ups that persist and persist are often evidence of something more complicated and may require professional help to manage. But most of the time, Old Grief comes and goes. And comes and goes. And comes. And goes.

Three types of Old Grief show up with frequency. Let's call them Cyclical Grief, Sneak Attacks, and Resurrected Grief.

Cyclical Grief

[Daniel] died on October 8, and for years during the first week of October I would relive that week with "This is the day I started feeling contractions, and this is the hour of his birth, and this is when he died, and this is the next day . . ." It was never gone from my mind during that whole week. This is really the first year that I didn't give it as much thought. The anniversary was two days ago, and it was already late in the day on the eighth when I thought of it.

—CECILE, seventy-three, whose infant son Daniel
died forty-five years ago, soon after his birth

For the first year after Andrew died, I shut it out and didn't deal with it. My mom's philosophy of grief was "Stay busy and don't think about it." She immersed herself in a graduate program, and I took the first job that was offered to me after school ended.

That March, around the first anniversary of Andrew's death, I was at work, and I did not know what was going on with me. I thought I was getting sick. I wound up going to a psychiatrist and getting some anxiety meds. She didn't directly link it to my brother's death. I even went to my brother's therapist, and she didn't link it, either.

The following year [in March], my foot was bothering me and I was feeling achy. I was getting worried that something was wrong with me, and then it escalated into paranoia and anxiety. I wound up taking a leave from work and spending six weeks in the hospital. Even then, several professionals missed what was going on. Nobody ever said, "You're having an intense grief reaction to losing your brother." I had to figure it out on my own.

—LINDA, fifty-four, who was twenty-one
when her older brother died in a car accident

My sister observes everything. Every time it's our mother's death anniversary, or our mother's birthday, she will make a point to mark it somehow and go to the temple and do something. I don't do that.

Mother's Day sometimes gets under my skin a little bit, like, the week before I'll start feeling blue, but I just don't necessarily want to make a big deal out of it. I don't know if I'm doing my kids a disservice by not doing anything. I guess I don't know, really, how to mark it in a way that's meaningful to me.

—PRIYA, forty-eight, who was in the second grade
when her mother died of breast cancer

CECILE, LINDA, and Priya: three women with three different losses, and three different responses to cyclical grief. Cecile's reminiscences about her infant son's death were a conscious and predictable annual ritual for many years. For Linda, an unconscious reaction occurred twice before she recognized its connection to her brother's death. And Priya continues to search for meaningful ways to mark annual events related to her mother's life and death.

Cyclical grief episodes have been a topic of scientific interest since the early years of psychoanalysis, when Freud wrote about them in *Studies on Hysteria* in 1895. His case study of Fraulein Elisabeth Von R. described how she had nursed several family members through their deaths at home, as women of that era often did. After each death, Ms. Von R. would keep reviewing the scenes of her loved ones' final days in chronological order, crying, and then consoling herself. In addition to these reminiscences, Freud observed, Ms. Von R. also "celebrated annual festivals of remembrance at the period of her various catastrophes, and on these occasions her vivid visual reproductions and expressions of feeling kept to the date precisely."

Sixty-six years later, C. S. Lewis eloquently described cyclical grief in his memoir, *A Grief Observed*, the story of losing his wife, Joy Davidman, to cancer. "For in grief nothing 'stays put,'" Lewis wrote. "One keeps on emerging from a phase but it always recurs. Round and round. Everything repeats."

With each turn of the cycle, the cumulative impact builds. Another year marks one more birthday a sibling has missed; one more Father's Day without a father to call or visit; one more Thanksgiving since the last time everyone gathered together to celebrate. This is an example of how the facts of a death *do* change. Bigger numbers and more years often carry more weight, not less. I almost never hear anyone say, "My father died twenty years ago, and twenty is a lot easier than ten." I do often hear people say, "My dad passed away twenty years ago, and every year on Father's Day I miss him all over again."

The anniversary of a loved one's death, popularly referred to as a "deathiversary," holds special weight, since it marks another full year since the person was physically present. It also stirs up memories of a loved one's final day. The shock of receiving unexpected news, the anguish of detaching life support mechanisms or saying goodbye, the crosstown or cross-country race to the hospital to try to arrive in time . . . all of this can come rushing back, especially when seasonal sensory triggers such as air temperature, the appearance of flowers and trees, and the hour of sunrise or sunset are also in sync.

As time marches on, we are also often left to observe or endure deathiversaries on our own. The social support that was available in the first weeks or months after a loss tends to have petered out by the one-year mark. This may be why adult mourners typically experience a noticeable decrease in functioning at the one-year anniversary and, after a year of steady and incremental recovery, typically face another dip at the two-year anniversary point. They're revisiting the loss internally, but by then they're often doing it alone. Death anniversaries for siblings, in particular, may be treated as overlooked or "disenfranchised" grief, since these occasions are often treated as the parents' loss rather than the family's as a whole.

A first death anniversary is just that: a first, and therefore a novel experience. A second anniversary, however, signifies that the absence is an ongoing and unchangeable reality. Facing this can bring additional sadness and even despair, Terrie Rando says. "Also, the expectation typically is that the reaction this time will be less intense," she explains. "Often the mourner is shocked when this is not the case, which only adds to his emotional distress, fuels his fears that he will never be able to master the loss, and presents him with yet one more violation of his assumptive world."

Western culture has intricate rituals for commemorating wedding anniversaries (paper for a first, wood for a fifth, china for a twentieth, and so on) but not so, not yet, for a death anniversary. An initiative by the Modern Loss on- and offline community to name the day as a "deathiversary" and a joint effort between Motherless Daughters and Seeking Ceremony to suggest annual rituals for mother loss have recently begun, but in the meantime mourners make plans and create commemorative rituals that have personal meaning to them.

"On her death date I try to do something to honor her, or do something for myself that I feel she would have liked me to do for myself," says forty-two-year-old Sabina, who was twenty-two when her mother died of breast cancer. "When it was the twentieth anniversary of her death date I created a legacy page for her, and I did an online fundraiser to raise money for charities for young at-risk kids, because when she was a social worker she worked for people at risk."

We tend to think of cyclical grief as tied to calendar dates, but it can also align with a time of day, day of the week, or season of the year. August and September, when the academic term begins in the United States, can be particularly difficult for parents who've lost children, and also for siblings missing a brother or sister with whom they would have started the new school year. Spring with its metaphor of rebirth, and autumn with its shortening of days and aura of decay, are also common times for flare-ups to occur.

As Linda's story illustrated, a cycle may need to recur several times before the conscious mind notices. My sister recently told me it took thirty years for her to realize that her discomfort at night was associated with being woken at 3 A.M. by our father saying, "It's over," on a morning in 1981. Adult Michele knew the likelihood of receiving such news again on any given night was slim, but Younger Michele dreaded the possibility and kept going into hypervigilant mode after the sun went down.

This tendency to take up silent residence has long been a curious feature of cyclical grief. Psychiatrist Barney Dlin wrote about an unconscious, internal calendar that quietly keeps time on its own, long after sadness has faded from the conscious mind. He believed that unaddressed trauma from the original event could get stored in the body as a "somatic time bomb" that waits to be set off by a cyclical event. In fact, trauma—meaning a sudden, disruptive experience that overwhelms an individual's capacity to cope using his or her existing inner resources, and causes states of powerlessness and emotional and mental paralysis—is considered to be the most salient factor in setting off an anniversary reaction. Early trauma that recurs around cyclical events has been linked to experiencing a parental illness or death, a sibling death, incest and physical abuse, and to witnessing or surviving accidental or intentional violence.

Historically, traumatic bereavement has been associated with deaths that include violence. But a growing number of psychologists believe that all forms of unexpected, sudden loss are traumatic to survivors, and some consider any loss during childhood to be a traumatic experience.

When cyclical grief leads to a traumatic recall of events, a mourner may experience emotional, psychological, behavioral, and somatic responses similar to those that took place around the original loss. Thinking, *This feels exactly like losing her all over again*, is a sign this could be happening. But for most mourners, Terrie Rando says, the most challenging element of cyclical grief is the awareness that it's bound to return. Thinking, *This will happen again, because it happened before and I can't do anything about it*, can send mourners into spirals of helplessness and hopelessness in the lead-up.

The anticipation, however, is often worse than the actuality. When we project into the future we can create a distorted picture of how a day or event might unfold. The Thanksgivings I start picturing each year in early November are always small, sad, lonely gatherings, nothing like the large, noisy tables of my childhood. This is why Thanksgiving is my least favorite holiday of the year now. Most of my friends travel out of town for the weekend or spend the holiday at their parents' or siblings' homes. A cyclical sadness always grips me two or three weeks before the holiday weekend, and lasts until Friday morning.

Now, I'm compelled to point out—we never had a terrible Thanksgiving at home as a nuclear family. But damn if I haven't spent every lead-up lamenting the absence of a large family gathering we can host or join.

Nancy, who lost her son, Lee, when he was nineteen and who now runs support groups for suicide survivors, recommends creating a concrete plan in advance of a dreaded day or event. The important part of having this kind of plan, she emphasizes, is . . . having a plan. By creating a clear picture in your mind of what you can realistically make happen, and taking steps in the direction of that desired image, you exercise some agency over the outcome. You also get to populate the day with things you might enjoy.

"I learned that if I was prepared, the wave of grief I was expecting couldn't knock me down as long," Nancy explains. "Or when it came I could accept it, let it knock me down, and then swim to shore. I tell people to have a plan for how to get through the first birthday, or whatever the holiday is, and to also be totally willing to throw the plan out the window on that day if the plan no longer feels right. If you have a plan, you'll think you're more in control of your emotions than you actually are, and that is comfort in and of itself, to think you have control."

Otherwise, you may wind up "holding yourself hard" against anticipated distress, says Allison Werner-Lin, a psychologist in New York City who specializes in adolescent bereavement. At the start of every school year, her teenage clients steel themselves against the predictable first assignment in English class to write their autobiographies. Structuring the story in their minds beforehand and pre-deciding what they do and don't want to include can reduce the homework's emotional charge when the day of the dreaded assignment arrives.

"In the beginning, I would type up my plan," Nancy remembers.

"I would have on it, 'Cry from eleven to eleven-thirty.' Really. And I would let myself cry and rant and rave and scream, and then it would be eleven-thirty and I'd say, 'Okay. Now what? Oh, we're going to meet Grant and Lisa and have lunch. All right. Go take your shower.' It enabled me to make it through the day. Now I make a much less detailed list. I might have three things on it, but they're still all about making it through the day."

Nancy also suggests lining up a social support network in advance. Friends and family won't know you're anticipating a flare-up unless you tell them. Choose a few trusted confidantes, people you know won't expect you to be "over it" and won't judge you if you're not. Ask them to input key dates into their calendars and check in with you around that time.

"It's a way of telling them, 'I'd like to talk,'" Nancy says. "Every year around Lee's birthday, one of my friends will call a week before and say, 'What are we going to do this year to celebrate the boy?'" In this way, Nancy is never left to commemorate Lee's birthday alone.

And that's especially important to her, because Lee's birthday is the day she has chosen for annual remembrance. "I'm finally moving away from the anniversary of his death," she explains. "Because no matter what the church says, there's nothing to celebrate there. I used to take flowers to his tree on the anniversary of his death. Now I do it on his birthday, because to me, he's more than his death. Also, on the holidays that he really loved I'll do something that relates to him. On his birthday I might send a cake to somebody that he liked or someone he never knew but I bet he would have liked. On the Fourth of July, if I'm at the beach, I'll look at the ocean and remember how much fun he had with crab races and swimming. Just a little moment of reflection sometimes is all it is, but it's pleasant. It doesn't take away the sting, but it smooths the ridges."

All anniversary dates don't have to be acknowledged. Dropping some isn't evidence you care less about the person. Sometimes it's a necessary form of self-care. Creativity is essential, too. Your method of coping with long-term bereavement is *your* method, and you get to decide how it's done.

I like to apply the "Where's the law that says . . . ?" test. As in, where's the law that says Mother's Day can't be a day for commemorating mothers who are no longer living? Where's the law that says a death anniversary has to be a somber remembrance? Where's the law that says we have to acknowledge that date every year?

Where's the law that says Thanksgiving has to be celebrated on a Thursday?

After a dozen or so terrible Novembers, it finally occurred to me that if all of our friends were occupied with their families on Thanksgiving day, we could celebrate our holiday on Friday instead. So now we have a small dinner together or with a few friends on Thursday, and the following night we open our home to all of our friends. Some years, as many as sixty people will show up with their Thanksgiving leftovers, often relieved to have a night with friends after spending a whole day and night with their extended families. The house fills with laughter, there's always an abundance of food, and we play Rolling Stones songs in the kitchen until late in the night. I actually look forward to Thanksgiving weekend now.

It's taught me that over the long arc, year after year, a certain type of resilience can start to build. The cumulative effect works in this direction, too. Each year, a little voice of confidence increases in volume. *You've got this*, it says. *You've done this before. You can do it again.* This is a way that time truly *can* heal. Time plus action, that is. What we do with the time is what matters.

Sneak Attacks

ON SEPTEMBER 11, 1974, seventy-two of the eighty-two passengers on board Eastern Airlines flight 212 died when the plane crashed on its approach into Charlotte Douglas International Airport. Among the passengers that morning were the father and two older brothers of television host Stephen Colbert. Colbert was ten years old at the time.

Forty-six years have passed since that tragic event. Nonetheless, certain and very specific shards of memory from that summer, Colbert says, can still pierce him in an instant. "The song of the summer was 'Band on the Run,' " he told Anderson Cooper in a 2019 CNN interview. "Do not play 'Band on the Run' around me."

When I heard Colbert say this, I immediately thought, *James Taylor. "Fire and Rain."*

The date was July 4, 1981. The place was the Belmont Park race track in Elmont, New York. I'd driven to the track with three friends that afternoon to hear James Taylor perform in a Sunset Series concert, an event that proceeded, rain or shine. In our case, lots of rain. When Taylor played the opening bars to "Fire and Rain" on his guitar, the crowd cheered in both recognition and solidarity. We all got soaked together as we sang along under a steady, unbroken curtain of rain.

Later that night I returned home to unequivocal evidence that my mother was much sicker than anyone had been letting on. Like, *much.* In just the eight or nine hours I'd been gone, her stomach had swelled to the size of a six-month pregnancy. That's a classic sign of liver failure, though I didn't know it at the time. She died eight days later. The burial took place in her family's plot at a cemetery in Elmont, New York, only two miles from the race track. The funeral procession passed right by the front gates. Just to rub it in, it seemed to me.

For a solid decade afterward, I couldn't listen to "Fire and Rain" without coming apart. I mean, those lyrics? Come on. *Just yesterday morning they let me know you were gone . . . But I always thought that I'd see you again.* I'd have to quickly turn off the radio or abruptly exit a room.

Poor James Taylor. It wasn't his fault that his song became a sensory trigger that would set off a grief response in me for the next ten years. The same thing would happen when I heard "Three Times a

Lady" by the Commodores, one of my mother's favorite songs. Or when I saw Good Humor toasted almond bars, which were her favorite—and only—ice cream choice. Or caught the lingering scent of Chanel No. 5 or Charlie perfumes after a stranger walked by. For longer than I'd like to admit, I kept a wide berth from the Chanel counter in every department store I entered.

These sneak attacks, sometimes called "pangs" or "stabs" of grief, occur when an associative memory is summoned, typically by a song, smell, place, food, forgotten object, or person who looks like the deceased. As one of the powerhouses of bereavement research, British psychiatrist Colin Murray Parkes explained in his 1985 article "Bereavement," "The bereaved do not forget the past; rather, they gradually discover which assumptions continue to be relevant and enriching in their new life situation and which have to be abandoned. However, the old assumptive world remains in the mind—a network of association into which the bereaved can again be switched by anything which brings the dead person to mind."

Sneak attacks activate that mental network, sometimes faster than we thought possible. The blade of memory cuts straight into the bone, exposing marrow to air. Time folds in on itself. We can't tell if we've been hurled backward or if a departed loved one has been suddenly pulled into the present.

Sneak attacks are, well, sneaky. That's what makes them so maddening. They can't be anticipated. They're completely out of our control. Who can predict what song will suddenly be piped into the elevator between floors six and eighteen? Who can prepare for the man sitting three rows ahead at a sports event wearing your father's favorite hat? Or for the restaurant server who appears at the edge of your table, looking just like you imagine your sister would if she'd lived into adulthood?

Even the most harmless interactions can expose a hidden landmine. Unlike cyclical grief, you cannot plan ahead for sneak attacks. You can only react when they occur.

"I remember riding the bus home from work one day," recalls

novelist Hannah Gersen in her 2016 essay "No More Dead Mothers: Reading, Writing, and Grieving." "It was a good day, I felt happy and free, and then I glanced at the passenger next to me—I wanted her to know I was getting off—and I saw a to-do list peeking out of her paperback novel, a list that began with, "Call mom." A hot arrow went through my heart. Why? This was the question I asked myself as I disembarked and walked the rest of the way home. Why, where does this pain come from? The heat? I didn't feel the presence of my mother's ghost that day, I hadn't been longing for her. It took a few blocks before I understood that it was the girl that I longed for, the girl who needed to remind herself to call the person who loved her most in the world; *she* was the girl I would have been if my mother hadn't died."

Sneak attacks—like anniversary events—can cut particularly deep when a loss involves unaddressed trauma. In such a circumstance, subsequent sensory triggers, especially those with sudden and abrupt onsets, can reactivate a traumatic response that's been stored deep in the central nervous system. The nervous system then responds to the sneak attack as if it were reexperiencing the original event.

Surprise associations are most likely to be painful when one's strongest and most defining memories of a relationship involve violence, loss, emotional pain, or absence. Bereavement covers three of those, and a violent loss all four. This is probably why, before I started therapy in my twenties, I felt a cold splash of adrenaline and an accelerated heartbeat every time someone asked about my mother, even in passing. For the longest time, that vision of her in a hospital bed at the end of her life replaced all of my memories of her for the preceding seventeen years. It took real effort to remember what had come before. Only when I developed a new internal relationship with her, one that wasn't focused on the trauma of her death, did my earlier memories of her return.

To lessen the impact of sneak attacks, lingering trauma must first be stabilized. This typically requires help from a therapist trained in trauma-informed bereavement work. Without this step, mourners will keep bumping up against a layer of trauma each time they try to access the bittersweet emotions of grief. A therapist may start by helping the mourner reconnect with positive aspects of the lost relationship through searching for memories and stories of connection. In this way, memories of attachment begin to balance out the images of trauma or violence.

When psychiatrist Edward Rynearson, founder of the Separation and Loss Services program at Virginia Mason Medical Center in Seattle, works with clients who've lost loved ones to violent death, he first assesses each client's capacity to feel physically and emotionally safe. About 10 to 15 percent of mourners experience traumatic bereavement in conjunction with separation distress after a death, he says. He works with these individuals to build inner resilience first, often through self-calming exercises and by sharing happy memories of the deceased. Otherwise, he explains, talking about the specifics of the death can retraumatize the bereaved and result in mental and physical distress in the form of heart palpitations, shortness of breath, panic and anxiety attacks, and intense fears of falling apart emotionally. Once resilience has been achieved, the bereaved are led through Restorative Retelling, a process Rynearson developed, to create a story about the death they can carry forward and a relationship with the deceased that's not dominated by images of violence.

Trauma can also cause an individual to dissociate a part of themselves, as if sending away the piece that's too painful to remain present. Therapists specifically trained in trauma-informed work can help bring those pieces back into the present.

"Some of the people who say, 'I feel like a piece of me is stuck in the past,' well, indeed there is a piece stuck in the past," explains Terrie Rando. "I have to go back with those people and find that little kid that got sent away when Daddy was murdered, and deal with it in the psychological sense and bring her forward."

The most common self-protective hedge against sneak attacks is to try to avoid obvious memory triggers. That also might be impossible. Is Hannah Gerson going to avoid ever sitting next to a woman on a bus again? Of course not. Just as I couldn't stop talking to people who might have inadvertently put the words "your" and "mother" together in a sentence. Because that would have meant avoiding, well, everyone.

Even when it *is* possible to get rid of objects, avoid specific family members or friends, or stay away from places that remind you of the deceased, the solution to one problem may only lead to another. "People who do that possibly miss some grieving, but it is more likely that their efforts to avoid grief create additional grief (grief for the lost memorabilia, grief over the home that they moved from in order to avoid feeling grief, grief over lack of contact with the living who are being avoided, and so on)," writes psychologist Paul Rosenblatt, a professor at the University of Minnesota. "It is also likely that grief work cannot be put off indefinitely, that an avoidance of certain reminders of a loss makes it likely that one will grieve later on, as one encounters still other reminders that set off the process of dealing with emotionally charged memories and hopes."

Even without trauma, intense memories can still be neutralized, though this process takes time. A memory needs to be summoned, and new associations have to be created. For example, I had a friend when I lived in Tennessee who sometimes wore Chanel No. 5 perfume when we went out in a group at night. The first time I smelled it, my body responded with a startle. I felt a wave of panic coming on. *That was then, this is now,* I reflexively reminded myself. *Then you were a child. Now you're an adult.* After a while, I started associating Chanel No. 5 with this friend, too. Now I keep a bottle on my dresser and occasionally spray it in the air to remember both my mother and my nights in Knoxville. I even wear it myself from time to time.

Most sneak attacks come and go in a short period of time, like my Levon Helm/supermarket moment in the car in chapter 1. But a response that lasts longer may indicate a need for professional assistance. If you're concerned about a sneak attack, consider the following questions:

1. Does the intensity of the response feel out of proportion to the precipitating event?
2. Is the duration of the response lasting for longer than feels bearable?
3. Is the response interfering with your normal daily functioning?
4. Has the sneak attack reactivated coping mechanisms that have a negative impact on you or others?

If the answer to one of more of these questions is yes, then individual therapy, bereavement groups for recent loss, or support for long-ago loss is recommended.

Let's also remember: Sneak attacks aren't exclusively negative events. Yes, they remind us of what was lost and of what can no longer be. But they also serve as bittersweet reminders of a love and a bond that was once shared.

A few years ago, Terrie Rando was sitting in a coffee shop when a woman walked in with her elderly mother. "Now, have I seen women come in with their mothers to various places over the course of my forty-six years without my mother?" she says. "Of course I have. But there was something about this, on this day, this woman, and how the two of them interacted. You would have thought that I lost my mother last month. I didn't make a scene or anything but the grief . . . I get tears in my eyes right now just telling the story.

"Would it be unhealthy if, after forty-six years, I'm like this all the time?" she continues. "Yes. That would be very unhealthy. But at the point this happened, I hadn't had an experience like this for years. I'd had little mini ones, where once in a while I'd see something or read something or my kids would say something and I'd get a little lump in my throat. But not like this. Personally, I would never want to get to the point where I would never ever again encounter something like this that could make me have a reaction like that. I don't want to spend 24/7 doing it, and I don't even want to do it real frequently, but I never want to be so blasé about this that once in a while something couldn't really touch me."

Because maybe these arrows to the heart, and these deep pangs of longing, aren't something that needs to be erased or fixed. Maybe we don't need to heal ourselves out of them but instead to welcome them as evidence of our capacity to love with intensity and passion. Maybe this is part of what makes us human. And if so, why would we want to give that up?

"It would be a mistake to think of grief as necessarily a bad thing," maintains Paul Rosenblatt in his essay "Grief That Does Not End."

> People may often welcome grief recurrence, and even if there is a sad or bitter side to it there may also be a sweet, affirming, and to-be-cherished side. The positive elements of grief may include memories of how important the person who died was to one or memories of a particularly joyous or profound time together. A widow or widower may remember times of intense passion, of youthful play, of caresses and kind words. A bereaved parent may remember a child's laughter, the tender feelings of holding a sleeping infant, or a child's creative mischief. Thus, recurrent grief is not like recurrent illness. It can be a link with the best of life, an affirmation of light and joy. This is not to say that recurrent grief is not difficult for many people but to say that there is much more to it than sorrow.

Resurrected Grief

LAST SUMMER our thirteen-year-old cat Timmy died after a cluster of tumors developed in his abdomen. I say "developed," though by the time an ultrasound was performed, the tumors had been nesting there for quite some time. The vet suggested putting him down that day. My older daughter, who'd brought him in, said no. Timmy had been a cranky, charismatic, hilarious member of our family for thirteen years. Everyone needed to say goodbye. She brought him home to live out his last days with us.

As Timmy was dying, a therapist asked me whether anything was coming up for me around the deaths of either of my parents. *What?* I remember thinking. *No. Timmy is a* cat. It seemed like such an odd question to be asked, given the context. But if I'm being honest, I had some culpability for Timmy's late diagnosis. He'd been ill for some time, losing weight and eating less than usual. When I brought him to the vet to be checked, his blood labs came back normal. At the time I was overwhelmed with work and family, and it was easy to convince myself that he was just slowing down, as aging cats sometimes do. Still. I could have pressed for an ultrasound then. I could have taken him for a second opinion. That's the thing about retrospect. Through its lens, there's *always* something more or something different that could have been done.

I tried to do right by Timmy near the end by setting up a kitty hospice in my bedroom, working from my bed on weekdays, holding the water bowl up to his chin to keep him hydrated, carrying him to and from the litter box. When we crossed the line from me helping him stay alive to me keeping him alive, we lay on the bed together and I explained that it was time. He didn't object. I told him I was sorry. I'd like to think he forgave me. Nonetheless. The guilt afterward had serious depth. And I realized that if I'd been carrying residual guilt from a prior death . . . well, maybe the therapist's question wasn't such a strange one, after all.

A new loss in the present has the capacity to revive elements of a loss from the past. That's the very nature of Resurrected Grief.

"One of the most significant reminders of previous loss is a new loss," Paul Rosenblatt has explained. "Thus, the fresh grief for a new loss may often be entangled in grief for other losses, and quite possibly, each recurrence of grief for one loss may set off grieving for other losses."

Certain aspects of a new loss might closely resemble those of an earlier loss, such as an illness that follows a similar trajectory or the death of a second parent or sibling. Emotions such as fear for the future or confusion about how to proceed may be so reminiscent of the past that trying to sort out what belongs to then and what belongs to now can feel muddy and uncertain.

That muddiness, however, can create opportunity to unearth and process pieces of a loss that you either weren't ready or weren't able to access before. That's what fifty-year-old Sasha discovered three years ago when she was dealt the double blow of the end of her marriage and the death of her older brother.

Sasha was twelve and the youngest of five siblings when their father died of heart failure. Five months later their mother died from complications of breast cancer. Her three older sisters were already out living on their own. Her brother Marcus, who was sixteen, went to live with relatives in the Midwest, while Sasha moved in with relatives on the East Coast. The five children would never live together in the same house again. Over the next three decades, their ties to one another loosened due to geography and lack of communication.

When Marcus died of heart trouble at age fifty, Sasha was a recently divorced single mother. "When he passed it hit me very hard," she recalls, "but it also, I think, forced me to confront a lot of my grief I thought I had handled along the way but had not. I had to make arrangements for my daughter to stay with friends and family, drive her there, and then drive to the Midwest for the funeral. I realized that even though I was well into my forties, I had never done that kind of traveling by myself before. I was trying to figure out how to do all that driving, and I was crying. I was a bit of a mess. I realized I felt very much alone. It definitely brought up a lot of things that were beneath the surface."

This specific, piercing type of loneliness was familiar to Sasha; she'd felt it when her parents died, and again when she divorced. As a child, she'd suffered from terrible anxiety, especially at night. As an adult, she could tolerate sitting with that feeling and even exploring it. "It took me a while to figure out that deep inside I had held onto a childhood wish that somehow I would connect with my siblings all together again," she explains, "and with my brother's passing, that was kind of like, 'Oh my God, it can never happen now.'"

Pieces of grief from Sasha's childhood were resurrected when Marcus died. She also experienced the secondary loss of a possible renewed five-sibling family connection. She hadn't even known that desire had existed until her brother's death brought it up to the surface. That specific piece of her original grief—the loss of close sibling relationships and the desire for reunion—had been buried all that time.

Neil Chethik, author of *Fatherloss*, has noticed that men who've lost their fathers tend to have papered over their grief quickly and moved on, and then come to a gradual recognition that's something's going wrong. Their marriage is floundering, or they keep getting fired, or they have a strained relationship with a child. A number of men interviewed for his book, Chethik observed, spoke openly of dealing with their fathers' long-ago deaths for the first time when one of these other losses arose.

"My sense is that men, being less schooled in our own emotional intelligence, won't think there's something wrong psychologically," he explains. "They'll just try to plow through it and get to the other side, thinking, 'It'll go away tomorrow' or whatever. It isn't until something like an alcoholic breakdown or a divorce comes along that they wake up to what's actually behind their struggle."

Pieces of grief can lie dormant for years, or even decades, before an episode of new grief reactivates them, especially if a legacy loss was mismanaged or suppressed. Resurrected grief may then show up when the next loss occurs. Or the next one.

Rhonda was fourteen when her mother died of breast cancer in the spring of 1969. "There was religion, but there was no support," she remembers. "There was no hospice. There was no counseling. You put up, you shut up, and you just closed off. My family was really rigid Roman Catholic, and the thing I always heard was 'It's God's will.'"

Rhonda married soon after high school, divorced a few years later, remarried, and raised two children into adulthood. Six years ago, her son and his girlfriend gave birth to Rhonda's second grandson. But the infant's mother was struggling with an opioid addiction, and when the baby was seven and a half weeks old she passed out in bed with him on her breast. Tragically, he suffocated while she was asleep.

Rhonda's shock and horror when she received the news felt painfully familiar to her. In an instant, she was emotionally catapulted forty-three years back. "I remember standing in the yard that night [after her grandson died], trying to be sick but I couldn't, and thinking, *Oh my god, it's 1969 again. It's going to be that bad.* But there were different ways, obviously, for coping with it. I was fifty-seven as opposed to fourteen."

As Rhonda discovered, what we've learned or accumulated between an original loss and a fresh one can determine what we make of Resurrected Grief. Even when our histories flash warning signs telling us grief is terrible to endure, even when we fear this time will be as bad as the last, we can acknowledge that we're not the same people we were ten, twenty, or—as in Rhonda's case—forty-three years ago. "It's going to be that bad" is the fear of the child, not the adult. Fourteen-year-old Rhonda had that thought, until fifty-seven-year-old Rhonda stepped in and took control.

"I didn't curse God this time," Rhonda explains. "I turned to him, and I know that if I hadn't I wouldn't have made it through the loss of that baby. It's amazing what all of those years can do."

Oh my god, it's 1969 again, It's going to be just as bad, It feels like losing him all over again—these are all classic statements of Resurrected Grief. They emerge from a deeply buried zone of helplessness, fear, loneliness, anger, confusion, guilt, panic, or trauma. If those emotions weren't addressed *at* the time or *over* time, they then lie dormant underneath thickening layers of lived experience until reactivated by a new loss. In those moments, it really *can* feel like reexperiencing the original loss again.

Resurrected Grief need not appear only when someone else dies. It can occur with any experience that involves major change and loss:

breakups, divorces, sending a child off to college or the military, launching a child into the larger world, loss of a job, loss of an identity, loss of an ideal. Threat of loss can resurrect past grief as well, as happened to many people worldwide as the Covid-19 pandemic started sweeping across the globe. Stories of thousands dying of respiratory failure, and of patients dying in hospitals alone, created a wave of Resurrected Grief among individuals who'd lost loved ones to lung-related illnesses or who hadn't been there to help with the passage.

In an April 2020 post on her Twitter page, feminist activist Michelle Guido shared,

> The aspect of our loved ones dying alone is very triggering to me. When I was 16 I was pulled out of my grandmother's dying arms in the hospital because visiting hours were over. She raised me. She was my parent my everything. My last memory of her is her begging me not to leave her alone. I was escorted out of the hospital. We knew she was going to probably go that night and that's why I stayed back. We got a call hours later. She was gone. I've suffered such trauma and guilt that she died alone & I know it wasn't my fault. But I can't count the panic attacks or sleepless nights I have had over it. & this aspect of this virus where no one can say goodbye. Where you can't comfort your loved one while they are dying is so triggering to me. It's brought a lot back up these few weeks.

Whenever panic, helplessness, intense confusion, rapid change, loneliness, or fear for the future become part of the equation, elements of a prior loss can be reactivated. And then we can find ourselves mourning the past, the present, and the past *in* the present simultaneously.

"Every new loss pulls up all those emotions and feelings," says Darcy Krause, who cared for her mother's parents toward the ends of their lives. "What changes is your viewpoint, which evolves as you constantly reexperience it. Not in a negative way, but in a way that's normal as we develop and grow and become who we are."

I could never have predicted the ways that my father's death in 2005 would reactivate such specific details of my mother's in 1981. He died from end-stage liver cancer, as did she, though his primary cancer was a tumor in his liver and hers had started in her breast. The final days of his illness mirrored hers with eerie precision as his body shut down, step by step. My siblings and I couldn't *not* notice the similarities.

The social and medical circumstances of the two deaths, however, couldn't have been more different. Our mother had died in a sterile, semi-private hospital room, attended to by impersonal medical professionals, and the hospital did us a favor by letting us sleep in the waiting-room chairs. It was a messy, panicked, chaotic few days with choices made largely by unfamiliar doctors and nurses. Details were still being withheld from her, right up until she lost consciousness.

Our father, on the other hand, made his end-of-life decisions himself, fully aware of how his disease was likely to progress. He died at home, with hospice care and a full-time aide who treated him like a declining prince. His children and grandchildren visited his bedside every day, and we slept at night on his upholstered couches. As terrible as it is to say goodbye to a parent who's suffering, any trauma I felt around his death was the reactivated trauma of reliving my mother's last days in such excruciating detail, and helping him die so differently healed some of the traumatic memories of her death. Giving him a peaceful, loving send-off went far toward reducing my anger and regret around the kind of death she didn't get to receive.

The Childhood Exception, Part 2: Developmental Grief

MELANIE HAS very little memory of the car accident that took the lives of her parents, older brother, and younger sister when a reckless driver crossed over to the wrong side of the road.

Tragically, at age three, Melanie was the only survivor in her family.

"I remember there was a really bright light, and I remember crying and feeling trapped and wanting to get out and lifting my arms up to someone," she says. "Later, I read in a newspaper that the woman who found me tried to open the door and get me out, and I was lifting up my arms. But I don't know if I've made that up or if it was real. It's hard to know."

At only three years of age, Melanie would have experienced her sudden and traumatic loss with immature cognitive and emotional skills. She wouldn't even have fully understood what "death" meant yet. Too young for abstract thinking or emotional complexity, Melanie could not have imagined a detailed future without her parents or siblings, or speculate about what that might mean. That would all come later. At the time, Melanie would have understood only that her family was gone and she couldn't find them.

Immediately after the accident, Melanie was adopted by a maternal uncle and aunt who embraced her as their child. They protected her from the public spectacle of the news cycle and trial, and helped her identify as a survivor rather than a victim.

"They were amazing," recalls Melanie, now a mother of two herself. "They're essentially my mom and dad, and my cousin is my sister. We're super tight. There's no way I could have gotten through this without their support."

The accident was never treated as a secret, and Melanie's adoptive parents helped her maintain a connection to her biological parents. Photos of them were always kept on display in the house. Still, Melanie was reluctant to talk about the accident or tap into her well of sadness. She was hesitant to feel different from her classmates, and the tragedy of losing her entire family made her *really* different from everyone she knew. But most of all, she was afraid of hurting her adoptive family by asking about her biological family, thinking it might make them feel they hadn't done enough to help her adjust and thrive.

These were now the concerns of a preteen, and no longer those of a toddler. Because as Melanie matured physically, her cognitive and emotional skills developed at a steady pace, too. With that development came an awareness of the enormity of her loss. And then along with that awareness came fresh waves of sadness about the family and the childhood she'd lost.

At age ten, losing her family in an accident when she was three had been an abstraction a preteen still couldn't quite grasp. By fourteen, however, Melanie had developed a deeper understanding of what the accident and the multiple losses must have meant to her as a child and found herself mourning on behalf of the little girl she'd once been. She fell into a deep depression that year. The remainder of her teenage years was a time of "grieving for a family that I'd lost and didn't really know," Melanie explains. "I was just too young to understand and process my feelings when it happened. In therapy it was explained to me that those feelings and thoughts were kind of frozen in time, and when I'd matured and developed they would come to the front and I'd be able to process and deal with them then."

None of this means Melanie grieved improperly at age three. It means she grieved as well as any three-year-old could, and then as well as any teenager could, and now she grieves as well as she can as a thirty-four-year-old adult. As a child's intellectual, emotional, moral, and linguistic capacities mature, so do their understanding of death, the meanings they make of an absence, and their ability to tolerate strong emotions.

What this means is that at different points along this continuum, children will understand and question different aspects of a deceased loved one's life and death. This is what makes children's grief a protracted, stop-and-start process, occurring in bits and pieces over the whole course of childhood. In this "shocks and aftershocks" model of children's bereavement, the death of a parent is revisited, reworked, and reinterpreted at successive stages of development. The further a loss recedes into the past, however, the less likely the adults in their lives are to understand that a child's behaviors in the present may be in response to a new understanding of a loss from the past.

Psychologists Nancee Biank and Allison Werner-Lin, who specialize in adolescents and bereavement, believe that in this developmental framework grief continues to be renegotiated but is never resolved. "Children may adaptively address each of the tasks of mourning at each stage," Biank and Werner-Lin explain. "Yet, as they grow and encounter nodal life transitions, they must begin these tasks again with a more mature set of tools . . . As children revisit the tasks of mourning at each successive stage they rework not only the death. They also rework their own formulations about the death from earlier developmental realms and their own beliefs about the hypothetical life they would have led had their parent survived."

Common junctures for developmental grief reactions are around age six or seven, when a mature understanding of death begins to develop, and again in early adolescence, when abstract thinking emerges and a child may get a vivid glimpse of what the loss will mean to them in the future, far beyond their current, everyday concerns. If the death was one of a parent, especially a same-sex parent, the midtwenties may be a time of reactivated grief as a daughter or son looks at their peers developing adult relationships with a mother or father and feels the pang of not being able to do the same. And remember: This is all happening in conjunction with cyclical grief, sneak attacks, and the potential for other losses, too.

"The grief is no longer intense and all-consuming, but it is still there," explains Phyllis Silverman, a co-principal Investigator of the Harvard Child Bereavement Study, in her book *Never Too Young to Know: Death in Children's Lives.* "Children have a longer life ahead of them, so they carry the meaning of this experience with them for a longer time than do adults."

A child like Melanie who was too young to have formed retrievable memories of the deceased may later feel confused about how or even whether she can grieve. How do you mourn a parent you can't remember or siblings you barely knew? At different points in development, these children may find themselves grieving a person's absence instead of the loss of that person's presence. They will grieve for what they imagine they've lost, while also mourning the secondary losses—no father to teach them how to shave, no sister to share adult jokes with—that occurred as a result.

Today Melanie is thirty-four and the mother of two small children. Motherhood, especially raising a young daughter, has brought her early losses to the surface again. "When I was younger I used to be quite flippant about my loss," she recalls. "It was all I had ever known and I couldn't remember my parents anyway; how could I miss them? To me they were just a photo in a frame. It wasn't until my daughter turned three, just after my son was born, that I realized the magnitude of my loss. My daughter was a confident, charming, independent three-year-old, and her dad and I were her whole life. She went through periods of desperately *needing* me, as every preschooler with a new sibling does, and it would get to the point where I would be feeding Alexander and she would be lying on top of me because she needed to be that close to me as well. It was during this time that I mourned the loss of my childhood innocence. I felt so desperately for the little girl I was at three years old and how much she had lost. All I wanted to do was go back and hold her tightly in my arms and tell her that everything was going to be okay."

Which brings us full circle, back to the NYU Library, Sarah Brabant's article, and the peculiar yet very common phenomenon of experiencing an old loss in an entirely new way.

CHAPTER FIVE

New Old Grief: One-Time Transitions

WALKING THROUGH the front door of Lili Bridals was like stepping straight into an icing factory. Swirls of white and cream blanketed the showroom floor, interspersed with layers of intricate lace and fountains of organza and tulle.

A salesman with a steel-gray moustache and a trim, tailored suit stepped up to greet me: "How can I help you today?"

A man. I wasn't expecting that. The previous weekend when my college roommate Susie drove me from bridal shop to bridal shop throughout the West San Fernando Valley, every store we visited was staffed by maternal, middle-aged women. They doted on me to such a degree, it almost felt as if they were trying to overcompensate for my minimal entourage. Grateful as I was for Susie's company, it was impossible not to notice how other customers were attended to by intergenerational cliques of what appeared to be mothers, friends, and possibly aunts. Each time a bride-to-be stepped out of the dressing room in a new gown to the appreciative murmurs of her audience, I found myself slipping into compare-and-despair thinking. *If only I were shopping back in New York with my aunts and cousins . . . If only my mother were here to do this with me . . . If only . . .*

But I needed to be realistic. I was getting married in California. If my mother were living, she'd probably still be in New York. Or maybe in Florida by then, like some of her friends. I'd most likely be telling her about dress shopping by phone and sending her photos and magazine clippings of the contenders. That's assuming we would have had that kind of relationship. Who knows what would have happened if she hadn't died? I could have been getting married any-where, at any time, or not at all. Or I could have been married for years by then, to someone else.

That's where my runaway train of hypotheticals came to a screech-ing stop. The thought of marrying anyone other than my fiancé, a man I waited so long to meet, was unimaginable. I had what I had, and it's what I wanted.

And so there I was in Lili Bridals on that Thursday at noon, com-pletely on a whim. I'd been driving east on Ventura Boulevard, run-ning late for a morning appointment with my obstetrician—I was ten weeks pregnant—when I noticed the store in a corner of a strip mall in Tarzana. On the way back, I pulled into the parking lot. Couldn't hurt to look, I figured. We'd just gotten engaged and the wedding was in nine weeks. At that point I needed something practi-cally ready to go, since I was tight on budget and also on time.

I was the only customer in the store at noon. I scanned the show-room floor. Glass display cases held arrays of sparkling jewelry and elaborate garters. An obligatory low pedestal sat in front of a triptych mirror for each bride-to-be to step up and do three-quarter turns. A half dozen or so upholstered chairs and loveseats were clustered around the staging area. There would be free coffee and tea some-where too, I knew.

"I'm looking for something off-the-rack," I told the salesman. "I'm normally a size eight, but my wedding is in two months and by then I'll probably be at least a ten. If you know what I mean."

He nodded. I detected a small smile. I'm sure I wasn't the only pregnant thirtysomething customer he'd seen that week—maybe not even the first one that day.

"Of course," he said. "Right this way."

I followed him into a small room off to the left, where the sale racks resided. Long strips of floor-length bridal gowns lined the walls. "Do you have a style in mind?" he asked. I didn't, I told him, as I started sifting through the hangers, but I knew what I didn't want, and maybe that was a start? Nothing strapless. No empire waist, even though everyone was recommending them for pregnant brides. No high collars. Easy on the sequins.

Over the past three weeks I'd fallen in love with only one dress, a sleek satin gown with an elegantly draped neckline and matching elbow-length gloves. Everything about it was exquisite, except the price tag. $1,200—more than double what I could afford. The saleswoman compared it to a pricier Vera Wang, but a budget was a budget. I was still looking.

I moved on to the second rack, flipped through a few dresses, and then—

This one.

The dress had a gentle scoop neck in front, capped sleeves, and a crisscrossed lace pattern overlaid across a sheer chest panel. The back neckline plunged down in a sharp V that ended at a cluster of three ornate flowers. The train was modest, nothing too cumbersome or elaborate. I could see just the smallest hint of sequins. The whole package was graceful and understated and just . . . *wow*. It was perfect.

"I'd like to try this one," I said.

The salesman flipped the tag over. Size ten. And the price had been reduced to a manageable $575.

Ten minutes later I was standing on the pedestal while a matronly saleswoman—aha! I knew it!—zipped me up in the back. She only needed to pinch about an inch of excess material in the back to make the dress fit. I was barely showing then, but in eight weeks I wouldn't need any alterations at all.

"Oh, honey," she said. "It's like this dress was made for you."

I turned my right hip toward the center mirror, then my left. She was right. It was like someone took my measurements and then created a dress to fit them. The salesman brought two veils over, one balanced in each hand.

By now another customer was trying on dresses in the fitting room. Her quartet sat on the upholstered chairs drinking tea from china cups and saucers while they waited for her to emerge.

"That dress is so *you*," the woman who looked like a sister said to me.

"Beautiful," the woman who looked like a mother nodded.

"You see?" the saleswoman said. "It's unanimous."

I stepped off the pedestal so she could position the first veil on the crown of my head. Gently but firmly she pressed the plastic combs into my hair. I slipped into a pair of size-ten white pumps the salesman brought me, and we were ready for the full effect. I stepped back onto the platform and turned toward the mirrors.

The reflection that stared back was me but not me. It was my face and my shape, but it was the image of a bride. And that's when I got it, really *got it*, that I was about to become a wife. And in seven months, a mother.

A wave of panic cartwheeled straight up my torso and lodged in my throat. How was I going to do this, any of this, without my mom? How could it be that she wasn't there to see it? It had been a long time since I'd felt anger or injustice about her death, but three words started flashing at me like a neon sign: *It's. Not. Fair.* To me or to her.

"Oh, honey," the saleswoman said when she saw the tears sliding down my cheeks. "Oh, honey. I'll go get you a tissue."

I wiped the heels of my hands against my cheekbones before anyone else noticed. I didn't want the attention. *I'm an adult now*, I told myself, fiercely. *I can control this. I can.*

But for God's sake, I chided myself—how was I not prepared? I'd been writing and speaking about early mother loss for *four years* at that point. I'd traveled all over the world to talk about its long-term effects. I knew what all the expected trigger points were likely to be. Preparation should have been my best defense. And yet, as it turned out, all of that intellectual prep work was meaningless. None of it could protect me from the emotional charge of seeing that image in the mirror as I stood on the pedestal alone.

The next bride-to-be emerged from the dressing room wrapped in layers of chiffon to the murmurs of her assembled little crowd.

"Thank you," I told the saleswoman as she handed me a folded tissue. "I'm okay now," I said. I told her I'd buy the dress. Of course I was buying the dress. "I'm fine," I said again as I headed back to the fitting room.

It was my most familiar and most reliable coping strategy. *I'm fine. I'm fine. I'm fine.* If I said it enough times, I might even believe it was true.

LIKE CHILDREN who can grieve only to the best of their abilities at whatever point they've reached in development, adults can only grieve to the extent of their accumulated, lived experience. It's unrealistic, and even a little absurd, to expect a sister to be able to grieve her sister's absence at a high school graduation that won't take place for another four years, or for a twenty-six-year-old son to grieve turning fifty-seven, the age at which his father died, thirty years ahead of time.

We can intellectually imagine these milestones. We might even engage in a type of anticipatory mourning when we envision the secondary losses yet to come. The young woman who's burying her father, for example, may be sitting at the cemetery already wondering who'll walk her down the church aisle at her future wedding. A sixteen-year-old boy may already have decided he won't celebrate his twentieth birthday, because it means he'll turn the age his brother was when he died.

But to truly experience, in advance, how it will feel to walk down the aisle on an uncle's arm or to walk it alone, or to wake up on a birthday morning and see the world through the eyes of a twenty-year-old—how can that be experienced ahead of time? It can't.

There was no way, truly no way, I could have pre-grieved the loneliness I felt when my prenatal yoga friends talked about their mothers' postpartum assistance while I was home alone with a colicky infant, or the sense of blistering incompetence I collided against as I began to parent a daughter beyond the age I was when I lost my mother at seventeen. The existential nature of a significant one-time event can only be experienced in real time, when it occurs. That's how we encounter our old losses in new ways.

Some grief simply can't be experienced until you get there. That's how this part goes.

Life Transitions: Maturational Grief

GRADUATIONS, WEDDINGS, first jobs, work promotions, new relationships, breakups, weddings, parenthood, job losses, divorce, retirement, grandparenthood: These are just some of many lifespan events that can populate a life story. Whenever we cross the threshold from one state of existence to another, from one status to the next—student to graduate; single to partnered; married to divorced; nonparent to parent; employed to unemployed—we may find ourselves longing for the comfort, reassurance, advice, support, praise, celebration, or camaraderie we imagine a deceased loved one would have offered. Such lifespan events may then contain both joy and sorrow, a bittersweet reminder of what is cherished and also of what was lost.

Fifty-three-year-old Kevin was almost eight years old when his only brother was stillborn. He had two younger sisters at the time. A few years later, his third sister was born.

"One of the ways Timothy's death haunted me in adulthood is that he was my only brother," Kevin explains. "My sisters have each other, and they go through major milestones as sisters. They have the shared experiences now of being wives, mothers, all the things that women go through together. At each milestone in my life that I hit, I couldn't help but think, 'What would it have been like if I had a brother who was here to share this with me, who I could talk to about these experiences?'"

An absence is often felt acutely when the loved one would have filled a culturally prescribed or expected role. The best friend who would have offered a refuge or a compassionate ear at times of distress. The brother who would have stood tall and proud as a best man, or the sister who would have been an attentive maid of honor. The grandparents who would have participated in rites of passage—a newborn's christening, a bris—and lavished gifts and love upon a new grandchild. To gaze around and see our friends and relatives participating in the kind of relationships we can't have, especially at times of transition, only pokes the fire more.

Sasha, who was twelve when her father died of heart failure and who then lost her mother to cancer five months later, remembers her high school graduation as a lonely, isolating event. She was living with an aunt and uncle by then, but they didn't attend. Her friends all had relatives present to witness their transitions, but no one in Sasha's family showed up to see her receive her diploma that day. She walked up onto the stage when her name was called without anyone sitting in the audience specifically for her.

"When you lose a parent, or both parents, you don't have someone who then thinks the way a parent would think, like, 'It's important that someone show support and be there for a graduation,'" Sasha says. "I think that's part of how grief continues on with us. There are milestone moments in life where there isn't the support that other people take for granted."

Sasha's father had been a minister, and as a child she'd always pictured him filling dual roles at her wedding: as both officiant and father of the bride. When she prepared to marry in her twenties, more than ten years after her parents' deaths, she was surprised by the emotional punch that came along with planning the event.

"All of a sudden a wave of depression came over me," she says. "I realized it was because it was going to be one of the happiest moments of my life but I couldn't share it with my mother. And then a whole other thing I struggled with and that caught me by surprise was how to plan walking down the aisle. It was like, 'Oh my God, what am I going to do? Who will be the person who will step into my dad's place?' I couldn't figure out who that would be. And so I thought, well, my heart belongs to the future, and I chose my two nieces to walk me down the aisle. They were nine and ten at the time."

With creativity, an absence can be turned into a presence at a milestone event. I've heard numerous stories about honoring a lost loved one this way, from affixing a photo to the flat top of a graduation cap, to wearing a father's watch or a mother's ring at one's wedding, to singing a song to a newborn that a deceased parent once sang to his or her own babies. It's a way to include them in the day in spirit, and to honor the ongoing inner relationships we carry forth. More than saying *You were important to me*, it says, *You are important to me still. Experience this with me. Be part of my special day.*

Just as with cyclical events, maturational grief can occur at the conscious or unconscious level. When I saw myself in the mirror at Lili Bridals, I knew what I was feeling and why. But when grief has been suppressed or repressed, especially due to family silence, New Old Grief can take us by surprise. In those cases, it may behave more like a sneak attack.

That's how Rhonda experienced New Old Grief when she was twenty-five. An only child, Rhonda had been fifteen when her mother died. To cope with her feelings of helplessness and sorrow, she stepped into a caretaking role for her father. She tried to build competence by taking over household tasks like cooking and packing up their house for a move. Her father was decimated by the loss of his wife and never talked with his daughter about what had happened to their small family. His modus operandi, Rhonda explains, was "don't think about it and it clears up." So, throughout high school and early adulthood, she never discussed the loss of her mother at age fifteen— not even with her close friends.

By age twenty-five, Rhonda had a steady job, a stable long-term relationship, and a home she shared with her partner. From the outside, she had all the markers of someone who'd successfully transitioned into adulthood and left her childhood loss behind.

And then.

"I can tell you the moment when the years of not dealing, of not opening the door, not looking at what happened to my mom came out," Rhonda says. It was exactly ten years and four days after her mother died.

"My boyfriend, who's now my husband, and I found out we were going to have a child," she explains, "and of course, we were ecstatic. We went out to breakfast, and we bought a TV, because we figured we'd be staying home a lot. We had a two-bedroom apartment, and when I got home I went upstairs to make the bed, and I don't know what came over me. It was like a tidal wave. I couldn't stop it. *I want my mother. I want my mother. I want her now.* I went from crying to sobbing to hysterically sobbing, and I cried until I fell asleep.

"It felt like I cried for hours. It was like all that crap was finally coming out. After that it became easier to think about her, longing and wishing she was there and thinking about how different things would have been if she had been. I started realizing it was a really stupid idea not to talk about it, so I would. I mean, I didn't bombard people with 'This happened to me!' but if the subject came up, I would share, 'Yeah, this is what happened.'"

Ten years of keeping grief at a distance came to their culmination on the day Rhonda learned she was pregnant. The enormity of that news made her long for the kind of maternal support she'd once had and wished she had still. I've heard similar stories from a number of adults bereaved as children. Only after their pent-up sorrow was released in an involuntary, cathartic rush, after which they felt cleansed, were they able to break through their own protective walls, access the longing and love they still felt toward their departed loved ones, and welcome those memories back into their lives.

As she prepared to become a mother, Rhonda was also longing for a parent who could witness and validate the significance of her news. When we lose a parent, older sibling, or beloved grandparent, we also miss out on the opportunity to be validated by that person as we mature. That's a powerful form of secondary loss. On the morning of my high school graduation, I looked in the mirror and wondered, *If a daughter graduates from high school and a mother isn't here to see it, does it really happen?* The real question might have been *If a daughter graduates from high school and a mother isn't here to see it, will that daughter ever feel like a high school graduate?*

We also lose the opportunity to feel the warmth of their adoration and pride. Priya, now forty-eight, remembers writing an essay for her college application when she was in high school, an early step in an important period of transition. The essay prompt was "If you could spend an afternoon with anyone, living or dead, who would it be and why?" She wrote about her mother, who had died of breast cancer when Priya was in the second grade.

"By the time I finished those couple of paragraphs, I was a mess," she says. "I was just bawling, because what tumbled out in the stream of consciousness writing was: What would she be like? and Would she be proud of me? I didn't have the sense of security of knowing what my mother would have thought of me, and becoming aware of that lack was very, very powerful. My wedding was another big watershed moment. I was a total emotional mess."

Like Priya, seventy-six-year-old Jack remembers how he longed for blessings and advice at key moments from the father who died of heart failure when he was fifteen. "I wanted to tell him about my girlfriends, and I wanted his advice about who I should invite to the prom," Jack explains. "When my first child was born, I wanted to be able to say, 'Hey, look at this, look at what I did, this is a good thing.' And of course he wasn't there."

When our elders aren't present to guide us across a threshold or welcome us into their fold, taking decisive steps into adulthood may feel like a type of role playing instead. A specific type of impostor syndrome may then develop.

"When I was in my forties, I recognized I had a basic belief I'd never really articulated, which was that I was just a big kid," recalls Terrie Rando, who was seventeen when her father died and eighteen when she lost her mother. "Even though I was assuming the adult responsibility of going all over the world talking to people and I'd written books and had two kids, deep down inside I felt that I was a big kid doing adult things. I just hadn't stepped into adulthood the way that somebody should have, and to this day I believe that the only thing that accounts for this was that I'd never been recognized as an adult by my parents."

As thirty-four-year-old Simone describes losing her mother at age twenty, "For her to die then felt like I'd never been given permission to grow up. It's left me sort of stuck in time. I'm very mature because of everything that happened, but also sometimes feel like I'm very immature because I feel like I'm still a twenty-year-old and always will be."

Let's say our self-image still corresponds with an earlier, younger identity, as often happens when trauma arrests pieces of development. If we don't receive external confirmation later that, yes, we *are* adults now from the adults who knew us as children, we may have trouble perceiving *ourselves* as adults, too.

Proxy Grief

A SUBTLE grief shift took place in my twenties, as I felt myself transitioning from being a daughter who'd lost her mother to also recognizing what my mother had lost by dying so young. "Out-of-time deaths," as they're called, mean a lifespan has been abbreviated, which in turn means our loved ones have missed out on milestones their peers will go on to experience without them.

The brother who never grew old enough to graduate high school, the sister who didn't get to marry her fiancé, the parent who didn't live long enough to retire. A particular kind of New Old Grief may arise at the time when an event should have happened and the person who would have been experiencing it isn't there. We may then feel a sort of proxy grief, causing us to mourn not for ourselves but instead on that loved one's behalf.

Steve, who was eighteen when his father died from stomach cancer, achieved a major personal goal two years later when he trained and ran in the New York City Marathon. He completed the race that

October morning to mixed emotions—triumph for having crossed the finish line and sorrow because his father wasn't there to see it happen. "I remember finishing and crying," Steve recalls, "because I thought of how proud he would have been to know I actually did this." The sadness Steve felt wasn't just for the twenty-year-old who didn't have his father there, but also for the father who had missed out on seeing his twenty-year-old son accomplish such a physically challenging goal.

Proxy grief is particularly poignant when a child has died, and all of the maturational events of adulthood cannot occur. When Nancy's son Lee was a child, she'd often imagined him into the future, as an adult—a husband and a father. That was part of her assumptive world. These visions were shattered when Lee died by suicide at age nineteen.

The desire attached to those expectations, however—for Lee to have been able to experience those milestones—never disappeared. Fifteen years later, Nancy experienced proxy grief when Lee's best friend from childhood married, and again when that friend announced his first child was on the way. Both times, Nancy found herself experiencing Lee's death at age nineteen in new ways, and mourning for both the husband and the father he'd never become.

New Old Grief asks us to mourn on two or three simultaneous levels: for what we lost, for what our loved one lost, and sometimes for what the next generation has missed out on, too. As a new mother, I encountered New Old Grief when my mother wasn't there to offer practical assistance or to share stories of her own early motherhood. I also found myself mourning her as a maternal grandmother for my daughters, who would never know her kindness or her generosity. They never felt this loss; for that they would have needed to experience her presence first. To them, their grandmother's death created an absence, or perhaps it was more of a vacancy, as they watched their friends being doted on and going to spend weekends with grandparents.

And there was more. My mother would have loved being a grandmother. She was good with children, and I have no doubt she would have been patient and kind. Sometimes I'm still angry that she never had the chance to experience that relationship for herself.

There's a world of difference, I've discovered, between acceptance and acceptability after a loss. I can accept that my mother died. She's not here; I accept that she's gone. But the circumstances and the timing of her death will never be acceptable to me. I won't ever find it acceptable that a forty-two-year-old mother would die before her children became adults and would never get to meet her grandchildren. And so now I grieve on her behalf. *My* milestones I've learned to walk through without her. *Her* missed experiences are the ones that are harder to bear.

Age-Correspondence Events

ALEXANDRA WAS fifteen years old when her mother died of sudden heart failure. Tragedy struck the family again when, ten months later, her father died from prostate cancer. Alexandra moved in with her aunt for the rest of high school, and the two had a close and loving relationship. Still, as she grew into adulthood, Alexandra found herself longing for ways to identify with and feel connected to the parents she'd lost. One way she could do that, she discovered, was to make some of the choices her mother had made, at the same ages—a phenomenon known as "life-pattern mirroring."

"As I came into the stage of my life of having kids, I discovered it was unexpectedly important to me to have my first child around the same time in my mother's life that I was born," explains Alexandra, who's now forty-three. "So around age thirty, I felt an intense pressure to be pregnant. I did get pregnant, at basically the same age that she was pregnant with me. It surprised me how strong I felt the need to connect with her life trajectory, to be able to step inside that same experience and feel that kind of connection."

Giving birth at age thirty helped Alexandra positively identify with the mother she'd lost as a teen. Like her mother, Alexandra gave birth to a girl. Which means that in two years, more life-pattern mirroring will occur.

"My daughter is now thirteen," she explains, "and I realize that the unexpected consequence of having her at thirty is that when I turn the age my mother was when she died, my daughter will be the age I was at the same time. And it will happen in the same year as the thirtieth anniversary of my parents' deaths." She calls this her personal triple whammy.

When she and her daughter both reach these watershed ages, Alexandra will be facing two "age-correspondence events" at the same time. This specific type of New Old Grief occurs when a mourner, or a close relative of the mourner (such as a spouse or a child), reaches an age that corresponds with a significant tragedy (such as a diagnosis or a death) that another person experienced in the past.

The main feature of an age-correspondence event is that it can occur only once, when that specific age is reached. But the lead-up to that age can also initiate a grief response, and the response can last for that entire age-related year. Also, as Alexandra discovered, one person can experience more than one age-correspondence event at a time.

Reaching the age of a loved one's diagnosis or death is a significant inflection point in a mourner's story. Women often travel long distances to attend the Motherless Daughters retreats I facilitate when they're approaching or have just reached their mother's final age, or when their child (typically a daughter in these retreat-specific cases) turns the age they were when their mothers died. They've found themselves struggling with fear, anxiety, and surges of sadness. They don't understand why this is happening, after all this time.

Watershed ages tend to burn brightly in our imagined futures, sometimes flashing in the distance like neon warning signs. We may approach these ages with trepidation, fearful that our life patterns will mirror those of our loved ones who died. We may complete that year with a sense of triumph, relieved to have exceeded the imaginary limit in our minds.

Sharon, now fifty-eight, was ten when both of her parents died in a private plane crash. They were on their way to a medical convention, and her father, a doctor, was piloting the small plane. "It was the first time my mom went on a trip with him and left me at home, and it kind of played into my superstition as opportunities cropped up when I was a similar age as her," Sharon says. "When my husband won a cruise, I refused to get on the boat. I was the exact age my mother was when she died, and it just spooked the hell out of me."

Fear of a foreshortened future is common among adults who lost parents or siblings when they were children. These individuals tend to fear being diagnosed at the same age and dying in the same or a similar way and at the same age—even when a cause of death isn't hereditary and is highly unlikely to occur again, as with a random accident or a rare disease. The identifications we form with parents and older siblings, especially of the same sex, can be that strong.

"For many, many years I dreaded turning forty-three, because that was the age when my mom died," says Cherie, now forty-four, who was eighteen when her mother died in an accidental fire. Cherie's mother, who'd been wheelchair-bound due to multiple sclerosis, had fallen asleep and dropped a lit cigarette, which started the fire.

"Of course, in my rational head, I understood that I didn't have MS, I'm not a smoker, so I'm not going to die at the same age in the same manner she did," Cherie continues. "But there was still that awareness that my mom died at forty-three, so here we go, tick-tock. And then forty-three hit, and then it was just like . . . okay. All right. I did it. I made it through that year. Once I hit that age, I could let my shoulders down a little and relax. But getting to that point felt treacherous."

It's not impossible, of course, for a mirror event to occur. Elvis Presley died at the age of forty-two, the same age at which his mother died. Winston Churchill famously died on the anniversary of his father's death. These are the exceptions, however. By no means are they the rule.

The statistical probability of dying at the same age as a loved one, and of the same cause, is very, very slim. But calculations offer little comfort. Age-correspondence anxiety is driven by emotion, not rationality. Until I reached and passed forty-two, you could have talked to me all day about my low risk of developing breast cancer in my thirties, or about how successful early detection was at saving lives. I would nod and smile and try to believe it, while in the back of my mind lived the solemn belief that my mother's destiny would inevitably become my own. I was genuinely surprised to turn forty-three without major incident.

For some the fear of dying young becomes a full-on expectation. This identification is particularly strong when a same-sex parent or sibling is the one who died. It's not unusual for bereaved individuals to postpone making decisions or taking major personal steps until they've passed a parent's or sibling's age of diagnosis or death. They then cross over into a zone of survival, where thoughts of dying young contain less emotional charge. Several of the people interviewed for this book spoke of calculating a parent or sibling's age at time of death down to the number of years, months, and days, and exhaling a sigh of relief when they'd outlived their loved one by a single day.

For others, the focus on a fixed future date serves as an engine for achieving personal goals and achieving them soon. That's what motivated forty-five-year-old Christopher, who was eight when his father died of a second heart attack at age thirty-eight. An inveterate explorer, by his midthirties Christopher had traveled to several dozen countries and lived in France for a number of years.

"Part of the fuel for a lot of the travel I did, and the different experiences I wanted to have, was the idea that maybe I'm not going to have too much time," he admits, "and so I'm going to do the things I really want to do, and that's not entirely bad."

On the other hand, the knowledge that he, too, could—not would but *could*—die in his thirties inspired him to accumulate life experiences over creating the kind of stability that most of his peers had chosen by that age. "When I got to my late thirties and realized I might be around for a while longer, I was like, 'I actually need to figure out what I'm going to be when I grow up,'" he explains. "And then I went through all of the craziness of 'Am I behind? What was I doing? I've wasted all this time,' and that noise can really eat you up."

As with cyclical anniversary events, age-correspondence events can occur at a conscious or unconscious level. Physical symptoms that mimic the deceased's can also develop as a significant birthday approaches. Again, directly addressing the underlying cause of distress—in this case, an age-related event—often allows the symptoms to resolve.

A classic example of powerful physical mirroring is found in the autobiographical account of French analyst Marie Bonaparte, who was only one month old when her mother died. Psychiatrist George Pollock summarized Bonaparte's age-correspondence episode in his classic two-volume 1989 book, *The Mourning-Liberation Process*:

Marie, who was named for her dead mother, was repeatedly told how her birth had been paid for by her mother's life. Throughout her childhood, she imagined she had really seen her dead mother. At seventeen years of age, she gradually became convinced that, like her mother, she had tuberculosis and that this fact was being kept a secret from her. Her mother had died at twenty-two, and Marie expected that she, too, would die of tuberculosis at twenty-two. Her symptoms began to mimic TB; she lost appetite and weight, and had frequent respiratory infections . . . Since her mother had died at twenty-two, Marie felt she had to pass this age before she would know whether she could live. Her sickness had the important function of discouraging her from marrying. If she did not marry, she would not become pregnant and therefore would not suffer her mother's fate. When she was twenty-two, her father pointed out to her that it was high time she found a husband and forget her imaginary illness . . . From then on her symptoms began to wane.

It's not unusual for an adult to live beyond a parent or sibling's death age, especially late in life. When a loved one dies young, however, we find ourselves approaching and crossing that threshold in middle age or earlier, out of sync with most of our friends. As we reach and pass that fateful age, a parent or younger sibling numerically shifts from being older than us to being, for one year, our peer. Then we move beyond them, in both age and experience. Our inner relationships, however, may remain fixed at that younger state.

"When I turned nineteen it was tragic to me," remembers Veronica, who was seventeen when her older brother died in a car accident, "because I was now at the age when James died. I still think of him as older than me, even though he was a mere nineteen years old when he died and I'm now thirty-four. I bring him into certain situations in my mind, wondering what he would do. If I'm dating somebody, I wonder what his reaction would be. Although there does come a point where the nineteen-year-old James probably doesn't have much to say about those things."

Reaching my mother's age at time of death was disconcerting enough. For one thing, it drove home how incredibly young she had been when she died. She'd gone to college, gotten married, held a job, had three children, dutifully ticking off most of the major milestones that still lay ahead for me. From the vantage point of seventeen, forty-two looked downright *old*. And then I reached that age myself.

At forty-two, my peers were teaching yoga, having babies, starting new careers. Forty-two suddenly looked extremely, tragically young.

My mother's imagined advice to eighteen-year-old me was still based on vivid memories. It's been harder to imagine what she would tell me now, since I'm so far beyond the last age she got to be. I've had to try to mature her in my mind, imagine how she might have changed and who she might have become, how world events and family circumstances might have influenced her, if she hadn't died. Sometimes I think I'm getting close. Sometimes I'm sure I'm missing the mark. Realistically? I could be her older sister now. Someday,

I hope, I'll be old enough to be her mother. That's going to be . . . even weirder, I suspect.

Both of my daughters are now older than I was when my mother died. Raising them beyond that point has been one of the biggest accomplishments of my life. A remarkable aspect of parenting is its capacity for time travel. Watching a child reach their milestones reactivates a parent's memories of reaching those milestones in their past. Because my younger siblings were fourteen and nine when our mother died, I observed my daughters closely at those ages. They were so young, still. I wondered how they'd cope if they were to lose me then. And then the present shifted to the past, and I wondered how my brother and sister had coped. Now is then is now is then.

And seventeen! At that age, I'd convinced myself I was mature and didn't need a mother anymore. When my older daughter turned seventeen, I was struck by how hard my seventeen-year-old self must have had to work to convince herself that this was true. I saw how much my daughter still needed a mother, even as she was pushing for autonomy. And then when my younger daughter turned seventeen, her birthday delivered to me the sudden, irrational thought that my work as a mother was done. Which of course was untrue. Still, having pressed forward on my own at that age, I couldn't help expecting her to do the same. That she wouldn't was irrelevant. That she didn't need to was obvious. That I had—that was the point.

When a child, especially of our own gender, reaches our age at a time of major loss, a triple identification occurs. We identify (1) with the child we have, (2) with the child we once were, and (3) with the loved one who died. When my daughters turned seventeen, part of me responded as the seventeen-year-old I'd once been, part of me identified with my daughter, and part with my mother, realizing how sad it must have been for her to leave her children when they were still so young.

Suppressed grief may rise to the surface, perhaps for the first time, as we imagine how our children would struggle through a major loss, and by association realize how much we must have struggled, too.

Feelings of compassion and curiosity toward that younger self often result.

That's how New Old Grief showed up for BBC Radio host Tony Livesey, who was thirteen when his mother died of cancer. In his article "Life after Mother," published in *The Independent* in 2010, he writes, "I'm 46 now and more than three decades have passed, but I've been thinking about it a lot lately. My own children are around the age that I was when it happened, and it's sparked some unexpected feelings and, in turn, a kind of reassessment of the effect her death has had on my life. My daughter is 16 and at college, and by all accounts pretty mature. But my son is 14 and daft as a brush, just as he should be, and as I was. If he'd lost me or his mother in the past year or two, I wonder how on earth he'd have coped. I have also started to wonder if I coped as well as I used to feel I did."

As we or our children reach and pass those fateful ages, a shift occurs from focusing on what we lost to imagining what the loved one and other family members experienced as well. When I was fifty-one, the same age my father was when my mother died, I could understand for the first time, truly understand, how hard it must have been for him to be wholly responsible for three children in addition to working every day to provide for their support. I'm not sure I could have grasped that at forty, or even forty-nine. It took reaching fifty-one to fully imagine myself in the same position.

When Abby turned twenty-eight, she reached the same age her mother was when Abby's father died. "Up until then it was always, 'Oh, poor me. I'm the girl who lost her father.' " recalls Abby, now forty-six. "It was how I identified myself until I reached that age. I remember being twenty-eight and realizing, 'At this same age, my mom was widowed with a four-year-old,' and there I was, moaning that I didn't have certain waitress shifts. That was the age when I was, like, 'Get over yourself, Abby,' because I had been pretty self-focused. Suddenly I woke up to 'Look at what my mom went through at this point.' "

We have no ritual for crossing these age-related thresholds, no culturally sanctioned way to acknowledge their significance. But do not let that minimize their importance: These transitions are significant. In the absence of ritual, we're free to create one of our own, to help us pass the milestone and step into the unknown years, the years our loved ones didn't get to see, with compassion and grace instead of fear.

In a culture that devalues aging, we must remember that aging is a privilege. It's a status that some, as we know too well, never get to achieve. I think about this often now that I'm in my fifties. Sometimes I see a photo of myself that looks older than I feel, or notice the sun damage on my skin, and I think, *Really? Already?* And then I remember that aging is something to be grateful for. I remember that I've gotten to see not just one but both(!) of my daughters graduate from high school—that I've even lived to watch one graduate from college—and then the whole world comes back into proper focus again.

Next-Gen, Next-Level

EVEN BY Southern California standards, it was a spectacular afternoon. Cloudless and unruffled, with a midday sun burning pure and bright. Our small entourage sat in a row on the aluminum bleacher: me and my husband, our younger daughter, Eden; and my sister, Michele. We rose as the opening bars of "Pomp and Circumstance" crackled through the loudspeakers at the corners of the football field. The music was so iconic and familiar, it could have been the same recording that played in the 1980s when I graduated from high school in the New York suburbs and again when my sister strode across the same grass three years later.

"Remember?" I asked her. But I didn't need to. Of course she did.

The procession of 170 graduating seniors came into view in alternating gowns of black and teal. *"Maya!"* we shouted. *"Maya!"* She couldn't hear us, but no matter. We yelled until we were hoarse anyway. We yelled for the people who weren't there, and especially for the one who didn't get to shout for us.

The students wove among the rows of folding chairs to take their seats. Some of them paused to give double thumbs-ups to the crowd. Families waved wildly at their graduates, someone had a bullhorn, and everyone was lifting cellphones sideways to capture the scene on video. The music wound down as the last students took their seats. Six hundred people in the bleachers sat back down.

That's when Michele and I both lost it.

Tears aren't unusual at a high school graduation. I know that. As a threshold ceremony, it symbolizes both a beginning and an end. The ritual can be a poignant rite of passage for students and parents alike. Michele and I weren't the only ones clutching packs of travel tissues that day.

My husband rubbed comforting circles on my back. After eighteen years, he was used to these emotional displays. I was always the mother at the preschool presentations and grade-school concerts who stood on the room's perimeter, simultaneously beaming and crying. The happiness, the grief, the longing, the gratitude, the awe: all of it involuntarily tumbling out at once. I used to embarrass my daughters so much with my crying that I'd have to promise to either stand way in the back or not attend.

Still, this was excessive even for me. And with my sister next to me, the effect was multiplied by two. By the time the principal was halfway through his address, Michele and I were full-on sobbing.

I reached out and squeezed her hand. "We did it," I said.

"We sure did," she said, squeezing back.

Neither of our parents got anywhere close to this graduation. Our father died eleven years earlier after a fierce, brief bout with liver cancer. Our mother didn't live to see any of her children finish high school. Our own high school graduations had been afternoons to endure in a family that had been struck down by grief and had never really risen up again.

In the high school bleachers that day, my sister and I were engaging in what I call Reparative Next-Generation Healing, or Next-Gen Repair. That's when what we didn't receive or couldn't do for ourselves at key moments in the past can be rectified through acts we perform for the next generation, whether it's for a child of our own, a niece or nephew, a student, or a younger mentee.

If you eloped instead of planning a wedding that a loved one couldn't help plan or attend, you can be the one to help a younger relative plan their wedding and make a toast to those who can't be there. If you struggled through infant care without help from family, you can offer help to other new parents when the time comes. By helping younger people in the present, we can address the loss in a constructive way that reflects our beliefs and values today, and also do retroactive, reparative work to heal deficits our younger selves encountered in the past. As long as our actions benefit the present-day recipients and aren't done with the sole purpose of healing ourselves, everyone wins.

Graduations are my personal thing. My own three ceremonies were dismal, poorly attended affairs. The first one, from high school, was still so soon after my mother died. My family didn't attend my college graduation because my father couldn't leave my siblings alone for the weekend and the cost of flying all three of them to Chicago was out of reach. I didn't even stay in town long enough after graduate school ended to collect my diploma. It arrived at a PO box on New York's Upper East Side on a completely ordinary Thursday afternoon. I remember opening the big envelope as I walked out of the building and thinking, *I guess I have a master's now.*

So I'm at all of my kids' graduations with a small but mighty entourage in tow each time and, for the big ones, a weekend packed with celebratory events. Do I overdo it sometimes? Maybe, but they seem to relish the fun. And it's my honor to be able to offer it.

To be able to be there at all.

For a long time, a part of me believed I'd die at forty-two, as my mother did. Michele feared the same. And yet there we were at

Maya's graduation, the two of us, both of us years beyond the age our mother got to be. Professional accomplishments, home ownership, retirement savings, vacation plans: All of it fell away like an extra, unnecessary skin. How much of that really mattered? Just *being there* felt like a miracle. For thirty-six years, neither of us had taken this for granted.

Other people on the bleachers were starting to stare at us by then. They were probably wondering what on earth was going on. But I know there were others who understood why Michele and I were crying. They knew it wasn't because we were sad. It was nowhere near that simple. We were crying because being touched by death at an early age taught us about pain and horror and anguish and beauty and mystery and elemental wisdom, and about the exquisite preciousness of life, and it all came together in one big rush right then, right there, under the blinding California sun.

This life. It's extraordinary. But for us to learn that and carry the knowledge with us for so long, someone we loved had to die.

Sometimes this feels like a burden. Sometimes it feels like an awesome responsibility. Much of the time now, it feels like a gift. Granted, no one ever said that the road from there to here would be easy. No one ever told us it would be so rich or rewarding, either.

* * *

CHAPTER SIX

The Rings of Grief

L ISTEN CLOSELY.
Can you hear it? It's the low growl of remote thunder, in harmony with a steady, whipping wind. The rumbling builds to a crescendo, until it explodes in furious cracks of lightning. Torrents of rain come hammering down.

It lasts for so much longer than you think a storm can last.

Then comes the slow retreat into remission, with fitful recessions across the plains. As the first timid rays of sun break through, you survey the damage left behind. Birdsong, now. Crickets. New, tentative green shoots soon appear. Watch them grow. Until the next gentle wind picks up and the aperture of the sky constricts again.

Do you hear it now? The dim rumble of distant thunder, heading this way. Again.

This is the nature of long-term grief.

A lock-step model of stage theory is, thankfully, a concept of the past. Newer models of bereavement—what I call "third-wave grief theory"—now rely on metaphors of seasons, spirals, cycles, layers, waves, or tiers to represent the extended, repetitive patterns of mourning as it progresses over time.

Twenty-first-century models are as plentiful (and as individual) as the minds that have developed them. I've chosen a few of my favorites below to demonstrate their variety.

Model Behavior

AFTER MORE than forty years as a therapist and educator in the bereavement field, Terrie Rando has come to view mourning as a multi-
tiered experience that involves a series of "drop-down actions."

She describes a cylinder-shaped children's toy with horizontal
levels inside. "Basically, each of the levels is a little floor with a hole
in it, and the objective is to get a marble to go through the hole and
drop down to the next level," she explains. "I think mourning is
very much like that. You go round and round, dealing with certain
issues to the best extent you can at a certain point in time and then,
boom. You drop down to another level. It might be weeks or months
or years later that you're going around and then, *boom*. Another
level.

"It's not at all linear," she continues. "Some of the same issues are
going to be revisited again and again but at different developmental
ages, especially for those of us who lost loved ones so young." Revisiting and reprocessing a loss from new and different perspectives allows us to reach these ever-deepening levels of insight.

For a while in 2017, a grief metaphor called "the ball in the box"
was circulating around the Internet. I first encountered it in a Twitter
post by a Canadian communications manager named Lauren Herschel, whose mother had recently died. Her doctor had introduced
her to the ball in the box metaphor to describe the chaotic yet evolving nature of early grief.

"There's a box with a ball in it," Herschel wrote. "And a pain button . . . In the beginning, the ball is huge. You can't move the box
without the ball hitting the pain button. It rattles around on its own
in there and hits the button over and over. You can't control it—it
just keeps hurting. Sometimes it seems unrelenting.

"Over time the ball gets smaller. It hits the button less and less but
when it does, it hurts just as much. It's better because you can function day to day more easily. But the downside is that the ball randomly hits that button when you least expect it.

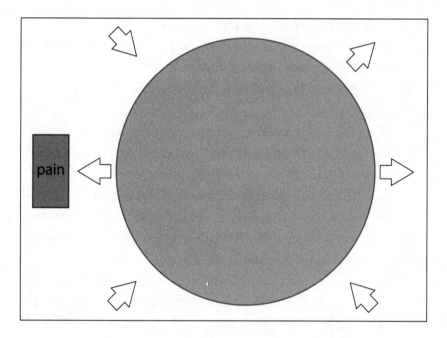

"For most people, the ball never really goes away. It might hit less and less and you have more time to recover between hits, unlike when the ball was still giant. I thought this was the best description of grief I've heard in a long time.

"I told my stepdad about the ball in the box . . . He now uses it to talk about how he's feeling. 'The ball was really big today. It wouldn't lay off the button. I hope it gets smaller soon.'

"Slowly, it is."

The majority of the 17,600 people who liked her post found the Ball in the Box metaphor helpful. "Thanks 4 sharing the BALL IN THE BOX analogy," one respondent wrote. "My daughter died in July and we are adjusting to life without her. I know that people process grief differently, and now I have a new analogy to share with my family. Currently we have different-sized balls and that's just the way it is."

"That is such an accurate description," wrote another. "My dad died in 1978 and my mum in 2013 but the ball hit the button out of the blue when my son got into university and I couldn't tell my parents. You don't 'get over' the loss, you learn to live with the absence."

One poster, however, offered a different response: "The ball will never, ever get smaller. The box is your life, when grief happens the ball takes over the box. Over time your life grows, changes, gets bigger making the ball seem smaller, but the ball always stays the same (IMHO)." Instead of a ball that shrinks, this person visualized a box that grows.

That's the benefit of multiple models. Some may speak to your experience for a while, some not at all, and others will capture it so exquisitely you'll wonder how anyone could have discovered a portal to the inner workings of your mind.

The bigger-box metaphor is similar to a concept that appears in the 2018 BBC video "How Does Grief Change Over Time?" In eight and a half minutes, a grief therapist named Cate draws a circle about the size of a melon in the center of a large sheet of paper.

"Imagine this is you," she says. "And everything about your life is contained within this circle." When a major loss occurs, she explains, every area of your life is affected by that grief. She fills up the whole circle with scrawls from her black marker to illustrate this point.

We used to think, she explains, that over time the messy scrawl in the middle of the circle diminished in size until it disappeared. "But the thinking now," she says, "is that [it] stays the same"—[she draws a larger circle around the original circle]—"but our life grows around it." Our grief remains at the center of our life stories, but proportionally, its size shrinks in relation to everything else around it. That is, until an anniversary, a birthday, or a special occasion occurs, and we dip back into that messy center well again.

Most mourners only care about two stages of grief: the stage where they feel really, really bad and the stage where they feel better. Renowned British psychiatrist Colin Murray Parkes popularized this two-step process in 1970, when he proposed that uncomplicated bereavement begins with states of distress and impaired functioning and moves toward a state of recovery, in which the mourner can function independently at a new and different level.

I appreciate the representations above for their creativity, simplicity, and authenticity. Mourners can tell when a model reflects actual experiences, as opposed to one that tries to force lived experience into an existing framework. Most models, however, imply that once a mourner has metabolized their most acute responses to loss, their grief will achieve a plateau. The ball hits the pain button with less frequency. Life grows large enough for the circle of grief to diminish in comparison.

But the Aftergrief extends beyond a return to optimal functioning. Bereavement can—and often does—lead to an even more expansive state of awareness. This is the place where meaning originates and develops, and where purpose is pursued.

I've been searching for a while for a unifying model of bereavement that can accommodate the plurality of grief responses and also provide containment for the breadth of long-term experience. It needs to be a model that grows out of mourners' real-life experiences and prioritizes their own perceptions of events. That's known as a "grounded theory" in the social sciences, meaning researchers methodically gather and analyze data—in this case, interviews and stories—looking for patterns and divergences. The scientific method poses a hypothesis and sets out to prove or disprove it with systematic research. Grounded theory, by comparison, relies on inductive reasoning to draw conclusions from the collected data.

That's how Nancy Hogan, Janice Morse, and Maritza Cerdas Tason developed what they called the Experiential Theory of Bereavement in 1996. They interviewed thirty-four adults—eight men and twenty-six women—who had experienced the death of a child, parent, or sibling. Seventeen of the losses had occurred as a result of chronic illness, and seventeen were due to sudden factors. The deaths were a mix of recent and historical, occurring anywhere from six months to thirty-seven years ago. Each interview began with the open-ended request "Tell me what happened," and the bereaved individuals spontaneously narrated their stories from there.

From the thirty-four transcripts collected, the researchers identified seven "Processes of Surviving a Death." These are:

1. *Getting the news.* This includes learning of a diagnosis, coping with shock, calculating the odds of survival, deciding upon a care protocol, negotiating treatment, enduring stress, maintaining hope, witnessing a decline, and ending the suffering. This first step applies only for death due to illness.
2. *Finding out* (about the death). News is delivered and mourners respond. This is the starting line for learning how to survive without the loved one. It's also the entry point in the list for sudden deaths.
3. *Facing realities.* This includes enduring states of numbness and confusion as mourners go through the social obligations of sharing the news, organizing a funeral or memorial, and facing constant reminders of a loved one's absence. The logical mind that knows the person died is now in conflict with the emotional mind that struggles to accept this new condition.
4. *Becoming engulfed with suffering.* This is the red-hot core of grief, where numbness and shock give way to missing, longing, hopelessness, guilt, anger, the physical pain of separation, fear, anxiety, and despair. We start letting go of our hopes and assumptions for the future that included this person. Sneak attacks occur frequently. We try to make sense of what's happened as we focus on getting from day to day.
5. *Emerging from the suffering.* This marks a transition into what philosopher Thomas Attig calls "relearning how to live in the world." Survivors experience more good days than bad, and begin dedicating more energy to the future than to the past. The loved one's presence is often felt in new and comforting ways.
6. *Getting on with life.* Humor, laughter, and hope return to a survivor's days. Confidence about moving forward without the

loved one develops, and new commitments toward future happiness are made. By finding courage to face occasional hard days, survivors build inner resilience. They still long for and miss the loved one, but can now hold the potential for happiness side by side with their sorrow, and they accept that they can experience these feelings simultaneously.

7. *Experiencing personal growth.* Hogan, Morse, and Tason noticed what other researchers have also found: Engagement with the acute pain of grief and the struggle to emerge from it are necessary ingredients for being positively changed by loss. If there can ever be a payoff from losing a loved one, this is where it's found. Hogan, Morse, and Tason found that mourners reported becoming less judgmental and more caring, tolerant, and compassionate. They described living more intentionally and deliberately with the raw knowledge that death could occur to anyone, at any time.

Although these processes are numbered, they're not meant to be unidirectional, and the researchers don't predict or prescribe how long an individual should engage with each process. The Experiential Theory also emphasizes the cyclical and recurring nature of long-term bereavement. Still, it's hard to visualize the ebbs and flows and fluctuations of grief that typify long-term survivors' stories. Despite this excellent analysis, I was still left searching for a model that represented the Aftergrief.

Then, while conducting the eighty-one interviews for this book, I stumbled upon one. Or, more accurately, the interviewees revealed one to me. Just as the researchers above had invited their subjects to start with the prompt "Tell me what happened," I began each interview with the open-ended invitation I've been using for more than twenty-five years: "Please start your story wherever you'd like to begin."

And here's what happened next: When I listened—really *listened*—to candid, uncensored stories of loss without trying to apply a structure or a framework to the mourners' experiences, an organic, common-sense model of long-term bereavement started to emerge. And it looked nothing like a list or a set of prescribed steps or stages. Instead, it resembled a process of retraction and expansion, retraction and expansion, like a slow heartbeat, over the course of a whole life.

In eighty-one out of eighty-one interviews for this book, this was the story I heard. Whether a loss occurred at age four or thirty-four, whether it was due to sudden death or death from a terminal illness, the loss of a parent or of a best friend, the stories all told of a sorrow that came on strong at first, loosened its grip for a period of time, took hold again months or even years later, only to loosen its grip again . . . and then seized up tightly once more. In the words of Buddhist nun and author Pema Chödrön, things come together and things fall apart. Then they come together and fall apart again.

About 90 percent of interviewees I spoke with began their stories with the details of how a loved one died. They detailed a diagnosis, a death, and a period of acute loss, tracking their movement from a pit of deep sorrow to a new approximation of normalcy. Quite a few of the stories continued into more nuanced and detailed discussions of how the mourner came to make sense of the loss and the meaning they draw from it today.

Nearly every story was punctuated by episodes of Old Grief and New Old Grief, in a back-and-forth motion between grieving and living and growing and re-grieving and living and grieving anew and living and growing again. The more time that had elapsed since the loss, it seemed, the more dynamic their processes had been.

From these stories, I started to visualize the flow of grief over time as movement among a series of concentric rings, like a bull's-eye composed of three nested circles. I call them the Rings of Grief.

The Rings of Grief

LET'S START in the middle.

The very center of the bull's-eye is the red-hot core of Active Grief. This is where we retract after a major loss occurs, the dimen-

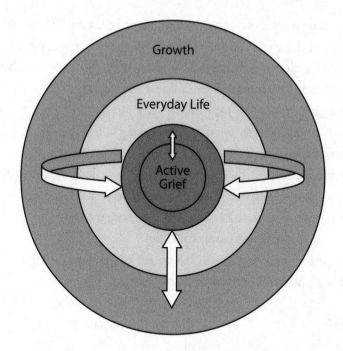

sion where the most acute and painful grief responses are felt after someone we love dies.

What does an average Active Grief reaction look and feel like? It's almost impossible to say. Some people express grief outwardly. Some don't. Some have extensive support networks, while others manage on their own. Different cultures have different rules and prohibitions for outward displays of mourning.

Active Grief is custom designed for each individual. My response will look different from yours, and yours won't look like anyone else's. There's no one-size-fits-all prescription. There isn't even a one-size-fits-two.

Active Grief is an elemental process. It strips away all that's superficial and exposes our most raw and vulnerable core. That's why I think of grief in terms of *elements rather than stages*. The elements of grief are an inclusive crew, making room for any possible emotional, cognitive, and behavioral responses that might occur after a loss. Numbness is an element of grief. So is anger. And relief. A bereaved person may experience many elements, or just a few. Some will flare up, fade, and flare up again at a later date. Others may not appear after this particular loss but will arrive in full force when a different loss occurs in the future. The defining elements of one loss may be very different from the ones that typify another. That's okay. Every loss is different, and so is every response.

Recognizing a high number of elements doesn't mean you're suffering more than another person or that your loss is worse. It could mean, however, that you're experiencing your grief in a more multidimensional manner than others do, or you are more in touch with naming or recognizing your emotions.

A comprehensive, though by no means exhaustive, grouping of possible elements would have to include:

fear	blame	sadness
anxiety	shame	sorrow
anger	regret	hopelessness
rage	embarrassment	irritation
numbness	guilt	helplessness
avoidance	self-reproach	terror
loneliness	disbelief	ferocity
despair	yearning	protest
magical thinking	shock	discomfort
liberation	escape	relinquishment
sleeplessness	agitation	isolation
depression	isolation	abandonment
panic	unreality	surreality
astonishment	outrage	contemplation
nostalgia	loss of control	introspection
self-recrimination	lightness	relief
rawness	tenderness	vulnerability
injustice	unfairness	determination
horror	heartache	denial
humor	rejection	revenge

withdrawal	restlessness	irritability
resistance	avoidance	denial
separation	distress	confusion

When we confront these elements we can almost feel our bodies contracting into an protected interior space, like an animal retreating into a corner to tend to its wounds. When a caterpillar enters its cocoon and disintegrates into a primordial puddle of goop? Active grief feels much like that.

Nonetheless, there *is* structural integrity in the chaos. The small white arrow inside the core of Active Grief—that's the oscillation of the Dual-Process model, representing how mourners swing back and forth between loss-focused and restoration-focused tasks after a loss, to protect themselves from overwhelming emotional pain.

The first year of Active Grief is filled with landmines as mourners encounter a series of firsts without their loved one. First holiday season, first birthdays, first spring, first summer, all the way up to the first anniversary of the death. It's also the period that's likely to include the most external support. Nancy, who lost her nineteen-year-old son to suicide, calls this twelve-month period "the Year of Shock and Making It Through."

"Basically, the first year is pretense," she explains. "It's like, 'If I pretend to be okay I can keep my job and my friends and my family won't worry about me.' So you pretend. Then the second year people back off a little bit, because you fooled them. You appear to be doing better than they thought you might be. This is good for the pretender, because you don't have to work as hard at the pretense. People aren't hovering anymore. But then it's just you and your immediate family working out the stuff that comes next. That was the year I was putting up Lee's Christmas stocking and I asked my younger son, 'Do you mind if we remember Lee during our holidays?' His answer was, 'Mom, it's okay. We should have Lee's stocking up. But I'm going to worry about you if you wrap presents and put them under the tree with a note that says, "To Lee, Love Santa."'"

So we worked it out. The rule was no presents under the tree but we can have a stocking, and we can celebrate the birthday."

The Middle Ring: Everyday Life

AFTER SOME time in Active Grief—and the amount of time spent here also varies from person to person—the majority of bereaved individuals slowly move outward into the middle ring of Everyday Life, where most of us spend the majority of our time. This is where we attend school, go to work, take care of family members, fold laundry, play Monopoly, fly off to the Caribbean for vacation, barbecue steaks with friends, binge-watch Netflix, tell stories about the funny thing that happened in the Costco parking lot last week, and make plans for next summer—all without feeling overburdened by grief. We reinvest energy in the wider world and become more accustomed to making and implementing decisions without a loved one's participation. The person is still present in our thoughts and often missed, sometimes deeply, but some—perhaps many—of our old rules of engagement have changed. We adapt as best we can to these new rules. Ideally, we encounter moments of joy and laughter again.

Crossing the threshold from Active Grief to Everyday Life can be marked by a distinct event, like the first morning you wake up and feel excited to greet the day. Sometimes it comes as a gently whispered "Hello, world. I'm back." Or a slight physical sensation of expansion, as if your lung capacity has just increased by 10 percent. The transition may happen so gradually that you barely notice it happening until it already has. No matter. You'll know when you're on the other side.

After Erin lost her mother to a car accident, a full three years passed before she was able to recognize happiness again, Erin says. Over the next decade she and her father developed a very close relationship, but when Erin was thirty, he died from complications from cancer treatment. "This time I was like, *I cannot lose three years on this*," Erin recalls. "But I also knew that first year was going to be miserable.

And it was. I was surprised by how hard it was to feel like an orphan as an adult. I felt super intensely sad, crying every day for probably over a year. But I can distinctly remember that at about a year and a half I woke up one day and was like, *Oh, I feel more like myself again.* You know how people talk about having a set point of happiness? I will always, eventually, arrive back to that set point, I think."

We encounter various ups and downs in Everyday Life, of course, but for the most part it's a place of relative emotional equilibrium where we experience more happy and neutral days than sad ones. This is where, often to our amazement, life goes on.

The Outer Ring: Post-traumatic Growth

FOR MOST of the twentieth century, psychiatrists and psychologists focused on the relationship between traumatic events and stressful outcomes, especially those that required psychiatric intervention. Grief therapy was mainly concerned with helping people transition from states of Active Grief back to baseline functioning in Everyday Life. "Recovery" was assumed to be synonymous with returning to the life of the living in the middle ring.

But in the 1990s, a pair of psychologists at the University of North Carolina discovered that the number of trauma and loss survivors who reported positive long-term outcomes as a result of their adversities was larger than the number of those who required psychiatric help. Richard Tedeschi and Lawrence Calhoun realized that a significant percentage of bereaved people were doing more than surviving their losses and returning to relative stability. Many of them were using adversity as a springboard to achieve personal growth. Some were reaching even higher levels of functionality than they'd possessed before.

Tedeschi and Calhoun's work launched a large body of research into what became known as "post-traumatic growth." Unlike resilience, which is the ability to encounter high-stress events without being damaged by their challenges, post-traumatic growth involves personal transformation. As individuals struggle to adjust to a stressful circumstance, they develop skills and insights that exceed those they had before the trauma occurred.

The transformative power of suffering isn't a new concept. It's been noted in storytelling and literature for millennia, dating back to biblical narratives and early religious texts. Ruminating about inner fortitude and the determination to persist beyond a loved one's death was a common theme among Romantic poets, too.

Wartime accounts and narratives of genocide have long included authors' musings about existential matters and the meaning of life. In 1946, soon after the end of World War II, psychiatrist Viktor Frankl published the groundbreaking book *Man's Search for Meaning*, in which he recounted his years as a prisoner in Nazi death camps. In the book he introduced the concept of logotherapy, in which Frankl maintained that humans are motivated by the will to live with meaning and purpose even under the most tragic conditions.

Nine years later, psychologist Abraham Maslow, best known for creating the Hierarchy of Needs, conducted research on what he termed "Deficiency Motivation and Growth Motivation" and noted that "the most important learning experiences reported to me by my subjects were single life experiences such as tragedies, deaths, traumata . . . which forced change in the life-outlook of the person and consequently in everything that he did."

Tedeschi and Calhoun's studies of post-traumatic growth are notable for several reasons. First, they prioritized survivors' reports of positive changes they'd recognized in their own thoughts, behaviors, priorities, and worldviews rather than relying on accounts from observers. Second, the researchers discovered that their subjects' growth experiences did not negate or replace distress. Their legitimate hardships remained stressful, but personal growth still occurred. In fact, the most growth occurred among those who identified both positive and negative outcomes of facing a major life crisis.

Positive change, it appears, occurs as a result of internal struggle. When an existing worldview—such as "the world is a safe place" or "my parents will always be here to protect me"—is shattered, our minds need to construct a substitute. This can lead to the creation of new and useful schemas. For this reason, post-traumatic growth is more accessible to teens and adults who've already established a worldview and are capable of changing it than children whose perspectives may be less developed or more rigid.

Positive changes can certainly occur among mourners with a recent loss, who are still actively grieving. That said, there's no quick or direct pipeline from the inner core of trauma and loss to the outer ring of growth. The struggle to adapt to one's new existence and create a new assumptive world to inhabit is work that's typically accomplished in the ring of Everyday Life. That's where we continuously bump up against the reality of an absence, test out new rules of engagement, revisit and reprocess events of the past, and restructure our expectations and dreams in a post-loss environment. All of this can deliver us into the outer ring of growth, where a new worldview can make room for life to be more complicated, surprising, and painful than we understood before, as well as more wondrous and meaningful than we otherwise could have imagined.

As Tedeschi, Calhoun, and other researchers found, individuals who report post-traumatic growth describe eight categories of change:

1. Increased appreciation for life in general
2. A changed sense of what's important
3. A radical shift in priorities
4. Closer, more meaningful relationships with others
5. Increased sense of compassion, tolerance, empathy, and sensitivity to the suffering of others
6. A sense of increased personal strength, as well as a recognition of vulnerability
7. Increased engagement with spiritual and existential matters
8. Change in identity from constructing new narratives that can accommodate the death

Post-traumatic growth tends to appear less in those whose worlds have been shattered by violent or sudden trauma. As Tedeschi and Calhoun point out, "We must also appreciate that trauma survivors often do not see themselves as embarking on searches for meaning or attempts to construct benefits from their experiences. They are either attempting to survive or trying to determine if survival is worthwhile." When transition from Active Grief to Everyday Life is effort enough, just getting to the middle ring and staying there is plenty.

We also must remember that time spent in Everyday Life, as well as expansion into post-traumatic growth, are rarely permanent migrations. In the course of a long and varied life, another loss or a painful reminder of a prior loss can send us hurtling back into the Inner Core at any time, sometimes faster than we thought possible. Birthdays and anniversaries are notorious catapults. Holidays, songs on the radio, even the scent of a certain flower. From that Inner Core it takes time for us to expand back out into Everyday Life and Growth again. Ideally, the core of Active Grief becomes a place we dip into and visit rather than a place where we reside.

That red-hot center isn't a comfortable place. Nonetheless, it's an important cauldron. What's brewed there is necessary for alchemy in the outermost ring, where the pain of bereavement can be transformed into something extraordinary for yourself or others. That's how, over the long arc, loss becomes gain and gain, under the right conditions, becomes growth.

CHAPTER SEVEN

* * *

The Power of Story

A T FIRST there is the story of a loss, and it's a story that wants to be told.

It's the story of a diagnosis that arrives without warning; of a phone call piercing the dark at 4 A.M.; of a door swinging open to reveal an officer in blue. The children are called in to the living room. The swirling lights of the ambulance are visible from two blocks away. The doctor was wrong. The doctor was right. The story of a loss is your version of *what happened* before your version of *what came next* and *what it means to you* begins.

The story of a loss might look something like this:

We lived in a split-level ranch house in a nondescript suburb of New York. My father drove to work in Manhattan every weekday morning and returned for dinner by 6 P.M. My mother, a pianist, had left her job as a grade-school music teacher when she became pregnant with me. She taught me how to play the piano, and accompanied me when I practiced flute. My sister played piano, clarinet, and baseball. My brother, the youngest, had just started learning the saxophone. He rode bicycles in a cul-de-sac adjacent to our street with his best friend after school every day. We had a dog named Candy. A cat named PJ. My father's favorite television show was *All in the Family*. My mother's was *Soap*. On Tuesday nights we all watched *Happy Days* and *Laverne and Shirley* back-to-back.

We were, I thought, as ordinary a family as ordinary ever was.

But then when I was fourteen, a routine ob-gyn exam revealed a lump in my mother's left breast. "It's just a cyst. And the doctor said not to worry," she told me. No one questioned how a doctor could know this without diagnostic tests. We were not a family in the habit of doubting medical authority. So when her allergist noticed swelling under her armpit a full year later and suggested she have it checked, she dutifully went for a mammogram. And then a biopsy. The results were not what any of us wanted to hear. But it was news that called for action, so a mastectomy came next. And chemotherapy, and multiple follow-up scans.

We all continued on as if treatment + patience = the road back to normal. I started dating my first boyfriend that spring. My sweet sixteen party was held in June. My mother told us her scans had come back negative, and we celebrated with Häagen-Dazs ice cream that night. Vanilla Swiss Almond. Her chemotherapy was adjusted. My sister turned thirteen. My brother turned nine. Ronald Reagan was elected president. John Lennon was assassinated and my friends drove into New York to leave flowers across the street from his building, the Dakota, on Central Park West. I drove my mother to the oncologist and read *People* magazine in the waiting room while she gave blood and got her shots behind a closed door. Her white blood cell counts were good, she told me, as she carefully assembled herself back into the passenger seat. Her next CAT scan results were clear. We didn't celebrate, this time. By now we were accustomed to good news. She was getting better, that was what mattered. Her medications were adjusted again. The calendar flipped over to 1981. The Iranian hostages were released. Someone tried to kill the president. Someone tried to kill the pope. I finished junior year with a 97 in English and an 84 in trigonometry. At the end of June, we drove my sister to summer camp in Connecticut in the family's blue Oldsmobile station wagon. The following week I went to see James Taylor perform outdoors, in the pouring rain, with three friends on the Fourth of July.

When I returned home that evening, something was wrong with my mother. Very, very wrong. Her stomach was suddenly all swollen. She didn't have enough energy to lift herself out of a recliner.

My father called the doctor from the kitchen and, after a few beats, called for her to pick up the phone on the bedroom extension. "What *is* this?" I heard her ask. Then, "Okay. Mm-hmm."

Each day brought another loss of function. She couldn't keep food down. She couldn't walk on her own. She became dehydrated. I was unclear about what was happening, and why it was happening so fast. On day five, my father left me in charge for a few hours so he could meet with a rabbi. This meant something important: My father was avowedly secular. He was not a rabbi-meeting kind of man. On day six, my mother vomited up black bile and the paramedics were called.

My father sat me down in the living room while we waited for the ambulance. *Your mother is going to the hospital, and she won't be coming back.* That's what he said. Also, *I've known for a long time.*

Wait. Known what?

Since the operation last spring.

What? But what about the scans?

Oh. Those. They hadn't been normal. They hadn't even been close to normal. They lit up like a Christmas tree every time. That's how he said it.

And the celebrations?

I know what you're thinking, he said. *Believe me, I've thought it, too. But how could I tell her, or you kids? When the surgeon told me he couldn't get it all . . .*

The ambulance pulled into the driveway. There was no time to make this new data compute. Neighbors seeped out of their houses and into the street. Everyone knew now. Or could guess. As the EMTs tried to carry her away, my mother cried out, "My wig! I need my wig!"

"Bring it with her nightgown!" my father shouted over his shoulder as they disappeared through the garage.

From behind the wheel of my mother's station wagon, I made a mad rush to the hospital, followed by a long wait in the ER, followed by another mad dash to the summer camp in Connecticut to bring my sister home. Relatives drove in from three directions to say their goodbyes. The next morning, my mother slipped into a coma. Two days later, in the middle of the night, my father woke me from a fitful sleep on the hospital waiting-room couch.

"It's over," he said, his voice catching on the second word.

I'd made him promise that she wouldn't be alone at the end, and he told me he'd been right beside her, holding her hand. But my trust had been decimated by then. I demanded proof, which he couldn't give.

When I sat next to her body to say goodbye, I did not cry. The nurse handed me the little plastic bag that held my mother's nightgown, wig, underwear, and a pair of cheap terrycloth slippers—"You don't want to forget this," she said—and still I did not cry. But walking across the dark hospital parking lot just before dawn, I caught a sharp, tangy whiff of freshly mowed grass and the injustice of it all leveled me, that something so recently living had been so unceremoniously cut down.

My aunt told me that my mother's last words were to my father. "Take care of my children," she'd said. I did not know what to do with knowledge of a love so powerful it could consume a final wish. I could not imagine ever loving someone that much. I felt certain no one would ever love me like that again.

A few hours later, the four of us (only four, now) sat around the kitchen table in the slanted morning sun and stared at one another. No one knew what the leading edge of our new story would be. What lay behind us no longer existed. Whatever was coming next was unknown. That morning of July 12, 1981, felt like my personal line of demarcation: the moment when the first half of my life ended and the second half began.

A Story Takes Shape

THIS WAS my original story of mother loss, which began forming in my mind soon after my mother died. I have a different story about losing my father in my fortieth year, and other stories for subsequent losses small and large. But the story of my first major loss is the one that's always held the most weight. Once you've carried your mother to and from the bathroom or kissed her cool, gray forehead goodbye, you can't ever not have done those things. Once you've discovered that human existence is a time-limited arrangement and for some that time will be short, you can't not know this ever again.

My mother's early death saturated my worldview moving forward, set my early expectations for what others were likely to offer at times of distress, and became the narrative I returned to most frequently for reflection and revision as the years passed. That first death was the one that taught me how stories of loss develop and, later, how they change.

I don't remember sitting down after my mother died and thinking, "This is the part where I create the story." The process was much more involuntary than that. The human mind naturally gravitates toward the familiar comfort of narrative. Story, after all, is the vehicle through which we think, imagine, build relationships, make sense of our experiences, and form our identities. "Narrative is present in every age, in every place, in every society," philosopher Roland Barthes has said. "It begins with the very history of mankind and there nowhere is nor has been a people without narrative."

A hunger for story echoes throughout every day. "How did work go?" "What did you do at school?" "What symptoms did you notice and when?" "What happened to your car?" Birth stories, war stories, relationship stories: all narratives. Stories of setbacks, achievements, triumphs, surprises, and loss: more narratives. We're surrounded by story all the time.

Almost as soon as an experience ends—and sometimes even as it's unfolding—the mind gets busy arranging selected facts, memories, and events into sequences across time to create stories with identifiable beginnings, middles, and ends. We cast our gaze backwards, seeking out cause-and-effect relationships, blazing a retroactive path to logically track movement from *there* to *here*. This happened, and then that happened, which—oh, yeah—led to *that*, which made me feel *this*, which now I see helped me realize *that*.

Creating a coherent story in the aftermath of a death offers a sense of control over what may otherwise feel like a set of unmanageable events. "I was trying to gather information, that was my big thing," says Evie, whose best friend died by suicide four years ago. "Because I felt powerless. I wanted to piece together the what and why. Who knew? Why didn't anybody do anything? Was there a way we could have stopped it?"

Especially after a violent or random death, survivors often comb through memories and facts and details in their minds, looking for a point of entry where someone could have stepped in and changed the course of events, searching for the pivotal moment when someone could have made a different choice and created a different outcome. When we can imagine that alternate storyline, the actual story, the one in which that decision wasn't made, then tracks in a way that makes sense. *That other thing could have happened but it didn't, and because it didn't that's how we wound up here.*

Organizing disordered thoughts into a coherent, manageable account is what helps us make sense of a crisis and fit it into a larger system of personal meaning. "Meaning is not something out there that is given to us," explains psychologist Stephen Joseph. "It is something we give to ourselves." This quest to find meaning through narrative appears to be such an important, instinctive, and uniquely human imperative that some bereavement experts have suggested the species *Homo sapiens* could just as well be classified *Homo narrans.*

At the same time, the shock and numbness of early grief often tax our capacity to craft a coherent story in the short term. Immediately after a death, emotionally charged memories and facts swirl around without shape or order, resisting attempts at control. New bits of information may arrive in random and scattershot fashion. We may have trouble focusing on a single image long enough to logically link it to another. When we can, the connections may feel comforting one moment and disturbing the next.

I don't understand. I can't wrap my mind around it. It doesn't make sense. This is the mind without story.

As the author Rebecca Solnit has written, stories are our "compasses and architecture, we navigate by them, we build our sanctuaries and prisons out of them, and to be without a story is to be lost in the vastness of a world that spreads in all directions like arctic tundra or sea ice." I remember so clearly the bewildering state of narrative limbo I inhabited during the first few weeks after my mother died. For sixteen months I'd thought I'd been living inside a story progressing toward her recovery and the resumption of normal family life. But that storyline had just been derailed by her swift decline and the facts disclosed in its midst—that my father had known she was dying but her children hadn't, and that perhaps neither had she. These new bits of information were so incongruent with what I'd believed until then that I had to revise my entire story to contain them, deconstructing my old version while simultaneously reconstructing a replacement version. But first I had to let go of my prior assumptions and replace them with new ones, in effect re-forming a worldview in which what had previously seemed impossible actually could happen.

Did happen. Happened. Past tense.

In that disorienting transitional space between the dismantling of my prior story and the formation of a new one—what psychologists call a state of "scriptlessness"—I tried out different versions of what might have happened, testing to see which iterations felt most plausible and, of those, which I was willing to accept. I'd been writing to a pen pal in Minnesota for several years, and one day I sat down and tried to tell her, in a handwritten letter, that my mother had just died. Each draft seemed more inaccurate and illogical than the last. Whenever I got to the part where she hadn't been told how sick she was, my mind would turn quick somersaults.

That's not possible, I'd think. *That couldn't have happened in our family.*

Could it?

And then, *Actually . . . I think it did.*

In the end I wrote something brutally reductive like "My mother died last week. She'd been sick for a long time." Those stripped-down facts were the only version I could count on to be true.

I didn't realize it then, but I was engaging in what social psychologist John Harvey calls "account making" after a loss. Harvey, who has extensively researched the intersection between bereavement and storytelling, identifies account making as the period after a loss when we repeatedly run the details of a death through our minds, fitting people into roles, working and reworking the facts and the connections between them until we land on a version that feels emotionally and intellectually complete. We then share that story with others. In this way, individuals make sense of a loss through negotiation and communication.

Account making after a major loss, Harvey says, is essential for creating a new sense of identity and to help us adapt to the practical and emotional changes that will lie ahead. It's far from a speedy process, though. Harvey and his colleagues estimate it takes between one hundred and two hundred hours of cognitive and emotional processing to adapt to the loss of a significant, close relationship that lasted for one year. How much effort must it take, then, when the departed was someone you depended on for much longer? No exact measurement exists, but Harvey speculates this would consume "a staggering proportion" of time and emotional energy.

That's because "seismic life events," as psychologist Robert Neimeyer calls them, rock our worlds so sufficiently that we need to fully revise, repair, or replace some of our prior assumptions and goals. This type of cognitive processing takes time, but the payoff can be large. The more effort we put into developing a narrative of loss and recovery, the more likely we are to engage with issues of meaning, and the more we engage with issues of meaning, the more we confirm and perpetuate that person's importance in our own life stories.

Just as grief is a culturally relative experience, so too is the way we construct life stories. Every culture offers unspoken guidelines for how stories should be shaped, which messages are to be emphasized, what kind of stories are discouraged, and which themes will be dismissed. Western culture, for example, loves to celebrate protagonists who are strong, independent, and invulnerable. Even better if they champion adversity and come through stronger and wiser on the other side.

Every culture offers its own master narratives to help mourners cope with trauma and make sense of loss. In Western society, we have the John Wayne narrative that focuses on muscling through adversity; the narrative of vulnerability that emphasizes sadness and fear; and the narrative of compassion, which emphasizes concern and caretaking of others. Western culture does not lack for bereaved protagonists in the heroes, heroines, and superheroes that populate fairy tales, Bible stories, Shakespearean plays, novels, and comics. Moses, Esther, Heidi, Cinderella, Snow White, Hansel and Gretel, Ophelia, Hamlet, the sisters in *King Lear*, Dorothy in *The Wizard of Oz*, Little Orphan Annie, Nemo, Elsa, Oliver Twist, Heathcliff, Jane Eyre, Pip, David Copperfield, Huckleberry Finn, Luke Skywalker, Princess Leia, Katniss Everdeen, Frodo Baggins, Harry Potter, Batman, Superman, Spider-Man, Captain America . . . the list continues on. And don't get me started about Disney films. When parent loss is positioned as the ultimate tragedy to overcome, orphans become nearly as common as villains. And villains can also be bereaved. Hannibal Lecter, Freddy Kruger, and Lord Voldemort are just a few.

Fifty-three-year-old Kevin remembers how he looked to his film heroes to help him cope after the death of his newborn brother. Kevin was seven when his mother went into labor on Good Friday and a babysitter came to the house to watch him and his younger sisters while his parents departed for the hospital. That night the children watched the first half of *The Ten Commandments* on television, featuring Charlton Heston as Moses. As Kevin prepared for bed, he thought of the new baby he'd meet in the morning. He hoped this time it would be a brother.

A few hours later, his father returned home with sobering news.

The baby boy had been stillborn. Before returning to the hospital he assured his children that their mother was fine, that it hadn't been anyone's fault, and that he loved them all very much.

Later that night, Kevin went back downstairs, unable to sleep. "The babysitter was silently crying in the kitchen," he recalls. "We sat down with bowls of popcorn and watched the second half of *The Ten Commandments*, which was all about God sticking up for his chosen people, about good triumphing over evil, and at that moment I went dead inside, because I knew that was a lie. I had always believed there was a cause-and-effect universe in which good people like me and my family wouldn't suffer these kinds of losses. I felt like God had abandoned us, that God had abandoned me, and that the universe was just entirely wrong."

After a brief, intense period of grief, his mother became pregnant again. Anticipation of a healthy birth shifted the family's focus to the future. But Kevin's earlier assumptions remained shattered, and he hadn't yet found a framework to support his new worldview. He was still searching for a context to help him understand how such a loss could occur. Today he looks back and says:

That summer after the death, I became close with two boys who had also suffered losses in their families, one whose father had recently died and another whose older brother had died before this boy had been born. We never really talked about this among ourselves, but we threw ourselves into movies, especially fantasies that gave us power over life and death, and we became sort of imaginary superhero figures.

I became obsessed with the *Planet of the Apes* movies that were re-released that summer. Charlton Heston was involved in those, too, and I felt in essence that I had gone to bed on Good Friday on the edge of the Promised Land, in a world where God took care of good people, and woke up in a forbidden zone where nothing made any sense at all, where everything was destroyed and apes were in control. Those movies articulated the kind of spiritual disorientation I was feeling at the time. And death was contextualized in those stories. They made meaning of it, and I craved a story that would make meaning out of loss, because the previous story I had relied on had been destroyed.

So that apocalyptic world of *Planet of the Apes*, in which the destruction of an entire world is contextualized within a mythic story in which the hero is just as angry and upset and full of grief as I was, right down on his knees saying, "Damn you all to hell! How could you let this happen!" validated and gave meaning to what I was feeling on the inside. And [those two friends] were right there with me.

Watching the films, rejecting and accepting different messages, and fitting his experience into a larger framework of meaning helped Kevin engage in the first part of account making, known as "story development." That's when we grind the facts over and over in our minds to come up with a version that feels true, and, though we are not necessarily aware of it, to select a mythic substructure to contain it. My original story of loss was the story of a woman who hadn't been told how sick she was, and of three children who suffered as a result. The teller of this story was furious with her father and the doctors, and didn't attempt to hide it.

After a sudden loss, story development is often marked by a search for information or justice. After journalist Roxanne Roberts's father died by suicide, "I read every book I could get my hands on about suicide," she explains. "I tried to make sense of it all, tried to find reason in an irrational choice."

Story development also can start before a death occurs, such as when an illness is diagnosed or trouble first arrives on the scene. For Alexandra, it was both. She was a sophomore in high school when her father was diagnosed with prostate cancer. Four months later her mother died of sudden heart failure, and ten months after that, her father died, too. In between those losses, she devoured whatever information she could find about heart failure and prostate cancer, collecting facts she could piece together into a narrative that made sense to her at that age.

"I had an intense need to better understand the medical aspects of things," she recalls. "My mom's family has a lot of physicians and nurses in it, so I had a lot of access to medical materials. I was voraciously reading about cardiac issues, prostate cancer, and cancer in general, everything down to the autopsy reports, trying to better understand. At school I was always drawn towards science, and so I think going into the science of it was maybe a distancing way to try to make meaning of it. You know, like, if I can understand the biology behind what happened, at least I can understand why her body stopped working and why she died."

Testing and Telling

THE NEXT part of account making—testing—occurs as we imagine sharing the story and receiving a response. Through this type of anticipatory storytelling, we engage in imagined dialogues with therapists, friends, loved ones, inner critics, our lost loved ones, and even our own conscience, letting structure and details emerge, trying out different versions of events. This is what I was doing in multiple drafts of letters to my pen pal, trying out different versions to see which one sounded and felt correct.

Testing can also be an interactive, reciprocal process. When someone calls with news of a death and our first question is, "What happened?" we're trying to collect facts for our story-development process. At the same time, whoever made the call is testing out a narrative when they share the details. The more calls made, the more opportunities for testing arise.

The final aspect of account making—referred to as confiding, or disclosing—occurs when the story is shared in oral or written form with an audience of one or more. "When the scaffolding is knocked down from beneath us, we have to build a new platform on which to stand," Robert Neimeyer explains. "And as is true in most construction projects, we do well to have others join us in that labor, maybe even some who are architects and know what they're talking about." They could be friends, partners, relatives, therapists—anyone with curiosity and compassion who can sit with us in our pain, offer empathy, show interest, and ideally help us reach new insights.

A story that's confided converts facts privately held or a secret concealed into an artifact that can be received with curiosity and contained by a community, even if that's only a community of two. A listener's acceptance offers validation that what happened was important, explains Mollie Marti, founder of the National Resilience Institute, which helps communities around the world prepare for and recover from tragic losses. It says, *What happened to you matters.* And then we might look back and think, *My healing started that day, when I felt that my story was heard.*

"It's the difference between carrying that pain within you and letting it eat away at you, versus bringing it to light," Marti explains. "So to the extent that we can create these safe environments and environments of connection and empathy for each other, we can play a role in helping each other heal. You don't need to be a therapist to do that."

Unfortunately, not everyone has the social or temporal resources to create accounts or confide in others. Both processes require open-ended time and compassionate others willing to devote the same, which are often hard to come by when abject survival must take precedence after a loss. Grief may then become congested or compressed.

"What happens to those people?" Harvey asks. "Our suspicion is that they suffer both directly and indirectly (sometimes psychosomatically), because they cannot address their pain and grief effectively." Unexpressed emotional pain, he predicts, ripples through a mourner's thoughts, feelings, body, and actions, building up until it finds a pathway for expression.

Account making is so important to coping after a death, Harvey maintains, that without it we cannot grieve to our fullest capacities. So important is this process that stories don't even have to be verifiably true to benefit their tellers. For example, if a loved one died in a car accident in which the use of alcohol was indisputably a factor but the storyteller resists accepting this and leaves alcohol out of the telling, he'll still find solace from crafting, testing, and sharing a story.

"Historical truthfulness is somewhere in the mix, but it isn't the critical ingredient," Harvey explains. "The work you do on the story and the public aspect of telling the story seem to be more important than having the exact facts down. And of course, in many cases, you can't have the exact facts. Because what are the exact facts of a loss?"

Death may be a definitive, verifiable event in the medical world, but in the interpersonal world one person's anguish or despair does not necessarily resemble another's. That's especially true in families, where pressure to conform to a shared version of events can easily conflict with different experiences and points of view.

I'm reminded of an anecdote I heard a few years ago from a woman I'll call Susannah. Right after her mother died, Susannah and her sister entered the hospital room to say their final goodbyes. Susannah walked to the left side of the bed and picked up their mother's hand. Her sister walked to the right side of the bed and picked up their mother's other hand.

"She's so cold," Susannah said, at exactly the same moment her sister remarked, "She's still warm."

Which sister was right? Which sister was wrong? Does it matter? While the facts of a death may be fixed, each person's interpretation of those facts will be individual and unique. A story of loss need not be true for everyone who hears it. It need only feel true to the teller. What matters, above all, is that it's told.

* * *

CHAPTER EIGHT

People, We Need to Talk
(and Write, and Paint, and Perform)

S HARING STORIES of loss has been a human salve for as long as stories have been told. Shakespeare knew this in 1606 when, while writing *Macbeth*, he had Malcolm encourage Macduff to "give sorrow words," lest Macduff's already burdened heart might break. Fifteen years later, English scholar Robert Burton, in his nine-hundred-page literary/scientific extravaganza *The Anatomy of Melancholy*, drew a direct connection between expressions of grief and improved mental and physical health.

This is the third component of John Harvey's account-making model: confiding. It's the performative, public part of the equation, and it involves presenting pieces of our stories to others who we hope will care about and empathize with our struggles, and offer support or perspective.

We grieve through story, but even more so, through story expressed. Studies conducted over the past forty years have found that mourners who confide in others, especially during the first year after a loss, ruminate less about the death when they're alone, have fewer health-related problems, and maintain more positive relationships with others. These benefits appear to come from the discharge of strong emotions, and also from establishing and reinforcing compassionate human connections.

"I'm here for you," a listener says merely through the act of sitting still and listening. "I'm here with you. You don't have to bear this alone."

When stories are told to others, tellers often expand beyond the factual to reveal the emotional aspects of their stories. Such higher self-disclosure of emotions is also positively related to personal growth after a traumatic event. This may be why mourners who have stable, consistent social support for confiding consistently score higher on post-traumatic growth scales. Supportive confidantes help individuals craft their narratives just by virtue of listening, and can offer insights and personal experiences that can be evaluated and even folded into the teller's story of loss.

I learned this firsthand when I reinterviewed seventeen women who'd appeared in the original version of *Motherless Daughters* in 1994. When we'd first met, most of them had never shared their stories of mother loss with anyone, not because they hadn't wanted to, but because they'd never been given permission—or never felt they had permission—to speak freely and at length about it before. Sharing their stories helped to diminish the power a previously unspoken story had over them. Many of them described the initial interview as both a relief and a release. All these years later, when they sat down to share the full arcs of their stories for this book, I was struck by how many of them mentioned our original interview in the early 1990s as a turning point in their larger story, a moment of personal expansion that encouraged them to continue to grow.

I remember how our interviews, just like the interviews for this book, became interactive affairs after a certain point. While the subjects' storytelling always filled the most significant portion of each tape, after a certain point the barrier between interviewer and interviewee would relax and they wanted to know as much about my story as I wanted to know about theirs. I would find myself sharing memories and anecdotes as well, which would inspire them to make new connections in their stories and reach for deeper personal insights. "I've never thought about it quite this way," they might say, or "I don't think I've ever put this into words before."

This was confiding at its most effective, as I would later learn. Because confiding is rarely a one-way enterprise. We tell stories to engage, interest, and entertain our audiences, even when an audience is a receptive listener of one. A listener, in turn, responds. In this way, telling becomes a collaborative effort.

It can also affect how we remember the events we're recounting. "Conversational remembering," as it's called, can shape what a teller remembers, how they think of their stories, and, by extension, what they think about themselves. That's because conversation demands that we reduce a complex event to a simplified form. When someone asks, "What happened to your father?" they are not requesting a thirty-minute blow-by-blow account of the past year. Answering the question requires a sifting, selection, and ordering of many small events into a compact summary. Then the follow-up questions people ask encourage a mourner to fill in gaps to bring the story to more completion.

How long was he sick?
What were her symptoms?
How did it happen?
Were there any warning signs?

Through this back-and-forth interaction, the bereaved also start inserting thoughts and feelings into their narration of the facts. At first, the story is made up of raw material and hard data. Listeners' questions will often encourage mourners to layer in emotional responses and thoughts they remember having at the time but may understand only in retrospect. *How are you holding up? What do you think happened?* In this way, a story of loss that adheres closely to the who/what/where/when facts of the matter starts to blossom into a story of loss that explores the impact those facts have had on the mourner. And then, revision by revision, this expanded story begins charting the mourner's individual arc of change and growth over time.

Storytelling, as a performative act, also demands that we tailor our narratives for each specific audience. We tell the same story one way to our children in the morning, another way to a group of colleagues around a conference table later that day, and a third way to a partner or close friend on the phone at night. The responses we receive are also dependent on the setting, the audience, and the relationship between the conversational partners. Through various forms of confiding, our stories develop in a climate of mutuality.

"Our listeners dispute details, complete our sentences, enthusiastically reinforce a good story, and clearly express boredom, disapproval, or confusion over a bad one," explains Monisha Pasupathi, a professor of developmental psychology at the University of Utah who studies how people recount past events through conversation. "Co-construction influences both which events are talked about and what sorts of interpretive statements, details, and emotions are connected with the event as it is discussed."

From having been listened to in the early 1990s, the motherless daughters I spoke to had absorbed the message that their stories were worth telling. Before we'd sat down with a tape recorder positioned between us, many of them had been holding on to unexpressed narratives, lonely with their stories, sitting with an assortment of facts that wanted to be shared.

Compassion and curiosity are key features of this kind of active listening. When confiders anticipate a listener's disinterest or disapproval, Pasupathi has observed, they're likely to hold back and, if they do speak, tend to tell shorter, less detailed and less coherent stories.

In addition, not every teller has the time or the opportunity to share their deeply emotional stories, or the inclination or desire to reveal their innermost thoughts. For some temperaments and personalities, silence is more comfortable than self-disclosure.

Gender differences play a role, too, especially when grief styles are involved. Women, who tend to grieve through emoting, typically confide more in their close friends than men do. Men tend to grieve through problem-solving and action, and also receive less cultural permission to offer emotional support to each other. Both men and women say they'd rather self-disclose to a woman than to a man, a preference that's already established by the early teen years.

"The day my mother died, one of my friends said, 'Come on. Let's go out,'" recalls Julian, who was twenty-one at the time. "I really wanted to talk about how I was feeling, and I started to talk, and then he quickly went, 'No, let's just drink.' I realized at that point, and it was really an eye-opener for me, that as much as I wanted to talk about it, no one really wanted to hear my story. At least, my guy friends didn't want to hear it. It was my burden to carry. So I kind of internalized everything at that point and never really opened up to anyone else, because I felt like I kind of got shut down." Today Julian confides in his wife and adult daughters, but he remembers his twenties mostly as a time when he felt alone with his grief.

Healing is facilitated when others listen to the bereaved's story, especially soon after a loss. However, friends and family who are uncomfortable with expressions of distress may actively discourage conversation from starting. So vulnerable are the recently bereaved, John Harvey has observed, that just one thwarted attempt to connect can shut down future efforts to confide. As in Julian's case, sharing may not occur until years later, if ever.

And this is a problem because without this confiding, the private aspect of account making still takes place but the public, interactive part does not. Without opportunity to disclose, a mourner may pull back from trying to connect with others and resolve to get through grief alone, which can lead to isolation and depression. The story then remains fixed in the mind of the bereaved unless another form of self-expression is found.

This may be why so many writers, artists, performers, and politicians have personal histories of trauma and loss. When psychologist Marvin Eisenstadt researched the histories of 573 notable individuals, both male and female, he found that nearly half (45 percent) had lost one or both parents by age twenty. Twelve presidents, from George Washington through Bill Clinton and Barack Obama, lost fathers when they were young, and a majority of British prime ministers experienced parent loss before age sixteen as well. Two U.S. Supreme Court justices are also what has become known as "eminent orphans"—Ruth Bader Ginsberg, who lost her mother at age thirteen, and Sonia Sotomayor, who lost her father when she was nine.

Is parent loss a reliable path to achievement? Not for everyone. Prisoners are two to three times more likely than the general population to have lost a parent during childhood. Both prisoners and criminal offenders are more likely to have faced multiple adversities during childhood. It's possible that early adverse experiences have a cumulative effect, and those who experienced several are less likely to have been able to overcome the sum of them. It's also possible that expression through art and public spectacle helps eminent orphans leverage pre-existing talents to transcend their early hardships.

As Donna Schuurman, the executive director of the Dougy Center, which supports grieving children and families in Portland, Oregon, has said, "Give sorrow words, yes, but also paint and glue, and music and play, and all other possible forms of expression, including silence."

Sometimes introspection, and even occupying the role of listener, is what a mourner needs in the moment. That's why every Motherless Daughters retreat that I help facilitate combines both speaking and listening in the program. The first morning is for Story Witnessing, during which each woman in the circle has five uninterrupted minutes to speak. Giving words to the unspoken is a powerful act, especially when one's voice has been silenced or suppressed in the past.

Afterward, women tell us that listening to others' stories was as important as sharing their own. "The best thing about listening to someone else's story of loss is that I can resonate with their story," Kaitlyn shared with me by email soon after attending a retreat. "When I'm doing the talking, a listener can agree or say they feel the same way, but when I hear someone else talk about an emotion I previously felt, I feel validated and understood. I realize I wasn't crazy for thinking that way when something similar happened to me."

By listening to other women speak and locating pieces of their experiences in the words of others, many said that, for the first time, they were able to feel less alone. "We crave normalization of our experience," explains Robert Neimeyer, "as well as community, identification, and mutuality. But very often we also want to lay claim to the radical particularity of our experience." Confiding in a group of like-minded others offers an opportunity to be unique without feeling isolated, to be special and ordinary at the same time.

The Cost of Silence

A story is told as much by silence as by speech.
—SUSAN GRIFFIN, *A Chorus of Stones*

IF SORROW yearns to be given words but no one ever comes along to hear them, what happens to a burdened heart? What happens to mourners for whom the act is dismissed, blocked, invalidated, hindered, suppressed, or delayed? I frequently hear from adults whose family or community members discouraged or even prohibited them from talking about a death or about the person who died. *Don't bring him up, or you'll upset your grandmother. Don't think about it, and you won't be sad.* (As if it's not already being thought about, all the time?)

After Randi's younger sister and older brother were killed in a car accident in 1976, the silence in the family contributed to what she calls a "two-fold wrongness." Randi and her three siblings were being raised by a paternal aunt and uncle after having already lost both of their parents in a plane crash seven years earlier. "It wasn't just the trauma of the [second] loss, but also the family not being able to recognize it or talk about it," she recalls. "When their names were said out loud, everyone stopped talking."

When medical doctor Vincent Felitti and his research partners went before an institutional review board in 1994 to receive approval for their groundbreaking research on Adverse Childhood Experiences (ACEs), they were initially turned down. The review board members were concerned that asking patients questions about loss, trauma, and abuse in their past would reactivate their trauma and cause vulnerable adults to break down, Felliti recalls. He went back and forth with the board for nine months before a compromise could be reached.

"Part of the agreement was that one of us had to carry a cellphone twenty-four hours a day for three years to take emergency calls from people who were going to jump off the San Diego Bay bridge when they were asked about their lives," Felliti ruefully recalls. "We never got one call. Instead, I had a stack of letters of thanks and compliments, including one from an elderly woman who memorably wrote, 'Thank you for asking. I feared I would die and no one would ever know what had happened.'"

This illustrates how deeply discomfort around trauma and grief has become institutionalized in America, Felliti says. "We've all been very effectively taught as children that nice people don't talk about certain things and, my God, certainly don't ask about them," he says. Children don't even have to be told not to ask, he points out. They'll respond to a variety of adult cues, subtle and overt, to clamp down on speaking about adversity, including but not limited to deaths.

And this is grievously unfortunate, because relationships that cannot be spoken of in the present become, as Felliti describes them, "lost in time," with no opportunity to mature as the survivors themselves adapt, grow, and change. This is how a forty-five-year-old man finds himself reacting to memories of his father, and to present-day father or authority figures, as a fifteen-year-old would. When he says, "It feels as if a part of me got stuck in the past," this is some of what he means. A part of his fifteen-year-old self, the part that was in relationship with his father, really didn't get to grow up. Their relationship will exist only in the past until it's consciously brought into the present, where both the sorrowful parts and the loving parts can be embraced together.

Without this, there's no place to have the love between them witnessed, says Lorraine Hedtke, co-author of *The Crafting of Grief.* The bereaved need to find private or public venues where stories can be told and emotional connections can take place, she suggests. This can take place through an act as small as wearing a piece of a mother's jewelry every day, or sharing a playlist of a brother's favorite songs.

"It doesn't have to be a vast public thing," she explains. "It's a moment where we say, 'My love for you is still present, and I can feel your love for me.' And that stands, politically and personally, against the discourse that says, 'You need to get over it.'"

What makes one person try to suppress another's grief? Sometimes the act is meant altruistically, as a way to protect mourners from additional distress. Sometimes it's a family's way of exerting emotional control, to keep the lid on expressions of strong emotion. Sometimes it's the listener's attempt to shield themselves from their own feelings of discomfort and helplessness—to shut others down in order to keep living in their own palaces of silence. Sometimes it's a failure of empathy. And sometimes all of the above.

If you're a *Mad Men* fan like me, you might remember a scene from Season 1 when Betty Draper, who's recently lost her mother, looks for comfort from her husband, Don, in a moment of sadness. His response is quick and mechanical. "Don't cry," he says.

Well, that's just about the worst advice possible, I thought. Then I remembered the episode was set in the early 1960s, at the height of "Don't think about it" messaging. And then I had to acknowledge how often this directive is still delivered today.

I can't help wondering what might have happened if Betty—or her daughter in Season 7, or any real-life adult today—instead were to say, "I *need* to cry, and I *need* to talk about it, and I'd like for you to sit with me while I do." How many husbands, wives, parents, siblings, or friends could manage this? Just to *be* with someone in a time of pain? How many would be brave enough to give it a try? A friend of mine recently told me that she'd just said to another friend, "It's okay that you can't see the light at the end of the tunnel. I'll just sit here in the dark with you for a while." Those were some of the wisest and most sensitive words of support I've come across in a while.

Grief can only be supported. It can't be fixed. And that's terribly hard for people to accept. Even experienced child psychiatrists admit how hard it is to acknowledge and sit with a mourning child's pain. If those with extensive bereavement training struggle, how can grieving family members and friends be expected to figure it out on their own?

Today, fifty-year-old Sasha can understand the context within which her aunt and uncle operated after both her parents died within a five-month span. Neither of them had suffered major loss before, and as an adult herself now she feels compassion for their lack of experience and also for the grief they must have felt when they lost a sibling and an in-law prematurely. Nonetheless, she also knows the silence that pervaded their household deeply affected her as a grieving teen.

> There was this myth that kids are resilient. That they'll adapt, they'll adjust, they'll be fine. I think the adults in my life had no idea how to deal with the fact that there I was, this kid who was traumatized. I was also kind of shy, and I wasn't the kind of kid to be like, "This is what I'm feeling. Let me tell you. Let me show you. Let me act out." I held everything in, almost waiting for someone to say, "Do you need a hug? Do you want to talk about it? How are you feeling?" and that didn't happen. It just wasn't that kind of environment. It was always made clear to me that I was not to disrupt anyone's life, and I just needed to kind of get through. Another thing is I was often told how lucky I was. I was lucky I had a roof over my head. I was lucky I didn't go into foster care. Lucky. That really screwed me up.
>
> So when I married it was very natural for me to go into the role of "My needs are . . . Oh, we don't need to talk about that! We'll focus on what you want to do. Where are we going?

How do I fit into your life, and how can I be supportive?" When my husband and I had our daughter our roles shifted, and that wasn't great for our relationship. Things kind of exploded, and that caught me off guard. I've come to learn, very clearly, through a lot of therapy and a lot of looking deeply into myself, that a lot of it goes back to when I was much younger and didn't have an opportunity to express my grief fully. It changed my personality. I felt like I needed to contain everything and just deal with it myself.

Emotional self-reliance became Sasha's main coping strategy as a teen. She contained her grief and anxiety so well that no one was aware she was still suffering. Except for her. Several times—at eighteen, when her aunt and uncle divorced; when she went through her own divorce in middle age; and when her older brother died—"it felt like the dam broke, and I became very depressed," she explains. In her forties, with the help of a therapist, she was able to finally express the anger and sadness she had suppressed when she was twelve.

"We all have faults. Nobody's perfect," she says. "But I still have a hard time understanding why the adults in my life didn't want to go near the sadness or the grief that I felt. It was almost as if there was something dangerous about it. 'Just keep it deep inside, don't let it leak out, and we'll all be fine.' Somehow, that was the goal. I think the twelve-year-old me deserved to just be, and not have that constant restriction on me, and not feel like I had to cover up part of me like it's something to be ashamed of."

Humans have an innate desire to transcend suffering, explains Thomas Attig. He believes that blocking another's expression of grief disrespects mourners by denying them the right to grow from their hardships. This misunderstanding of suffering actually increases a mourner's loss and hurt, he says, by creating and reinforcing feelings of helplessness, powerlessness, shame, and guilt. "And it withholds support from, breaks connections with, isolates, and abandons the bereaved in their sorrow," he explains.

Silence leads to isolation. This may seem obvious, but it's important enough to repeat. *Silence leads to isolation.* And isolation breeds the perception of being alone with one's experience, of being different from everyone else, and of existing in a world where no one understands. During my senior year of high school I felt separate and apart from nearly every other girl in our class of six hundred–plus. I categorically *was* different from every other girl whose mother was alive, which is to say nearly every girl in our grade. Only one other was motherless, that I knew about. On top of this, in our medium-sized suburb my mother had been an active community member with a large circle of friends, and people I barely recognized would take me aside in public to express their condolences. Sticking out in a crowd, and not in a good way, was poison to a teenager. At least it was to me back then.

But the silence at home was even more disconcerting than public attention. Something huge had happened and left me traumatized and confused. My response felt in proportion to the magnitude of the event, yet I couldn't get anyone else to acknowledge this was actually a big deal. Wasn't it? It seemed to be; any mention of my mother immediately reduced my father to tears. But maybe it wasn't, if I was the only one who felt this way. The external reality was so out of sync with my thoughts and feelings that there were days when I seriously questioned my sanity. To hide this, and to protect my father, I deliberately silenced myself. And from there a domino effect began, in which silence reinforced my sense of feeling different, and feeling different bred a kind of shame.

I know. I know. It doesn't make sense. There's nothing inherently shameful about losing a parent. The event was out of my control, I knew that, and a death in a family shouldn't be an automatic black mark on someone's future. But I felt so terribly alone in the experience, and my lonely sorrow became a source of private shame.

Self-silencing is, regrettably, not unusual in families where one or more central members are perceived as fragile or on edge. If a sibling has died and parents look like they're barely holding it together, who wants to risk behavior that could undermine them further, especially when they're the adults in charge? A Rutgers University study of thirty-four adults who'd lost brothers and sisters before the age of nineteen found that 76 percent—more than three out of four—said they hadn't shared their thoughts or feelings about the death with anyone after it happened and hadn't talked about it for a long time afterward. That's a lot of children folding unexpressed grief into their development. Maintaining that silence then becomes part of their young identity.

Just one compassionate confidante, however, can minimize or even prevent an adverse outcome. Numerous bereavement studies have found that children who have one stable adult who listens and provides guidance or mentorship after a parent dies fare better in the long-term than those whose stories become congested or stuck. This confidante often isn't and sometimes shouldn't be a parent or guardian.

Thirty-two-year-old Chelsea was four and the youngest of three children when her mother died of breast cancer. Her father moved the family across the country, where a counselor at Chelsea's new school worked with her for a session or two. "I remember sitting on her lap and writing a letter to my mother," Chelsea recalls. "But other than that, we didn't talk about our grief or our sadness." Just before Chelsea's twelfth birthday, her father died in a car accident. A neighborhood couple stepped forward as legal guardians, enabling Chelsea and her sister to remain with the same teachers, neighbors, and friends.

Chelsea was in middle school by then, a transitional, wobbly time even under the best circumstances. "You had to play it cool at school, so I was literally making jokes about my situation," she recalls. "[Our family] didn't talk about the fact that we were moving in with the Jacksons. We just did it. My grandparents cleaned out my dad's house and most of it went into the Jacksons' storage unit."

During her junior year of high school, Chelsea started dating a senior named Gray. He became the first person in whom she confided the stories of her parents' deaths and the effects she'd experienced. "He really listened, for the first time," she says, "whereas with everybody else I kept that sadness tucked away." The two fell deeply in love. But then—just before his graduation—a car accident claimed Gray's life, too. By age seventeen, Chelsea had experienced three major losses. This time she couldn't hold back her distress. She raged, she cried, she spent all of her free time at Gray's parents' house.

"My whole senior year, I was just a complete mess," she recalls. And still, the message from her guardians at home was to "move on." "For me, that was the hardest part. I hated those two words, because I didn't want to move on," she says. "I wanted to sit in my grief. I wanted to be sad. Gray had *just* died."

By then, the counselor from her grade school had moved to another town thirty miles away, but she heard of Gray's death and sought out Chelsea on her own. "Any time you want to talk, just let me know," she offered. Chelsea drove to meet with her informally several times. Those hours in the counselor's living room became a time and place to confide her thoughts and feelings and receive validation from an adult.

"The thing I most remember her saying was, 'Not everyone you love is going to die,'" Chelsea says. "Because it sure felt that way after Gray." That message helped her rebuild the faith to connect with others, eventually to marry in her twenties, and to become a mother. We spoke soon after her third child was born. Seventeen years after Gray's death, Chelsea expressed gratitude to that counselor, the one person, other than Gray, who'd provided a place for her teenage self to speak without fear of judgment.

Sharing a story of loss involves elements of risk. We never know for sure how we'll be received. Will the person on the other end be engaged, distracted, or having a bad day? Will his or her response be compassionate, distant, or—it's possible—horrified?

Alex, now twenty-five, lost both of her parents when young and has engaged in enough of these exchanges to recognize familiar patterns. As she writes in an essay she published on Medium in January

2020, "My conversational partner may scrunch up their face and grit out some verbal expression that indicates they are kicking themselves. As if they should have known. As if they should have picked up on the aura of orphan that they can faintly see now. They may apologize profusely, as if they've just reminded me that my parents are dead. *No one ever forgets that their parents are dead.* They may simply go blank, pale with panic. Or they may make a wounded expression, seeping with pity for my misfortune."

Alex's impulse, in these moments, is to take on the pain of others. Then she'll try to save them from their own discomfort. Her social mask is a veneer that displays a culturally acceptable countenance. Her true feelings remain hidden behind it.

"I offer something in the way of reassurance," she explains, "a mentioning of how good things are now, a redirect to my family members who are alive, a disclaimer that I'm *okay* and things are *okay* and it's really *okay* that they're not here and they're not coming back, though that last one could not be further from the truth. It will never be okay. It will only be true."

Disclosing to others poses a special challenge when details of a death are violent or traumatic, such as when a suicide, murder, natural disaster, or disfiguring accident occurs. These storytellers learn how to judiciously assess when, how, whether, and in whom to confide.

"People have no idea what they're getting into when they ask, 'Where's your mom?'" forty-four-year-old Cherie explains. "If I say, 'Well, she died.' Then it's, 'Oh, I'm sorry. How did she die?' and I'm thinking, *You don't want to know the answer to that.*"

Cherie's single mother was wheelchair-bound due to multiple sclerosis. One afternoon when Cherie was eighteen and at work, her mother's cigarette ignited a house fire that claimed her life. The circumstances of the death were so traumatic and painful, Cherie says, that moving forward she avoided any mention of her mother at all. If someone she'd just met asked about her parents, she would practice self-talk in her mind, reciting, *Okay, you can do this. You can answer without crying*, and even then she'd share only the most superficial facts.

Easier to keep details simple and vague, survivors often decide. The inquiry "What does your father do?" results in "Oh, he's not around anymore." "How many siblings do you have?" leads to "I grew up in a family of three kids." "Are your parents coming to graduation?" "My father and stepmother will be here at noon." Some become skilled story acrobats, tumbling away from direct questions and toward shiny objects of distraction.

Let's talk about something else.

My family's boring. Tell me about yours instead.

Which is unfortunate, because compelling research suggests that congested or "stuck" stories can affect mental and physical health over the long term. "If you don't create a pathway for grief to come out in a constructive way, it will come out sideways or will be carried within," explains Mollie Marti. "I see this all the time. When people are provided an environment to connect with each other and talk about what's going on, it begins a healing process. We can then provide tools that empower them to be part of the solution. These opportunities to connect, repair, and contribute as part of a community take care of so many things that if left unattended might well require additional mental health support. People are so hungry for this."

Vincent Felitti and Robert Anda's research in the Adverse Childhood Experience Study (ACES) has revealed that unexpressed emotions around childhood trauma and loss can produce chronic toxic stress, creating inflammation that later puts individuals at higher risk for ailments ranging from depression to diabetes to cancer. Similarly, Harvey and his colleagues found that failure to confide a story of loss results in higher incidences of hypertension, prolonged anxiety, difficulty coping with future losses, and repeated stress responses. It's long been known that silence creates inner conflict if the risk of speaking up overpowers an urge to disclose. Now there's evidence this exacts physical tolls as well.

The Good Kind of "Letting Go"

ALL OF this raises an intriguing question: If keeping a story of trauma or loss bottled up can affect one's health later, can telling one's story now *prevent* mental and physical distress in the future?

That's what psychologist James Pennebaker and his colleagues at the University of Texas at Austin set out to explore in the mid-1980s. Pennebaker's team already knew that people who experience early trauma are more likely than others to have health problems as adults. They also knew that when the natural human desire to share painful information is blocked, stress and illness are more likely to show up later in life. They wanted to know if unblocking the desire to disclose could have a positive effect on health. So they devised an experiment using what they called "expressive writing" and recruited forty-six undergraduates as subjects to test their theory.

Their methodology was simple. First, they divided the students into two groups. The first group, the control group, was asked to come to a classroom and write about a neutral topic such as their dorm room or their shoes for fifteen minutes per day over four consecutive days.*

Members of the second group, the expressive-writing group, were also asked to come in and write for fifteen minutes per day, but these students were encouraged to write freely about the most deeply upsetting or traumatic events in their lives so far. As their instructions explained, "Ideally, it should be something you have not talked about with others in detail. It is critical, however, that you let yourself go and touch those deepest emotions and thoughts that you have. In other words, write about what happened and how you felt about it, and how you feel about it now."

---

*There was no hard science behind the fifteen-minute and four-day structure. A set of rooms on campus happened to be available for four consecutive days, from 5 P.M. to 10 P.M. only. When the experimenters divided the amount of available classroom time by the number of subjects, they were left with fifteen minutes per student.

At first, researchers were concerned that the expressive-writing students might not open up emotionally in a sterile classroom setting, so they were surprised by what happened next. Many of the subjects cried as they revisited their past traumas in writing. The essays they produced were rich in detail, with prose that expressed deep emotion. Over the four days, this group reported frequently thinking about and even dreaming about the topics in their writing.

Researchers had anticipated that students who released pent-up emotions through expressive writing would feel a decrease in sadness and anxiety after each writing session, followed by an increase in euphoria. But again, the expressive-writing subjects surprised them. They reported feeling emotionally worse at the end of each expressive-writing session rather than feeling better. The feeling, the students said, was similar to what they might experience at the end of a sad movie. Nonetheless, in the days that followed, the expressive-writing students would stop Pennebaker on campus to thank him for letting them participate in his study. They felt they'd walked away with long-lasting, positive benefits, even if they couldn't articulate them at the time.

The control-group students had a very different experience. Writing about their dorm rooms and shoes seemed to have no demonstrable or lasting effect on their emotions. From all appearances, they'd sat down in the classroom, written about their neutral topics, and then continued on unchanged. From this, the researchers concluded it wasn't the simple act of writing that had produced positive results. It had to be the *kind* of writing the students were doing that led to the different outcomes.

Then the results became even more interesting. For the next six months, the researchers tracked how often both groups visited the student health center. Expressive-writing students were making only half as many doctor visits as their control-group counterparts. Either the expressive-writing students weren't feeling sick enough to warrant clinical visits, or they just weren't getting as sick as often as the other students were. Or perhaps, the researchers theorized, the experience of reorganizing and reframing a traumatic event had helped the students' bodies self-regulate better.

Pennebaker and his team were intrigued. What, exactly, had expressive writing facilitated in these students? Were the results real or coincidental? And could they be replicated?

In subsequent, similar studies, subjects who wrote expressively about past traumas showed evidence of enhanced immune system functioning for up to six weeks after the experiment's end. These subjects also continued to visit the student health center less often than control-group writers. In follow-up questionnaires, 80 percent of the expressive-writing respondents said the writing sessions had helped them achieve helpful, lasting insights.

Again, the kind of writing they'd done mattered. In subsequent studies, students who merely vented their emotions, page after page, didn't experience positive benefits. Actually, they tended to fare worse than other subjects. Writing what they thought about the trauma in a rote, intellectualized manner wasn't very helpful, either. The magic occurred when the two were integrated: when students wrote what they thought about their feelings, and how they felt about their thoughts. Cognitively processing their emotions on the page led to measures of personal growth. Later studies found the same results occurred from similar processing through conversations.

Until this point, Pennebaker's subjects had been writing about emotional upheavals in the past, including everything from parental divorce to the death of a grandparent to the loss of a beloved pet. They'd also been writing their stories instead of speaking them. But then, purely by chance, Pennebaker had a chance to observe the effects of confiding a story of death to another person, out loud.

It happened one afternoon when Pennebaker was having lunch with a former student named Latoya. Latoya was visibly upset during the meal and explained that today was the one-year anniversary of her parents' death in a private plane accident. She shared her distress with Pennebaker, and after lunch the two headed back to campus to talk more. On the way, Pennebaker had an idea. He asked if Latoya would participate in a skin-conductance test in his lab to measure stress levels when she talked about her loss. Latoya, who was familiar with these kinds of studies, was intrigued. She agreed.

What the pair discovered that afternoon was, as Pennebaker describes it, "fascinating."

The first anniversary of her parents' accident was clearly stirring up painful emotions for Latoya. One might think, then, that talking directly about the topic would cause her body to feel stressed. In the lab, however, when Latoya talked about her parents' deaths her skin-conductance levels dropped, which indicated that her body was "letting go" of stress. When she talked about trivial or neutral topics her skin conductance increased, an indication that stress was building up in her system. Put most simply, Latoya's body experienced more stress on that day when she *didn't* talk about her parents than it exhibited when she did. It was as if her body wanted her to talk about her parents on the anniversary of their deaths, and holding back her thoughts and feelings about them and their deaths required a stressful effort.

Would the same results have occurred on a different day? It's hard to know. What we do know is these results occurred on a day when Latoya wanted to talk about her loss, and that her body experienced stress when she was told to avoid the topic. Would expressive writing, instead of speaking, have the same effect? Those results are less compelling. Several studies on the effects of written disclosure on the bereaved found that the best results were under certain conditions and for certain groups of people, including those who reported feeling high levels of hopelessness beforehand; those who had lost loved ones to sudden death, especially suicide; and individuals who can successfully regulate their own emotions.

Nonetheless, Latoya's experiment offered scientific evidence that consciously suppressing a story of loss can cause physical stress, and that confiding in a trusted other can release it. Pennebaker's earlier research revealed that integrating thoughts and emotions through self-expression—for some individuals—could offer lasting emotional benefits.

Cherie may have experienced both on the twenty-fifth anniversary of her mother's death last year. That year, for the first time, she decided to post about the anniversary on her Facebook page where relatives and friends would read it. "I started by remembering my mother," she recalls, "and then I kind of went on a long . . . it wasn't really a rant, but I wrote about how people think you should get over it. I wrote, 'It's not something I have gotten over. It's not something I foresee getting over, and I don't feel like I should have to get over it. It was something that was difficult and continues to be difficult. It changed me, and it's a part of who I am. I don't want to forget it or her, and I want to acknowledge and remember her today, and I want other people to remember her, too.'

"I actually got a lot of positive feedback," she says. "It was helpful for me to write that all out, and helpful, I think, for friends and family to better understand, even if it was twenty-five years later, how I really feel."

For Pennebaker's student subjects to achieve lasting benefits, for Latoya's stress levels to decrease, and for Cherie to achieve a deeper sense of healing, three elements were necessary: (1) a storyteller; (2) an audience, real or perceived; and (3) the story itself. "None of these," states the sociologist Arthur Frank, "could be what it is without the others."

CHAPTER NINE

* * *

Six Exceptions in Search of a Narrative

I F YOU see the phrases "story development" and "coherent narrative" and your mind impulsively bucks, dodges, or goes blank,
you're not alone. About 30 percent of the loss narratives I encounter
are nonconforming, meaning they resist following a classic story
structure. That may be because gaps in memory or missing facts have
created blank spaces that can't be easily filled. Or perhaps because
the cause of death is ambiguous or was kept secret, generating more
questions than answers. Or it may be a story that's hard to make
sense of for other reasons, in which case a loss that already feels stigmatized or marginalized winds up feeling doubly so.

When a mind attempts to shape facts and details into a narrative
soon after a loss occurs, the typical default structure it aims for is the
Aristotelian story arc. That's the dramatic structure Aristotle observed
in Greek tragedies from the fourth century B.C. It's essentially a three-
act structure with a clearly defined beginning, middle, and end.

The classic Aristotelian arc in a simplified linear form, with a couple of writing terms added in, looks like this . . .

Classic Story Structure

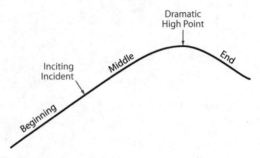

In which

- The Beginning functions as an establishing shot of the world of the story, showing us what the main characters are up to before story action begins.
- The Inciting Incident is a disruptive event that sets the story's action into motion. Put most simply, *something happens.* Everyone would have kept on existing indefinitely in the world of the story if not for an Inciting Incident. A key feature of an Inciting Incident is that it makes the protagonist of a story (in this case you, or your family) want something they didn't want before. This new desire is the engine that keeps the story running.
- The Middle is where the bulk of a story takes place. It contains all of the developments and complications that must be faced and overcome on the way to getting or not getting, achieving or not achieving this new desire.
- The Dramatic High Point is a story's moment of peak drama. This is where the conflict introduced by the Inciting Incident is resolved. Meaning, it's where the main character(s) either get what they want, get something different, or discover they'll have to live without achieving their goal.
- That brings us to the End, which reveals the fallout from the Dramatic High Point. It gives us a glimpse of characters learning to live with or without achieving their goal. It's no surprise that a grief experience is often marked by a search for *"resolution,"* since that's another name for the End of a story arc.

My original story of loss in chapter 7 follows a classic story arc, as do many stories of long-term illness that track from an initial symptom or diagnosis through treatment and hope of remission or cure, all the way to recovery or a death. We were an ordinary family doing ordinary family things in the Beginning, blissfully unaware of what was about to come. Then, one day in the spring of 1980, my mother came home from a doctor's appointment with news of a malignant tumor in her breast (the Inciting Incident, which set this story in motion). This caused everyone to want her to recover. Sixteen months of treatments and attempts at normal family life then followed (the Middle, in which chemotherapy appointments were made and kept, scans were done, and the family rejoiced in her supposed improvement). Then came the summer of 1981, when her disease crossed an irreversible threshold, the truth about her illness was revealed, and she died on the morning of July 12 (the Dramatic High Point, in which we—the protagonists—did not get what we hoped for). We returned home from the hospital as an altered family unit. As we sat at the kitchen table that morning (the End, in which we protagonists started adjusting to our new world), it felt like my life had been divided into segments of before and after, and that nothing in the after would resemble what had come before.

As hard as it may be to review events after a loss, creating a story about it is how we ultimately find meaning and adapt. In this process, we first try to make sense of what happened; second, we find benefits in the experience, despite its tragic nature; and third, we experience a change of identity. Mourners who can do all three appear to experience less intense symptoms of acute grief and suffer fewer incidences of complicated grief.

To get to benefit-finding and identity change, however, we first have to be able to create a story that makes sense. Which can be frustrating, because at first, story development relies on a mourner's knowledge and accessible memories to create a coherent accounting of events.

At least six types of stories resist fitting into a conventional narrative structure. No matter how the brain tries to create a three-act story with a beginning, middle, and end, stories in these six categories won't comply. If your loss falls into one or more of these categories, the narrative you'll create will inevitably follow a different pattern. That's okay. For you, a more creative definition of "story" may need to emerge. Just like your grief response, the story you tell and the way that you tell it will be uniquely yours.

Stories of Sudden Death: Narratives Compressed

DEATHS THAT occur instantaneously—due to an accident, suicide, murder, aneurysm, heart failure, stroke, or other acute health event—subvert the classic story structure. A sudden loss offers no opportunity for a logical progression of cause-and-effect relationships that lead to an inevitable conclusion. The story is not one of momentum building; it's about a single moment in which a building explodes. .

As Joan Didion wrote about the shock of losing her husband to a heart attack during a dinner at their home, "Life changes in an instant."

When a fatal event results in immediate death, an Inciting Incident and a Dramatic High Point collapse into the same moment. The result is a story of loss without a middle, and a story without a middle may not feel like much of a story at all.

This is one reason why, very often, the aftermath of a sudden death is marked by a survivor's fervent attempts to find a different Inciting Incident. *If only*, the thinking goes, *If only I can find the place earlier in this story where I could have stepped in and prevented this outcome. If only I can identify the moment when a crucial choice was or wasn't made, then* maybe *this story will make sense.*

When a sudden death is the result of a fleeting, random moment, arbitrary and unpredictable, the story is one of a tragic occurrence that can happen to anyone at any time, without warning. That's a hard story to bear. Choosing a different, earlier inciting incident opens up space for the story to have a middle, and the progression of events that fill it can then give the story a sense of logic and progress. What happened makes sense, and events that make sense are events that can, the thinking goes, be prevented in the future with proper foresight or creative planning.

In this alternate, virtual story a survivor can also play a role instead of being helplessly relegated to the sidelines. Even occupying a role of omission can feel better than having no role at all. Could the flu she had last month have weakened her heart? (*Why didn't I tell her to go to a cardiologist? I should have insisted that she go to a cardiologist.*) If only Dad hadn't let him take the car, the accident could have been avoided. (*I told Dad to say no. Why didn't he say no?*)

Soon after her best friend Carla died by suicide, Evie felt an overwhelming sense of powerlessness. She began calling Carla's friends and colleagues in an attempt to understand what happened and to uncover any clues to Carla's mental state that may have been missed or ignored. "I wanted to find out: Who knew? Why didn't anybody do anything?" Evie recalls. "Her boss said, 'I knew she was having some issues, because she had dropped a ton of weight' and he knew she was doing drugs. The hardest part for me was trying to come to grips with 'Why didn't anybody *do* anything?'"

Immediately trying to reconstruct the story of the death—also known as the "death reenactment story"—is a common response for survivors of a sudden, unexpected loss, especially those who didn't witness the event. When Hillary's mother died of a sudden, ambiguous health event at home fourteen years ago, Hillary and her sister soon "became obsessed," in Hillary's words, with recreating the events that took place on the morning of the death. Their father had been home when it happened, and they grilled him for all the details.

"I was trying to find out where the prevention could have come in," explains Hillary, now fifty-one. "'*Did she see a doctor? When was the last time she saw a doctor? When did th* . . .' It really annoyed my dad. He was in a horrible place at the time and was unequipped to deal with my questions. But I had that idea of 'If I can take this back far enough to a time where this could have been prevented, by a doctor or someone else, then either I can make more sense of it or it will not have happened.'"

Their fixation on finding a different narrative also offered Hillary and her sister a distraction from what would have been a harder and more painful version of the story: the possibility that by minimizing their mother's symptoms that morning, their father may have contributed to her death. You see, a long-standing, recurring pattern in their family had been for their mother to exaggerate her health concerns and for their father to assume she was overreacting. Until that fateful morning, the latter had always been true.

"I think we were probably trying to escape from knowing that my dad didn't take her seriously and didn't call 911 until after she was dead," Hillary explains. "That was a truth that we didn't want to go anywhere near. There was too much blame wrapped up in that, so I think we believed if we ran through the events over and over and over again we could somehow make it so that wasn't true."

The quest for illumination and meaning is particularly difficult, and especially heart-wrenching, when a death occurs by suicide. In the absence of a suicide note, and sometimes even when there is one, ambiguity often persists. By combing through all the facts and memories and details, by recreating a chain of probable events, survivors search for opportunities for intervention that they or others may have overlooked, trying to find a plot point where the story could have taken a different turn. Having any plausible explanation feels more satisfying than having none, even if it means laying oneself on the altar of blame.

This may be one of the most difficult aspects of a story that involves suicide: that the loved one prioritized their story arc over yours, and the Dramatic High Point they chose left their loved ones with a tragic story to bear.

Too Young to Remember: No Conscious Memories to Draw From

RONNIE WAS four years old when both of her parents died in a private plane accident on their way home from a vacation. Having been so young, Ronnie has few memories of their time together and no memory of the events around their deaths. From her older brother she learned that the four children in the family had made their parents a "welcome home" banner that day, but almost everything else she knows about her early childhood has been pieced together from other sources, such as artifacts, documents, and other people's recollections.

"I don't know if it's just part of child development, having been only four years old and not being able to remember being four years old, or if it's something that's been blocked in my mind to protect me," Ronnie now says.

The answer could be either or both. The average adult's earliest memory usually dates back to between ages three and four, about the age when the hippocampus, the part of the brain that's responsible for memory storage and retrieval, matures into an advanced state. At age five, a child can typically recall preverbal and sense-based memories that go back to as young as age one. By age seven, however, the majority of those memories are lost through a phenomenon called "childhood amnesia."

A 2014 study conducted at the University of Minnesota sheds some light on how this process works. The study, which spanned several years, involved eighty-three preschool-aged children and their mothers. Researchers asked the kids to speak about recent events in their lives and recorded their responses. In follow-up sessions a few years later the same kids, now between ages five and seven, could recall only 60 percent of what they'd talked about at age three. By ages eight and nine, their recall had dropped to 40 percent.

That's probably because, around age seven, an adult-like distribution of autobiographical memory starts to develop. As a result, memories from age seven onward tend to remain more accessible to us as we age. But after age seven, just as with adults, a child's earliest memories will date back only to about three and a half years of age. Memories that can still be recalled at age nine, the researchers speculated, are likely to persist into adulthood.

The Minnesota study revealed two additional findings: First, even accounting for their more expansive vocabularies, older kids talked about their earliest memories differently than they had when they were young. Their eight- and nine-year-old narratives were more detailed and more complete, incorporating information about time, place, and cause-and-effect relationships.

Second, the researchers observed that the three-year-olds whose mothers encouraged them to elaborate on their memories with prompts like "What happened next?" and "Remember when?" became the eight- and nine-year-olds who remembered the most details, indicating that talking about experiences with an adult from a very early age may help cement memories for later retrieval. In other words, kids whose parents or caregivers engage them in remembering tend to remember more, and to be more likely to have retained those memories into adulthood. So if you were very young when a family member died, and no one spoke with you about that person afterward, your memories of time spent together may be hard to access for that reason.

We don't know exactly why certain memories are lost, but we do know a bit about which are retained and why. Emotionally charged memories—both good and bad—are the ones that tend to stick. My older daughter was seven when her grandfather died and now, at twenty-two, can recall a few vivid, verifiably true incidents from the two very emotional weeks we spent with him in New York before he died. But my younger daughter turned three on that trip. When she was five she would often reference how she saw me cry the morning my father died, an emotionally charged moment for her, but now she says the memories she retains from that time—of snow on the ground, of a man lying in a bed—may be ones that have been implanted from photos, other people's stories, or her own imagination.

We also remember things that were out of the ordinary: outlier moments, unexpected events, and disruptions to the normal routine. Single moments may poke through the veil of consciousness like a spoke of light in a field of indiscernible gray. Very young children can often remember the announcement of a death, including where they were when they were told and how they felt. That single memory, because of its emotional charge, may remain discernible for the rest of a mourner's life. It may even cause trauma responses later when exposure to similar sensory details occurs, such as seeing hospital scrubs or hearing an ambulance's siren.

The sons, daughters, and siblings I interviewed for this book who were very young when a loved one died describe a particular kind of sadness around having lost access to memories of their time together and frustration around not being able to retrieve them. *How could someone have been such an important part of my every day, and then vanish from my memory?* they'd wonder. "I wish I had just one memory of being hugged, or being put to bed, or of playing together," they'd say. It feels as if crucial bits of their history have been lost, pieces that they need to form a stable, consistent identity.

When the loss occurred in a preverbal stage of development, memories of early time together may be stored somatically rather than with language or in memory. Even when we do have language to wrap around an experience, loss is still experienced by structures in the brain that respond to emotional stimuli and reinforce behavior—known as the limbic system—explains psychologist Robert Neimeyer.

"We recruit the resources of language and conversation to get through [a loss] and make sense of it," he says, "but at a core level what are assaulted are really our senses of self and other, and those are the kind of things of which an infant can be aware. It has to do with our sense of security in relation to people. Can I trust that others will be here for me? What happens now that I face a difficult world alone? Those questions may never be framed in language, but they can be lived out themselves even by a very young child."

Only later, when the child becomes proficient in language, does the human impulse to explain and make sense of what happened through narrative emerge. Without memories of their own to draw from, very young survivors later engage in a historical piecing-together process to craft their stories of loss, relying on documents, photographs, videos, and whatever family members, friends, or healthcare professionals are later willing to share. The contributions of others can range from a steamer trunk of helpful information all the way down to, well, no shared memories at all. Some of the most poignant stories I've heard on this subject come from sons and daughters who snuck around a parent's or sibling's former bedroom, searching for any small clue about the deceased's life and death. *Who am I if I don't know who they were? And who I was in relation to them?* they wonder.

"We like to think that we know ourselves through what we remember, but it may be just as true that we know ourselves through what we don't remember—the erasures in our narratives, the ellipses, the lacunas of our personal history." That's the first sentence of an email that landed in my inbox one evening while I was writing. It came from a woman I'll call Nina, whose mother died of a brain aneurysm, and was part of a short essay she has titled "Unremembered."

"I was six, old enough to remember her, yet when I try I am met with an unsettling blankness," Nina writes. "How can it be that I have forgotten the person who gave me life? I must be storing memories of her somewhere within my subconscious. I've even entertained the idea of seeing a hypnotherapist and would if I didn't fear what I might say. Maybe I'm afraid to discover that I deliberately chose to forget her, that I out-hurt the hurter, punished her for leaving me, not sensing the future harm I might cause myself."

Not only did Nina grow up with an absence after her mother died but that void cannot be filled with her personal recollections. Although early experiences with her mother may have been imprinted on her consciousness and carried forth in her body, without access to memory they feel inaccessible and lost.

All I remember about her are the stories of her death. Sitting on my Grandpa's brown leather recliner watching reruns of *Star Trek*, my father came in from a track meet and, through tears, informed me that my mother had died. Because I was only six years old, he relayed the cause of her death in terms I could grasp: there was a bubble on a vein in her head and that bubble had burst causing her death. My father explained to me that she was at a job interview, that when they finished, she stood up to shake the man's hand and then she fainted. The man could tell she was dead before she hit the floor. This last detail, a memory passed to me from my father, became the haunting visual of my childhood: a young woman, thirty-one years old, my mother, dying mid-faint.

Twenty-eight years later I discovered the truth about my mother's passing. Through a circuitous sequence of events, I came into contact with my mother's boyfriend at the time of her death (my parents had been separated for a few years), and he told me that my mother died in his arms. To be more precise, they were making love. Out of all the people who knew her, I am the only one who knows what happened to her when she died. No one else knows because no one else ever asked him. Not even my mother's own parents.

In my late twenties, I asked my grandmother to tell me about her only daughter, and she replied, "Who can remember?" The irony was not lost on me that she was trying to forget what she remembered while I was trying to remember what I had forgotten.

Memory is like a prism. The person looking through the glass determines the colors and shapes that we see. Despite the potential for distortion, I prefer the faulty recollections of others to the nothingness of my own memory. From their flawed memories, I cobble together a sense of my mother, a sense of myself. From the void of memory, I become who I am.

In this way, a story of very early loss may not be a factual accounting of events but instead a story of what a child could not retain. Those blank spots in memory become an essential part of the survivor's story of loss. The narrative is shaped both by the absence of a person and by the absence of memories that include that person. Regardless of what's missing, a narrative of trying to remember is a valid story, too.

Too Young to Understand: Magical Thinking and Retrospective Upgrades

MOST CHILDREN develop a mature understanding of death—meaning that it's irreversible, inevitable, and will happen to everyone—by age eleven. Before then, a child can only make sense of a death according to the degree of understanding they've achieved by the time it occurs. When details are explained but are beyond the child's ability to grasp intellectually, they can be interpreted in a distorted or fantastical manner. The result is what's known as "magical thinking."

Magical thinking is the belief that one's thoughts, actions, words, or feelings can cause events in the external world. It can occur among adults, too. In children, magical thinking often results in fantasies created to make sense of the world around them. These stories may or may not be grounded in truth or even in physical possibility.

Even when given the most honest explanations possible, children's ability to make sense of death is still limited by immature cognition. Those facts will need to be revisited again and again, at different developmental periods, ideally with help from an adult, for a mature understanding of death to develop and stick. Otherwise, the fantasies of magical thinking can persist as emotional imprints, long after the child's developing intellect knows they can't possibly be true.

Noted child psychologist Jean Piaget, in his studies of children's cognitive development, pinpointed the stage between about ages two and seven (known as the preoperational stage) as peak years for magical thinking. Those are the ages when children learn to distinguish between fantasy and reality.

Now in his early fifties, Kevin, who was seven when his brother was stillborn, still remembers the magical thinking he relied on to cope with the big, unanswerable challenges he faced after the death. Even though his parents reassured Kevin and his sisters that the stillbirth was not their fault, Kevin could not understand why it had occurred at all, and why God would have permitted an innocent baby to die. These existential questions taxed his seven-year-old intellectual capacities, which were grounded in binary divisions of good and bad, right and wrong.

"I was still in that cause-and-effect mentality where bad things happen to bad people," Kevin explains. "Children are moral purists, and they aren't intimidated by big ethical and moral questions. They engage in them directly in their own innocent way. So I was stressing over that. I thought something went very wrong in the way the universe worked, because I couldn't see that my parents or sister had done anything bad. So then I thought maybe it was something I had done. Maybe I'd caused it somehow, maybe I hadn't prayed hard enough, maybe I hadn't been a good enough kid."

That sense of potential responsibility stayed with Kevin long after he developed a more mature intellect that understood such simple cause-and-effect logic couldn't possibly have been true. Only years later, when his mother shared details of the birth with him, was he able to fully let go of the seven-year-old's belief. He was then able to piece together a story based on scientific fact rather than fantasy.

"My mom had difficult births in the past," Kevin explains. "She had repeated contractions without a break that didn't allow the child to get enough oxygen. My sister had almost died when she was born, and then my brother did. In retrospect, Mom could see there were things the hospital did that were wrong. They put her in a room alone at night without anyone to monitor the contractions, even though they knew about her history. So that did impact me, knowing the hospital could have done things differently."

Like Kevin, Alisa, who was six when her father died after a long struggle with cancer, convinced herself that she was somehow responsible for the death. She was the youngest of four children, and the details of their father's illness were kept hidden from her and her next older sibling. Alisa doesn't remember ever hearing the words "die" or "death." She's not sure she would even have understood what those terms meant at the time.

On the morning of October 28, Alisa's school held its annual Halloween parade. She went to school dressed as a devil. That afternoon, her mother gathered the children at home to tell them their father had died earlier in the day. Alisa quickly took in this information, reviewed the day's events in her mind, and landed on a conclusion that made sense to her at age six: Her father's death was her fault.

"I remember going back in my room and grabbing my costume," Alisa recalls, "and running outside with it and shoving it into the trashcan and having a big fit. That stuck with me for many years, the idea that I was bad, that I was a devil that year and that's what made my dad die. Of course, no one took my idea seriously, but it was a very, very serious thing for me for about ten years. I put it [his death] on myself in a really big way, and it was kind of damaging for a while."

During her teen years, Alisa was able to revisit and revise her story with a compassionate adult. She corrected the faulty logic of her earlier version, and acknowledged that she, as a child, didn't have power over her father's life or death. Addressing the guilt she'd held on to for a decade, however, took longer for her to work through.

"Just because you're young doesn't mean you won't look for a cause-and-effect relationship," Alisa says. "You're just going to do it in your child mind, which is probably more creative and imaginary than an adult brain is."

In addition, children lack agency to make choices for themselves during and after a loved one's death. Whether that means witnessing a loved one's deterioration, learning the details of the death, or attending the funeral or memorial, children are at the mercy of other people's choices. They become, in effect, emplotted in the stories that adults decide to write for them. Later, they become cast into stories others tell about their past. For this reason, it's hard to know for sure whether any narrative you construct about an early loss is fact based or shaped from the subjective and often unreliable accounts of others. Any current version you tell may include other people's memories, mixed in with facts you've uncovered on your own, plus more mature insights that an adult filter inserts later.

186 : THE AFTERGRIEF

These layers are evident when forty-six-year-old Abby tells the story of her father's death. Abby was just four years old when her father died by suicide. She has no accessible memories of her own from that day. Instead, she has pieced together an account that includes her mother's version of the story, research she did as an adult, speculation, some blank spaces, and her adult perspective today.

> The way the story goes is this . . . she picked me up from preschool, we came home, and she noticed [his car in the garage]. She went right into the house, and I guess I let myself out of the car, because she knew. And she went upstairs—this is the way she tells the story, I don't remember—and she was at the top of the stairs and I was at the bottom, and I said, "Mommy, why are you screaming?"
>
> She ran down the stairs and grabbed me and we ran out of the house, because she didn't want me coming upstairs, and this I totally understand. There were two elderly women who lived on our street who were retired nurses, and she ran to their house. She was thinking, "If they're home, everything is going to be okay."
>
> Of course, they weren't home, but it wouldn't have mattered if they were. From then on, I don't really remember what happened. I think she sent me off to my grandmother's while she reestablished her life, and we moved away pretty soon after. So age four is, like, the delineation of two lives for me.

As a very young child, Abby would not have been able to form a coherent account of her own. It's not just that children that young can't understand death; they also can't yet grasp narrative. Children younger than five are rarely able to place events in sequential, chronological order. Before age five, children have little sense of time, and the stories they create move around in time and space. By age six, time starts being related to personal experience (e.g., *I go to bed when it's nighttime*) and the concepts of clock time can be grasped. This is why most schools start teaching students how to tell time in first or second grade.

By age eight or nine most children can grasp the basic elements on a calendar. Still, the ability to shape a coherent, chronological narrative continues to mature in sync with intellectual development, including higher forms of abstract thinking. Which is to say, an understanding of narrative isn't fully developed until about age ten or twelve.

School-age children who suffer a loss may be so overcome by the event that they're more likely to be focused on adjustment and survival than on shaping an account of the loss. That quest may not surface until years later, and then only if and when a search for meaning becomes urgent. It's not unusual for this to take until midlife to occur. But these individuals may not be revising a child's immature version by that time. The iteration they create at midlife may be their first attempt at a comprehensive account.

Stories of Silence, Secrets and Lies: An Absence of Truth

FAMILIES CREATE their own realities, resulting in what's known as "the family world." After a member dies, a shared account of the loss typically develops. The degree to which conversation about this story occurs depends on a family's culture and also, very often, the opinion of the most powerful or dominant family member.

A true consensus, in which everyone agrees upon every detail and its meaning, is rare. "Family members may agree in some basic way about certain meanings but then each member seems to add his or her own twist," explains Janice Winchester Nadeau, a psychologist in private practice in Minneapolis and the author of *Families Making Sense of Death*. In an ideal family system, both a family narrative about a loss and individual members' different versions can peacefully coexist. That's not always the case in a real-life family, though.

The number of ways to interpret the same set of facts equals the number of people in the room. One person's fact can be another person's secret, and one person's secret may be another person's shame. Some members may be more able or more willing to speak freely about a death, depending on their individual temperaments and grieving styles, their individual relationships with the deceased, and how they feel about the facts of the death. That's how we often see family members in disagreement about what a death means, even when the facts are incontrovertible.

Family narratives may be formed and agreed upon quickly, and may become a version that the family is deeply invested in telling themselves and others. But that story may or may not correspond with medical records or police reports, and it may or may not pass the test of time.

"I've been living inside my family's agreed-upon story for so long, I'm not sure I even know what the real story is," one of my clients once said about the aftermath of her mother's death. "I feel like in my forties I'm finally starting to piece it all together."

When a family blocks conversation about the deceased or the death, the family's shared process of making meaning suffers. Each individual is left to engage in private account making, which is likely to result in different versions of the story, some of which may be contradictory and even wholly inaccurate.

In addition, specific details about a death may be withheld from certain family members. Children, for example, are often shielded from facts about a violent or painful accident. Facts may be withheld in a broader sense, too, as when a family covers up a death by suicide. At the same time, a family can remain deeply invested in holding on to a shared or public version of events and punish members who break from the ranks to create a separate version of their own.

Constructing a coherent narrative can be frustrating when information exists and you know who has it, but your search for an objective, verifiable truth keeps bumping up against refusals and firewalls. In such instances, the only part of the story that's known for sure is the Dramatic High Point. A loved one is gone. How, when, why, where, and because of whom? That information may not be easily accessible.

I've met individuals who've had to order death certificates to find out how their parents died because surviving relatives remained committed to keeping the cause of death secret. Sometimes that's because the circumstances of a death—as with a parent who dies in the presence of a lover, or a teenager who dies due to drug use—may be too painful for a family to accept. Causes of death that have been stigmatized, such as suicide or AIDS, may be discussed only in vague terms, or lied about to reduce feelings of shame among survivors.

When my mother was diagnosed with breast cancer in 1980, cancer was still being called "the big C," and no one wanted to say "breast" in public. That's almost unimaginable now, but in 1980 those taboos were very real. People didn't talk openly about cancer and, as in my mother's case, sometimes not even with the patient. In some cultures, such concealment is still the norm. This practice was depicted in a 2019 film called *The Farewell*, in which a Chinese American woman travels from the United States to China with her extended family to see her beloved grandmother, who has been diagnosed with terminal lung cancer. The family decides not to tell their matriarch about her prognosis because of a cultural belief in China that those who are told about their illnesses will fulfill their prognoses more quickly.

Raya, now fifty-one, was twelve when her younger brother became seriously ill. Her family had recently immigrated to the United States after seeking political asylum, and their first year in America was a tumultuous time for them all. In the midst of it, as Raya recalls, her parents began driving her brother to a major medical center for treatments, an hour's drive in each direction, and leaving her and her older sister alone in their new home.

"All they said was 'Oh, there's something wrong with his blood and he's sick,'" Raya recalls. Yet something wasn't adding up. She knew that, even at twelve. Maybe it was the amount of time each week her parents were spending at a hospital with her brother. Or how drawn and frightened her parents looked each time they came home. Raya tried to find an explanation on her own, but whatever narrative she created refused to make sense. No one had spoken to her about either a diagnosis or a prognosis. She didn't know what Inciting Incident to look for, or what to hope for other than in the vaguest terms. All she had was her parents' explanation that something was missing in her brother's blood.

"So I started going to the library and researching, reading about [blood diseases] just to find out what the hell was going on," Raya says. "At one point I figured out that my brother had leukemia. That it was a cancer of the blood and my parents weren't telling me the truth." From her library research, Raya also concluded that her brother's disease was serious, and he might not survive. Sadly, this was accurate. He died the following year.

Raya says she does not blame her parents for the secrecy. As a parent herself, she believes they were trying to shield her and her older sister from devastating news while they were struggling to acclimate to new social, academic, and geographic environments. Still, I can't help thinking of that twelve-year-old girl sitting alone in her local library, searching for clues about her brother's illness. And I can't help being moved by how determined and how resourceful she was, how she needed the truth badly enough to seek it out herself, and how her efforts delivered a story she didn't want but that finally made sense.

Raya was old enough to enter a library and seek out information on her own. Younger children are unable to do this type of investigative work. They also tend to be less willing to ask questions they sense may cause upheaval or distress in the home. Which is unfortunate, because young survivors who do not receive accurate details about a major loss are at risk for additional distress later in life. A 2013 study of thirty-three adult men and women in the United Kingdom who experienced parental death before age eighteen found that those who came from families that had not communicated clearly and honestly about the death struggled in adulthood with issues of trust, intimacy, self-esteem, self-worth, loneliness, isolation, and emotional expression.

The study's researchers also observed that families in which members were not allowed to discuss a deceased parent set implicit rules for how members should communicate about all of their thoughts and feelings after the loss. Those families often stopped functioning as a unit, to a point where members wound up feeling like "individuals in a family" instead.

Children tend to have piercingly accurate lie detectors. They know when they're not being told the truth, even if they don't know what the truth might be. Kids who can't obtain information from an adult, or who receive only small bits of information that can easily be misinterpreted, will often make up a story to fill in the gaps. This isn't the same thing as magical thinking, which involves a component of fantasy. Rather, these workarounds are the products of existing facts pieced together in a manner that make sense to a young child *at that time*.

Grace, now fifty-eight, still recalls in vivid detail the day her classmate Lynn disappeared from kindergarten. "It was after Christmas and before the March break, during the winter," she says. "Everybody was wondering, 'Where's Lynn? Where's Lynn?' The teacher and my other friends' parents just said 'She's out, she'll be back.' But she didn't come back, and the kids in the class got more and more afraid of what was going on."

Lacking answers to their questions, Grace's classmates tested out narratives that seemed possible to them. "One kid said that Lynn had been bitten by a squirrel in the park across from the school and got rabies," she recalls. "Another boy in the class said, 'No, no, she doesn't have rabies. She got kidnapped by the blind man who walks up and down the street at pick-up time'—without understanding, of course, that a blind man couldn't kidnap a child. We were just freaking out. I ran home, hysterically crying that my friend had rabies. My father, who was a surgeon, turned to me and said, 'What are you talking about?' He found out that Lynn had bone cancer, and that she'd had surgery and lost her leg. She was undergoing chemotherapy and radiation and was at home. None of the parents in the class wanted their kids to know how sick she was or what had happened."

Grace's father quickly stepped in to gather information, calm his daughter's fear, and help her understand her friend's illness. She was able to periodically visit Lynn at her home and maintain the friendship until Lynn died.

Without such adult guidance, children will often hold on to the illogical narratives that have helped them make sense of a confusing situation.

"Those meanings stay a lot longer than their utility," explains Allison Werner-Lin, an assistant professor at the University of Pennsylvania School of Social Policy and Practice. "And those meanings are a core part of the child's life when the child is developing aspects of their personality, aspects of their attachment ideas, aspects about their self-worth, and about their value as individuals."

If questions of *What's going on?* or *What just happened?* become overwhelming for the child, and the child doesn't have an environment that can help them understand or process the facts of a loss, that confusion may become part of how they understand themselves in the world. Global messages of *You're not worthy of understanding what's happening around you, You have to make sense of everything yourself,* and *You're on your own here* can then become internalized and get carried forward.

Just like adults, children will later need to unpack the stories they created for themselves and revise and update lingering messages. This can create a sharp distinction between "the story as I understood it then" and "the story as I understand it now."

That was what happened to Darlene, who suffered long-lasting repercussions as a result of secrecy and silence around a loss that occurred when she was eight.

Darlene, now forty-five, was the third of four children, two of whom were adopted. Her brother Joseph was just a few months older than her and had joined the family after spending his first seven years in an orphanage in the Philippines. Darlene's younger, adopted sister had been born in Vietnam, and she also had an older biological brother.

For Joseph's first eighteen months with the family, he and Darlene were inseparable. "We were like twins," Darlene remembers. "We went everywhere together, we did everything together. He was my best buddy."

One weekday morning, as the children were preparing for school, their mother told them Joseph would be staying home that day. The announcement was unusual but not, in Darlene's recollection, cause for alarm. When she returned from school that afternoon, she saw the adoption agency's van parked in the family's driveway.

Another sibling! she thought. *That must be why Joseph was kept home. To welcome our new sibling!*

Instead, as Darlene approached the front door Joseph came walking out with a suitcase.

A woman from the adoption agency led him down the front steps and put him in the van. Darlene never saw him again.

The last thing I remember seeing was his face pressed up against the window of the van, just looking at me waving. He was just bewildered. I mean, the look on his face was like, What happened? I remember sitting on the top step by the front door. I was only eight, but somehow, I knew that something horrible had just happened. I sat there and I sat there, and I just kept thinking, *If I stay here long enough, they'll turn around and come back*, but they never came back . . .

I went upstairs to the top floor. My sister and I shared one bedroom and then my brothers shared the bedroom right across the hall from us, and that's all there was on the top floor of our house. I went into his bedroom and all of his stuff was gone. Everything was gone.

When I came back downstairs, my mom refused to talk to me. She wouldn't say anything about it, and within a week, my parents sat us down and told us that my dad was moving out and that they were getting divorced, and for the rest of my childhood we were forbidden to ask about Joseph. Every picture of him, every trace of him, was removed from the house, and I got in trouble every time I tried to bring him up.

Because the adults refused to speak about Joseph, Darlene and her two remaining siblings, ages five and fourteen, tried to create a plausible account among themselves. Their father must have rejected Joseph, they decided, because he wasn't his biological son. Also, they determined that because Joseph had been blinded in one eye during his early years in the orphanage, their father must have been ashamed of his disfigurement. They'd seen how their father had been harder on Joseph than he was on his older son, so this explanation tracked logically in their minds.

Within a week, their father moved out and, before long, took a job in another state. Their church turned its back on their mother for being divorced and she fell into a deep, prolonged depression.

"After Joseph left she managed to function enough to keep us moving forward, but she was never a mom to any of the remaining kids after Joseph left," Darlene explains. "I became the mom to them at that point."

The fog of secrecy and silence surrounding their brother's departure, and the stories Darlene and her remaining siblings created to make meaning of the loss, led to an extreme worry about what might come next. If a parent's love could be so conditional, could a biological child be equally vulnerable? Darlene wasn't sure, and she wasn't willing to take the risk to find out.

"Joseph's leaving also triggered a dark fear in me for my little sister," Darlene recalls. "I spent most of the next ten years lying for her, shushing her, telling her that she needed to be perfect and quiet and compliant and have good grades and do everything Dad said or he might send her away, too. I was frantic. I became absolutely pathologically perfectionistic in an effort to keep what was left of my family together. I wasted an awful lot of time and energy running scared, trying to be perfect, trying to be sure my sister would be safe and that we were going to be a family forever.

"It took me a really, really long time and many, many hours of therapy to get over this feeling that I had to be perfect for people to love me," Darlene continues. "And that I wasn't going to be discarded if I fucked up somehow, because that was the reality I lived in as a kid."

To this day, Darlene does not know the real story of what happened to her brother or why. Over the years she's received different and contradictory explanations from her mother, all of which put the blame on her father, and none of which passed the test of truth. Darlene's mother now suffers from Alzheimer's disease, and her father has since passed away. She may never know, she acknowledges, whether Joseph found another adoptive family, or where he is today. All of her searches for him have led to dead ends. The middle of her story remains full of speculation, and the final echo of ". . . and I still don't know what happened" attaches an ellipsis instead of a period to the very end.

But Darlene can now distinguish between the story she told herself as a child—the one that served her so poorly—and the version she tells now, which she imagines is closer to the truth. This is the one that her adult mind has pieced together from facts she was able to gather over the years.

At eight, she did not yet know that her father also had a biological son just a few years older than her, or that when her mother found out about him she'd asked for a divorce. That event may have been the precipitating factor of Joseph's departure, Darlene now believes.

"I think what happened is we had a two-year or eighteen-month foster period before we could do the full legal adoption," she says. "And when my parents decided to divorce the adoption agency may have decided that Joseph needed to go somewhere more stable, with two parents." She thinks it's possible her mother shut down because she couldn't bear the guilt of the consequence of her decision to divorce.

While compassion for her mother factors into Darlene's story today, so does her commitment to telling an honest, true, balanced version of events, to the best of her ability, and to holding both of its personal truths side by side. "I'm at the point where I feel that it was an amazing experience to have had as a kid, to have seen my parents open their hearts and their home to these children and have them be part of our lives," she says. "But I also saw how it broke my mom when Joseph left, and unfortunately, the domino effect was that it broke the rest of us, too."

Stories with Missing Pieces: The Search for Resolution

PEOPLE LOVE to have answers, love to satisfy the incessant urge to know *why*. As much as we crave mystery, we also seek closure. Especially when death is involved, the human survival instinct longs to know what happened, so we can prevent the same thing from happening again.

Yet sometimes the information a story needs to be brought to completion just can't be obtained. The cause of death may remain inconclusive. Or a body was never found. Or the case is labeled cold. Was it an accidental overdose or a suicide? An accident or a homicide? How can we ever know for sure?

When these questions remain unanswered, the middle of a story contains critical gaps and holes, lacking the kind of sequential, cause-and-effect relationships that help a mourner make sense of a death and find meaning. Tellers are forced to hop from known fact to known fact, inserting disclaimers along the way—*No one knows what happened next, but then . . .* —and filling in blanks with speculation. Deaths by suicide, accident, or murder are most likely to fall into this category, although details of an illness can be enigmatic or ambiguous as well.

What impact do these perpetual question marks have on survivors?

"If I don't know what happened, I can't know how to feel about it" is a common refrain. This speaks to how crafting a story of loss is both a cognitive *and* an emotional process. Intellect steps up quickly to assemble a story that makes sense, while grief waits offstage for its cue to enter.

When intellect is given an impossible task, however, grief can get stuck backstage. There in the darkness, it can become blocked, postponed, displaced, or misdirected. Or it can attach itself to the missing pieces of the story rather than to the pain of absence.

That's when survivors devote an outpouring of effort and energy to investigating a cause of death, or working nonstop with police or private investigators to recreate events. Intellect keeps combing through facts and memory in repetitive loops, searching for new information, revisiting the plotted action, trying to stitch together disconnected facts to create a comprehensible narrative.

Mourners who try and try to figure out what happened actually show more evidence of trauma than those who thoroughly avoid thinking about the death. In this case, what you don't think about really can't hurt you as much as thinking about it incessantly does. Immersing oneself in the facts and facing multiple failed attempts to find meaning may also result in higher incidences of depression and intrusive thoughts.

So why do we do it? The urge to frequently think and talk about the details may be an attempt to create order and control over ambiguity and to discharge stress. An obsession around piecing a story together also offers a welcome distraction from the pain of grief. The search for elusive information always has the potential, however small, to achieve a clear and satisfying resolution.

For more than thirty years, Olivia has dipped in and out of searching for details to explain how her sixteen-year-old sister, Jeannie, died. Jeannie went missing from their home on the East Coast one day and was found less than twenty-four hours later after falling from the top of a high-rise hotel on the other side of the country. Olivia has worked with private investigators and consulted with mediums, and she and her aunt have run through the known facts over and over and over again over the past three decades. And still, nobody knows why Jeannie flew across the country, why she might have checked into that hotel, or what happened on the roof that night.

At the time, Jeannie's death was ruled a suicide and the case was closed. But Olivia has long suspected that the missing details might reveal a different story, and that this new story might offer the truth.

When she died, Jeannie had recently returned from a six-week summer program in Europe. It had been a "miserable trip" for her, as Olivia describes it. While she was in Europe, Jeannie had gained fifty pounds very quickly. She'd returned home changed in several other ways, too.

To re-create the narrative leading up to Jeannie's death, Olivia has to weave together what she and her family could remember, additional details that were uncovered later, what she thinks *might* have happened, and her acknowledgment of which pieces are still missing.

My grandparents' fiftieth wedding anniversary party was coming up and [Jeannie] had to get a dress for it. My mother gave her a credit card, and she went to the mall, but she never came home. We know she went shopping, because a Gap bag was found in her car, but the next morning the police and a rabbi came to my parents' door at 6 A.M. saying that Jeannie had died. She had taken a flight [across the country] and checked into a hotel. A lot of the details here are from private investigators. She left the hotel for about five hours and was seen with someone, came back to the hotel, and they said that she jumped from the roof or fell from the roof.

Even after hiring a private investigator, we still don't know exactly what happened. I've done a tremendous amount of work with suicide specialists and professionals over the years, and this is a very atypical suicide story for a teenager. My parents were able to accept that Jeannie's brain just snapped, but I've never accepted that. So, for me, it's been a really long time of having to, wherever I am in the story, accept whatever I know at the time.

For Olivia, the story of Jeannie's death has become a thirty-year odyssey of searching for the truth about how her sister died, and making peace with what she knows after each minor revision. At the same time, she acknowledges that not knowing everything may offer some protective benefits. "It's like, what you don't know can't hurt you," she says. "The final act was extremely violent. So the leading-up to it is what I've focused on—the reason why she went to California. Maybe there had been a rape? Maybe she was pregnant? I'd like to finally stop the perseverating about what could've happened.

"I don't know if I'll ever have resolution. I'd like to think I will. Maybe there's just something that will click for me one day that will say, 'Okay, I'm at peace with this.' But in the meantime, I can't just let it be and accept it, because I don't know what I'm accepting about it."

Olivia may never be able to recreate the completely plotted action of the last fateful day of Jeannie's life and solve the mystery of what happened to her sister. The more time passes, the harder it's become for her to find people who might remember that night. The story of Jeannie's death may never find a detailed, emotionally satisfactory Middle. At best, Olivia may eventually find some peace with the ambiguity surrounding an event that's so deeply personal to her.

At the same time, it's important for Olivia to recognize that her story of loss, the story of her search for information and justice for Jeannie that acknowledges its missing parts, *is* a narrative. Its portions of uncertainty offer an honest accounting of her experience with both the known and unknown facts of Jeannie's death. It's a story of incompletion, of questions that have not yet been answered or can never be answered. The story of a loved one's death may never find its resolution. But acknowledging and accepting the incompleteness and ambiguity in *your* story of loss may be what finally helps it feel whole.

Traumatic Loss: When Memories Are Fractured or Blocked

FIFTY-EIGHT-YEAR-OLD SHARON says her memory of the day both her parents died still comes back to her in pieces, like separate shards of glass.

"My two older sisters and many people from our church were in the house," she says, "and everyone was crying and screaming and carrying on loudly. I still to this day don't recall anybody personally telling me my parents were dead. I remember sitting under the table by myself, knowing something was dreadfully wrong. I know trauma can do this. Trauma can really slice up an event. It's kind of like a black-and-white PowerPoint slideshow [when I remember it] now; definitely not like a movie camera."

When both of her parents died in an accident, Sharon would have likely experienced what's known as a "shock trauma." Psychologist Ernst Kris coined the term in 1956, along with "strain trauma," and the distinction he made between them remains useful today. Shock trauma occurs as the result of a one-time experience like an accident or homicide, when the harsh reality of a death abruptly intrudes upon an individual's existing worldview. Strain trauma occurs when long-standing stressors build up to an unmanageable degree over time and culminate in a crisis, such as when a loved one is ill and deteriorating for a long period of time before death.

Trauma fractures memory in the way that Sharon describes because trauma fractures experience. When the brain is flooded with stress hormones, especially cortisol, it operates in a climate of intense confusion. This creates a breakdown in the brain system that forms autobiographical memories, and also interferes with the part of the brain—the hippocampus—that's responsible for storing memories in

a way that allows them to be retrieved in a narrative fashion, as positive memories are.

This means that at times of extreme stress, images and sensations
aren't always stored and assembled in a coherent manner. Traumatic
memories, when we have them, often occur as sense memories, of
specific sounds, textures, and fragrances. Persistent, chronic stress,
such as the type associated with complex PTSD, can have a similar
effect, creating patches of white space in memory from the time period of the trauma.

Trauma also floods the brain with neurotransmitters that imprint
vivid sensory images of the event on our brains, such as the flashing
lights of a police car or ambulance or the sound of a siren. Those images become intertwined with the corresponding emotions of fear,
panic, or helplessness that were experienced during the event. Together, they're stored as fragments that exist outside of conscious
memory and can intrude on our awareness, without warning, long
after the event itself. That's what we typically refer to as a flashback.

Trying to fit those disparate, isolated images into a plot structure,
Robert Neimeyer explains, while simultaneously struggling with the
massive invalidation of a prior worldview, involves a good deal of effort. Some trauma survivors find themselves obsessively trying to
piece together a story out of fragments of memory and intrusive sensory details as they come up. Edward Rynearson's Restorative Retelling program as well as Narrative Exposure Therapy, a short-term
psychological treatment for post-traumatic stress disorder, both guide
survivors through this process—to help them stabilize the trauma
and turn a fragmented account into a more cohesive story.

Trauma can also wipe clean (for a period of time or permanently)
the recollections of the time before, during, or after a specific, traumatic event through a phenomenon known as "autobiographical erasure." This is most common in younger victims and also those who
didn't receive support from a trusted adult at the time, but autobiographical erasure can happen to teens and adults as well.

This may help explain why I have so few memories from the four or five months that followed my mother's death. No matter how hard I try to recover them, I remember almost nothing from July through November of 1981. It's like a heavy curtain comes down between the me of today and the me of 1981 whenever I try to remember. I know I was working two jobs that summer and that I went back to school in the fall, so I must have taken classes? Helped around the house? Had friends? Honestly, I can't remember, and not just because it was almost forty years ago. I can't remember, most likely, because of the way my memories during those post-trauma months were stored.

Memories that aren't stored properly can't be retrieved properly, either. As psychologist Peter Levine explains in *Trauma and Memory*, when memory works properly we store two kinds: explicit and implicit. Explicit memories include the superficial details of an event or encounter, such as who said what, what happened when, and what everyone was wearing. Implicit memories are the recollections of what we thought and felt during those experiences. Sometimes implicit memories can be stored as physical sensations and surface later as somatic responses.

Together, explicit and implicit memories create a full picture of an experience. Both are essential to story development. Trauma, however, can seriously interfere with this process. Trauma scrambles both the storage of explicit memories and the emotional processing that's essential to forming implicit memories. When we try to remember an event later, we may not be able to pull up both types of memories of it. Or we may not be able to access either one. This leaves mourners feeling as if they have access only to one layer of a significant piece of their past, or none at all.

Survivors of trauma also may temporarily lose their recall of the event, only to regain access much later—often in bits and pieces and sometimes without warning. It's disconcerting when this happens, and professional assistance is often needed to calm down these intrusions.

Ordinary memories are dynamic, fungible, and subject to constant revision. They can be recalled in a chronological narrative form. Traumatic memories tend to be dissociated and disorganized. They lack sequence and may be missing important details. It's hard to fit them into a story for this reason.

Traumatic memories also tend to be static and fixed. When a memory has been erased and recovered, it tends to be accurate, because the mind hasn't changed what it couldn't retrieve before. It's a bit like taking a time capsule out of deep storage after forty years and discovering that the contents that went into the box for burial haven't changed even a bit. If memories have been fractured, the pieces might come through as fragments or splinters, or as intrusive thoughts, images, or sensations that could reactivate a PTSD response and thrust you into a personal crisis. This is why it's important to be very careful about your own mental health when recovering memories.

All this said, it's still unclear whether memories that become lost in time like this are truly inaccessible as the result of the trauma itself, or whether something called "functional avoidance" is at work. This is a built-in, self-protective mechanism that may keep us from accessing painful recollections, and that can cause a search for specific memories to stop at the level of generalization to keep a mourner from being overwhelmed by the details. For example, a memory might be of being neglected frequently during childhood without recalling a single, specific, or vivid incident of a time when that happened. The higher the level of stress at the time a memory was formed, the lower the incidence of specific details when that memory is stored and retrieved. Without functional avoidance, a survivor risks becoming retraumatized by their own memories.

Creating a narrative about a traumatic loss is a delicate process that needs to be undertaken carefully. Therapeutic support that helps a mourner stabilize the trauma response first may be necessary, and carefully choosing compassionate listeners who help you test and confide is essential. The narrative of a traumatic loss may also benefit from creating an extended resolution: The End of a story (in the Aristotelian sense) often leads right into a new narrative—one that includes the processing of the trauma, as well as stories of post-traumatic growth.

Because that's how a story of loss evolves. The End of one story is always the Beginning of another, in an overarching, never-ending chain of cause and effect. A story of loss leads into a story of survival. A story of survival sparks a story of adaptation that, under the very best circumstances, becomes a story of growth.

CHAPTER TEN

* * *

Reauthoring Your Story of Loss

T HE BOXES still held their original shape, but the thick strips of packing tape had already yellowed and peeled with age. I hadn't seen these boxes since I'd carefully packed them up in New York City and shipped them 2,800 miles to California more than two decades earlier. When my husband handed them down to me from the opening to our attic, I recognized them immediately. Seeing them again felt like a reunion with a pair of old friends.

Inside the two boxes were all of the articles, notes, and interview transcripts from my first book, neatly lined up in manila file folders labeled by subject matter and chapter. I opened up a thick file of transcripts and skimmed through the jagged pile. I'd interviewed ninety-two women for my first book, and here were all of their stories in my arms again.

For three years in the 1990s I'd lived with these stories every day. I'd gotten to know many of them almost as well as my own. Now, twenty-seven years later, I was hoping to talk with some of these women again, to learn how their stories of loss had changed over time. I needed the original transcripts for comparison. And here they all were again.

I'd been searching for these boxes for months, had even emptied out our entire garage, item by item, in my quest to find them. I'd been so single-mindedly focused on the interview transcripts they contained that I hadn't stopped to imagine what else might be stored inside. So I was not prepared for what I found inside a file that was labeled, very simply and in my own handwriting, "Notes."

The single document it contained was four pages, single-spaced, with my name printed in the upper left corner. The title was "After the Talking Stopped." The font was an old one I recognized from my very first computer and printer. 1991? 1992?

What is this? I wondered, and I started to read.

"My mother died in the middle of summer, with everything in full bloom," it began. "She died just before dawn."

The pages were an early prototype for the introduction to my first book, I realized. I kept reading. The story followed the same arc as my original story of loss, the one that's reproduced in chapter 7. Then it kept going. From what I could tell, this must have been written about ten years after my mother died. It wasn't the story I was telling soon after. Neither was it the story I'd tell now. No, this was some kind of intermediary version, a transitional account. I'd just found a copy of my story of loss in motion.

Snapshots in Time

A STORY of loss captures a moment of conscious awareness, like a single snapshot in time. Early versions typically gather and arrange facts in one place to answer the basic questions of what, when, where, why, and how. They're like episodic first drafts in which an author tries to get the beats of the story onto the page. In narrative therapy this version of a story is called a "thin narrative" for its attachment to the superficial details of cause and effect. *This happened, then that happened, then she said this, and then he said that.*

Only later do we layer in the emotional aspects and "thicken" the story to move it beyond a rote recitation of events. These additions create a more nuanced and multidimensional account of how *we* responded, adapted, changed, and grew as a result of being exposed to those events. It also fills in the story of our relationship with the deceased. This is how, throughout the Aftergrief, the story of someone's death matures into a unique and individual story of loss.

This ongoing process of "interpretive reconstruction," as John Harvey calls it, requires us to periodically revisit and reprocess the same set of facts. It's like returning to the same well over and over, and pulling up a slightly different bucket of water each time. The well doesn't change much, and honestly, neither does the bucket. What changes is the composition of the water we extract. Each time we pull up the bucket full of facts, we're choosing which ones will float to the top and which can drift to the bottom, and we'll deduce a different meaning from each new extraction.

It's *all* in the perspective. In writing workshops, when students are ready to move beyond episodic first drafts, I like to quote Vivian Gornick from *The Situation and the Story:* "What happened to the writer is not what matters. What matters is the large sense the writer is able to *make* of what happened." Viktor Frankl said basically the same thing about human behavior when he maintained that what happens to us does not determine how we react. What ultimately drives our behaviors, he said, is the meaning we make of what happened.

Meaning making is a process of constant engagement (and re-engagement) with the facts. Memories and feelings form a temporary version of events that persists until we reach a new level of development or acquire new information. Then the story may change again. But a story of loss is only as flexible as we allow it to be. We must be willing to let it change. And that's not always easy. It may be tempting to reject information that doesn't fit into an existing worldview, or that threatens an identity that's attached to an existing story. This is often a problem in families where different members have their own versions of the facts.

When a story becomes fixed and rigid, it can calcify into what I call a "dominant life narrative." That's a single, organizing story that starts to define the entirety of a life and becomes central to one's sense of self.

Told and told again, this type of story of loss becomes a well-rehearsed performance. The details are rattled off mechanically, almost automatically. The storyteller knows which facts will make eyes widen, and which points they should emphasize or de-emphasize to achieve a desired effect. As the delivery is perfected, the story risks becoming an artifact rather than an organism.

"That story felt like *mine*," admits thirty-five-year-old Gala, whose story of mother loss at age ten underwent several significant revisions when new sources chimed in with different accounts. "It felt like a security blanket I'd traveled around with. Granted, it was old and ratty and rarely, if ever, washed or examined closely, but it was a comfort. When I met someone new, I could launch into my autoplay of the life-story highlights. I knew where to inflect to make sure my listener didn't get too sad. I knew at what moments to expect the sharp inhales from an audience, when an *'awww'* was coming, and I had sarcastic one-liners to keep the flow of the story somewhat buoyant."

I see this in writing workshops also from time to time, when a student has been working on the same childhood memoir for years or even decades. They'll register for class after class, rewriting the same events, remaining prisoners to their story's current content and meaning. Sometimes this is because attempting to write the story has become such a part of their identity they don't know who they'll be once they resolve the struggle to tell it. Sometimes it's because confiding is their main goal, and they want to keep being heard and validated. And sometimes it's because the story, in that form, has become so central to their identity they're afraid to let it go.

"To change [our stories] feels like we're losing our identity," explains Stephen Joseph, the author of *What Doesn't Kill Us: The New Psychology of Posttraumatic Growth*. "To rebuild that sense of self, we need to craft new stories that reconstruct our values, our expectations, and our place in the world."

Stories in Motion

RECONSTRUCTING A familiar, comfortable story can be an act of courage, Robert Neimeyer reminds me when we speak by phone. Sometimes we have no choice but to begin the process, he points out, because we need to build a new platform to stand on. Other times, we undertake the mission as a conscious choice.

If reauthoring is a fluid, ongoing process of constant renegotiation and reevaluation, do we ever settle on a final version? Maybe, at the end of a long life. Until then, I believe, our stories remain in transition, steadily evolving as we continue to learn, mature, investigate, and experience. This transitional process seems, to me, like a figure eight, or a giant infinity sign. We stand at the point right in the middle—where our present-day consciousness resides—as we cast back into the past to retrieve memories, bring them into the middle where we synthesize them in the present, and then cast forward into our projections of the future. Through this process, the stories we tell ourselves about ourselves continue to change. Transitional stories retain elements of past versions, and also keep layering in new insights and experiences. This is how we continuously write our way into a new and different future.

A story of loss in transition might look something like this:

My mother died in the middle of summer, with everything in full bloom. She died just before dawn. I walked out of the hospital alone, carrying her last few possessions in a white plastic bag: a nightgown, a wig, a cheap pair of terrycloth slippers, and the underwear she'd been admitted in. Walking across the dark parking lot, I caught a sharp, green tangy whiff of freshly mowed grass, and it seemed terribly absurd to me that anything should grow just to be cut down.

My mother was forty-one when she was diagnosed with cancer, and forty-two when it took her in the night. I was seventeen. My sister was fourteen, my brother nine, and my father at a complete loss regarding how to handle us all. Nobody had told us how to mourn, and we did not do it well. We did not do it at all. We simply began eating microwaved dinners with a television set on the table where my mother used to sit, and instead of discussing our respective days at work and school we pretended to be absorbed in *Wheel of Fortune* reruns. We had lost all comfort of speech. When my sister and I talked, it was usually to argue in simple sentences over petty household chores—It's your turn to set the table, your turn to collect the dirty clothes. My brother withdrew to his bedroom. The empty Scotch bottles began to multiply on the kitchen counter, and none of us dared knock on the closed door to our father's room at night.

My father and I maintained a purely functional relationship, designed to keep the house running in order, and when we spoke, we stuck closely to the facts. What time was the appointment for Glenn's haircut, and how did Michele do on her last algebra exam? When were my college applications due and how much money did I need for the fee? Those kinds of conversations. Hadn't enough already been said? The hour before my mother entered the hospital for the last time, my father sat me down in the living room to tell me she was going to die. "I've known it for a long time," he said. "Since the operation last spring. But how could I tell her, or you kids? I know what you're thinking," he said. "I've thought it, too. But when the doctors told me they couldn't get it all . . . They told me she had a year. We've had her for fifteen months. We've been lucky."

"Who's been lucky?" I ask him a year later, in the car on the way to the airport. At 10:57 A.M. I will fly off to a college eight hundred miles away.

"What are you talking about?" he says. He doesn't know what I mean.

Or does he? I can't tell.

"You're lucky," he says. "You're heading off to a whole new life."

We speed underneath the Bronx, across the Triborough Bridge, past Rikers Island, and escape seems to require little more than a plane ticket to Chicago and a couple of suitcases filled with clothes.

But in my dorm room that evening, I unpack memories that fill my drawers. Every piece of underwear reminds me of the little plastic bag—"Here," the nurse said. "You don't want to forget this"—and I roll my socks into little balls the way my mother showed me. At night, when the women in my hall line up to call their mothers from the pay phone on the wall, I sit cross-legged on my bed, feigning interest in the orientation schedule, and my anger fills the room.

My mother died in 1981, at a time when cancer and death were supposed to have begun losing their mystique, and doctors were supposed to tell their patients the truth. Supposed to. Doctors were not supposed to do what my mother's doctors did.

On sunny afternoons, I would drive her to the oncologist and read magazines in the waiting room while she gave blood and got her shots behind a closed door. "My white blood cells are good," she'd tell me, smiling as we got back in the car. (Later, I learned the doctor called my father from his office with the heavy mahogany desk and the diplomas hanging on the wall. "We're worse than last time," he said. "What should we tell her?")

It's the "we" that stings me every time I remember this. Who was the "we"? My father, the oncologist, the surgeon, even the allergist who found the lump under her right arm and suggested she get it checked out. All of them men, all of them secretly discussing among themselves the fate of the woman whose body was slowly failing. "They're switching my medication," she told me as we sat together at the kitchen table, eating peanuts and dumping the shells into a big, green Tupperware bowl. "They say I'm ready to try something new."

(My father took the call at his office that day. "We're losing her," the doctor said. "We have to try something new.")

She came home from the CAT scan, tired but still smiling. "All clear," she said. "Good news."

(In a side room the radiologist told my father the tiny spots were everywhere: her lungs, her ribs, her bones. He mentioned a slight shadow on the liver.)

"Goddammit!" I wanted to scream at her later, much later. "Why didn't you look at the screens yourself?"

At the end, we had two last weeks of silence. My sister was dropped off at summer camp. What happened next happened quickly. My mother became dehydrated. My brother was sent to stay with a friend. Her stomach began to swell. My father called the doctor from the kitchen and yelled at her to pick up the phone in the bedroom. "What's going on?" I heard her ask. "I look like I'm six months pregnant." When my father went to meet with the rabbi, I carried her back and forth to the bathroom, a useless trip each time. But it kept me busy. It kept me from focusing on how bad this was, and how it was probably going to get worse. It kept me from remembering that the last time my father had spoken with a rabbi was his wedding in 1960.

In the morning my mother called out to my father, who helped her lean over the side of the bed. When he saw her vomit was black, he called the ambulance. That's when he called me into the living room and told me to sit down.

When the attendants arrived, they tried to carry her away. "My wig!" she shouted. "I need my wig!"

"Put it in a bag with her nightgown!" my father called out over his shoulder, as they all disappeared through the garage door.

The house was quiet for the first time in days. As I walked upstairs to find the wig, I stopped at the edge of the living room. I looked at the silent couch and the upholstered chair, facing each other in a position that said confrontation. I didn't know it then, but I would revisit this setup many, many times in the following years. In a therapy session in Tennessee I would sit on a make-believe couch and face an empty chair, remembering the words spoken on that afternoon before the talking stopped. *I've known it for a long time. Since before the operation last spring. But how could I tell her, or you kids?* In Tennessee, I screamed and threw pillows, and called my father a fucking liar and a snail. I stamped my feet and threw more pillows, hurling them past his invisible head, and watched them bounce off the wall. I cursed at him for never allowing my mother to know she was going to die.

After the ambulance arrived at the hospital that afternoon, my mother lay on a stretcher in the emergency room and cried with her eyes closed, tears squeezing through the corner cracks. "I'm so afraid," she said. "I'm so afraid I'm going to die." And then, when my father stepped beyond the curtain to fill out the insurance forms, she pulled on my arm and pleaded. "Tell me, Hope," she said. "Tell me I'm not going to die."

What does a daughter owe her mother in this last moment alone together, before she is whisked off to an empty bed upstairs? I looked down at her, her body swollen and bald. Her hand gripped my wrist tightly. Even now, she had perfectly manicured nails. I was the helpless, disorganized one here. In that crucial moment, I was no longer certain if my loyalties belonged with the living or the dead.

"I'm not going to leave you," I told her. "I promise, you won't be alone." But even as I said it, I knew I was missing the point, and I felt that I had failed.

What happened next happened slowly, over three or four days, but it seemed to cover weeks. I drove to Connecticut to retrieve my sister from summer camp. When we returned, our mother was in a coma. A social worker appeared and backed me into a corner, with her hand pressed against the opposing walls.

"Your mother is dying," she said, with urgency, as if this were breaking news.

"This is a nightmare, a total nightmare," I told my aunt as we sat together on a black vinyl couch in the waiting room, "and I'm surrounded by clowns." I was mixing my metaphors, but no one seemed to notice or to care. My aunt stared at the linoleum tile on the floor, tiny squares of unequal size fitting together to form larger blocks. "The last thing your mother said to your father," she told me, still staring at the floor, "to anyone, was 'Take care of my children.'"

I was sleeping on the same black couch the following night when my father woke me just before 3 A.M. "We lost her," he said. Already, we were speaking in euphemism. I had made him promise she wouldn't be alone, and he said he was sitting next to her, holding her hand, but my trust had been destroyed by then. I demanded proof, which he couldn't give.

When I went into the hospital room to say goodbye, I did not cry. At the funeral, I did not cry. A cousin delivered the eulogy, and kept stopping to wipe his glasses as he talked about her strength and her courage in spite of her impending death, and at that moment I realized that nobody knew. I wanted to stand up and shout out, "But she didn't know she was going to die! No one told her! And she never had the chance to say goodbye!" But I kept quiet. It was a funeral, after all. Months later, I began to let it out in my journal. MY MOTHER DIED WITHOUT DIGNITY WITHOUT DIGNITY WITHOUT DIGNI, I wrote, and my pencil broke on the final T.

READING THESE pages today, I'm struck by how furious I was at my father and those doctors, and how distant that anger feels now. I'm also struck by how much more insight I had a decade later than I'd had at seventeen. The original version of my story of loss in chapter 7 was all about the facts as I perceived them soon after the event itself. This later version contains more emotion and context. It's coming from a more mature perspective, but it's still a story I was trying to figure out and work my way through, even as I wrote it.

Stories of loss can change for a number of reasons. From the interviews for this book, and especially from the eighteen follow-up interviews with women who participated in *Motherless Daughters* in the early 1990s, I've observed how new information arrives, often without warning, to change the plotting of events. We're then thrust back into the story-development phase again, to run through the facts and events in our minds to create new and perhaps even more authentic accounts. On occasion, that information may even come from the deceased themselves, in the form of letters or journals we discover after they die. Sometimes another person's account causes our perspective to shift, or a source whose reliability is questionable introduces doubt. We might reach a new state of maturity and suddenly see the same events in a different light. Or we might make a willful decision to change a narrative because the story we're carrying has become burdensome and no longer serves us well.

Claire Bidwell Smith, who lost both of her parents by age twenty-five, was in a master's program in psychology, learning about issues of identity, when she had a revelation.

"I started thinking about the story I was carrying around," she recalls, "and wondering, Did it really have to be, all the time, about what I'd lost? I realized that I was skewing everything toward negativity and toward something I didn't have. I was constantly looking at my life like a negative image. And I thought, *Wow, that's a choice I'm making, to look at it that way.* That's when I started doing exercises of basic gratitude, as cheesy as it sounds, to remind me there was more. Because I didn't want to walk around like that. It was so painful and sad all the time, and it made me so miserable. So I had to ask myself, *Does this make sense?*"

The big shift in my story occurred when I was in my late twenties, visiting my mother's best friend, Sandy, in Florida. We were sitting in her kitchen and talking about the end of my mother's life. Sandy could tell how angry I was at my father for concealing information from us all. She saw how I was depicting my mother as a victim. Anyone could see that, at the time.

I remember how Sandy leaned forward a bit when she spoke next. "You might be selling your parents short, Hope," she said. "I wouldn't overlook the possibility that they had an unspoken agreement for your father to get the news and decide what to tell your Mom. I knew your mother since she was thirteen, and I'm not sure that she was strong enough to know she was dying. You may have gotten a couple of more months with her than you would have if she'd known the truth."

Oh. *Oh.* I'd never thought of that possibility before. Not even a little.

For a decade, so much of my identity had been wrapped up in being my mother's champion, in avenging her for a single, dramatic wrong. That was very much my seventeen-year-old point of view, coming from the girl who saw everything in black and white, who didn't yet know how much of adult experience occurs in shades of gray. Only as an adult could I begin to imagine what Sandy meant, and to acknowledge that it might be true. And to consider how terrible it would have been for my mother to take in that news, and that she might not, as Sandy said, have been able to live with it for long. I could begin, then, to understand why she might have gratefully handed that responsibility to her husband.

There wasn't any way I could have possessed that insight or that empathy at seventeen. Not because I wasn't an empathetic teenager, but because I didn't have the maturity to imagine that adults might make such choices, or to cope with how that knowledge might make me feel.

Sandy was a reliable source, someone who'd known my mother as a woman and not just as a mom. Her opinion seemed like more than just speculation. When I opened myself up to its possibility and allowed my story to change, its sharp points began to soften. I realized I'd been carrying around an immature version of a story I'd needed in adolescence in order to survive. Righteous anger had served me well for a while. Energizing and purposeful, it had kept me from plummeting into despair.

That afternoon in Sandy's kitchen was the day I outgrew the story of loss I'd been carrying and began crafting a new one, one that could become richer, more detailed, potentially more confusing, and also exquisitely complex. And over time, I began telling that new story with less anger and blame.

I was lucky in that Sandy was a trusted and reliable source, and that she'd generously agreed to talk with me that day. Sometimes when a bereaved individual approaches a relative or family friend, that person is happy to share what they know. Perhaps they've even been waiting and hoping for permission to talk about the deceased, too. In that respect, the request is received as a gift. But there's also a risk that instead the response will be "Why do you want to know about that?" or "Can't you leave the past in the past?" This almost always says more about that person's long-term adjustment to the death or grieving style than it does about your request.

If you have more than one person you can approach, try another, and another, until you find someone who'll receive your request as a gift. And remember: Other people's memories are subjective, and their perspectives may be faulty or self-referential. You don't have to fold everyone's memories into your story. You're not writing by committee. As we say in the writing workshop, take what you want and leave the rest.

The Story of Now

JUST AS we can only grieve to the best of our abilities at any point in our development, our stories can only reflect the degree of awareness and maturity we've achieved and the information we've accumulated at a given point in time. I hadn't known, in the early 1990s, that the story I'd titled "After the Talking Stopped" was a temporary version, or that excavating it twenty-five years later would feel like meeting up with a younger version of myself.

I feel deep compassion now for that younger woman, still so bound up in her outrage and her pain. She won't talk with Sandy in Florida for about another year. In the meantime, I want to put my arm around her and tell her, "I know that anger feels empowering now, but you won't need it forever. Good things are coming. They'll soften your story. Let that happen."

It wasn't hard to notice, as I was reading her words, how much my telling of the story has changed since then. The facts? The same. The meaning? Different in so many ways.

If I were to build upon her scaffolding to create an accurate snapshot of today, the new version would include a context and a perspective that it lacked before. It would include compassion for the other characters and myself, which took a long time for me to achieve.

That new, present-day story would read something like this:

My mother died in the middle of summer, with everything in full bloom. She died in the liminal hours between midnight and dawn. I walked out of the hospital alone that morning, carrying her possessions in a white plastic bag: a nightgown, a wig, a cheap pair of terrycloth slippers, and the underwear she'd been admitted in. Walking across the dark parking lot, I caught a sharp, green tangy whiff of freshly mowed grass and it cracked my heart open, to be encountering such a vivid example of vibrant life cut short.

My mother was forty-one when she was diagnosed with cancer, and forty-two when it took her in the night. That's almost imaginable to me now. Forty-two seemed old to me at seventeen. Now that I'm thirteen years older than she ever got to be, forty-two seems heartbreakingly young. At the time, my sister was fourteen, my brother nine, and our father was at a complete loss regarding how to raise us. How could he possibly have known? Our parents modeled a division of labor in the 1970s that fell along strict gender lines. A father who worked outside the home and paid the bills. A mother who took care of the house and the kids. I'm not sure my father even knew how to use a microwave when his wife died. There was so much he would have to learn. It must have felt overwhelming to him, at the time.

Also this was 1981. Cancer was still referred to as "the Big C" and no one would say "breast cancer" because of the public embarrassment of saying "breast." It was not uncommon, still, for physicians to hide diagnoses and prognoses from patients. We were also in the dark ages of grief support in the United States. Nobody reached out to us in our grief, and so we mutely soldiered on. We began eating dinners with a television set on the table where my mother used to sit, and instead of discussing our respective days at work and school we pretended to be absorbed in *Wheel of Fortune* reruns. My family became emotionally distant yet highly efficient. What we lacked in connection we achieved in productivity. We managed to fill the dishwasher, collect the dirty clothes, make sure haircuts and doctor's appointments occurred (more or less) on time. I focused on what I could control. The best grades I ever achieved were the ones I earned in school the following year.

As the empty Scotch bottles began to multiply on the kitchen counter, my father withdrew further into his own pain. The hour before my mother entered the hospital, he had sat me down in the living room to tell me she was going to die. "I've known it for a long time," he said. "Since the operation last spring. But how could I tell her, or you kids? I know what you're thinking," he said. "I've thought it, too. But when the doctors told me they couldn't get it all . . . They told me she had a year."

I was angry about this conversation for a very long time. I carried that anger with me everywhere, took it out frequently and ran my fingers over its familiar surface until it felt like a smooth, polished stone. The anger energized me. Rallied me to activism. Made me fierce in my conviction to never let men make decisions on my behalf. I would live, I firmly believed, in a way that my mother never got to, because the men around her took away her freedom of choice.

But this became a hard story to carry, this story that pitted oppressor against oppressed. Being my mother's champion after death meant hewing close to that outrage, all the time. It eventually became exhausting. At times the anger felt corrosive and confusing. Was I making choices that were good for myself, or choices that vindicated my mother? Sometimes I couldn't tell.

Perhaps it was a result of becoming a mother myself, or of reaching the age my father was when he lost his wife, but at some point, I realized how terrible it must have been for him to have had to conceal such a secret, to have lived every day with the knowledge that his wife was dying, that his children would soon lose their mother, and not be able to talk about it with anyone else. I knew what not knowing had done to me. I thought I knew the price my mother had paid. But I'd never stopped to think about what those sixteen months must have taken from my father. All those empty Scotch bottles now seem less like a weakness and more like attempts to cope.

For a long time, I saw the story of my mother's illness and death as a standoff between the men who possessed critical information and the woman who was kept in the dark about her body and her survival. That position became harder to maintain when I read the medical records from her surgery and a social worker's post-op notes. The therapist had tried to tell my mother how extensive her cancer was, and about the gravity of her prognosis. Her repeated attempts to convey this were shut down by my mother's insistence on "getting back to life." The notes revealed the social worker's growing frustration.

Someone tried to tell her. She didn't want to know.

Not long after I'd read the records, I told my mother's best friend, Sandy, about what I'd learned. She didn't seem surprised.

"I knew your mother since she was thirteen years old," Sandy told me, "and I don't think she would have been strong enough to handle that news. I wouldn't rule out the possibility that your parents had an agreement, even if it was unspoken, that your father would get the medical results and decide what and whether to tell her. I think if she'd known, you might have lost her sooner. Maybe by not knowing, you got to be with her for a few months more."

My mother wasn't told that she was dying. Also, my mother may not have wanted to know that she was dying. Two things can always be true.

When the end arrived, it happened quickly. On July 4, I was attending a James Taylor concert outside in the rain. On July 8, the ambulance brought my mother to the hospital. Early in the morning of July 12, she was gone. At the funeral, I did not cry. As my family walked down the aisle behind the coffin, I gripped my brother's hand and told him, "That isn't Mommy in the box. It's just Mommy's body. Her spirit has already moved on to somewhere else."

Even as I said the words I wasn't sure I believed them—it sounded more like something an adult should say to a nine-year-old—but I believe them now. I feel my mother everywhere. I do. Her body was lowered into the ground that afternoon, but the rest of her—that's the part I've carried with me, everywhere I go.

Stories of Loss Are Also Stories of Lives

EMBEDDED IN every story of loss is also the story of a life—the deceased's—and also the story of a shared relationship, no matter how brief. My mother lived for forty-one years before she was diagnosed with cancer. The disease spanned only her final sixteen months. Yet after she died, those last months occupied most of my mental space when I thought of her. Their influence remained that strong.

It took me a long time to remember that my mother was more than a woman who died. She was also a woman who lived. She conducted an elementary school winter concert with a slim black baton; checked on dinner's progress by lifting the lid of her flowered Crock-Pot; regularly sat side by side with her daughter on a piano bench, demonstrating how to practice scales.

I'm fortunate, I know, in having an abundance of memories of my mother, and exponentially more of time shared with my father. So why am I so quick to overlook nearly all of those memories when I tell my stories of loss? What is this eagerness to emphasize their departures, to prioritize the effect their deaths had on my story and identity over the effect of their lives?

As Lorraine Hedtke explains in *The Crafting of Grief,* grief therapy tends to place an overwhelming emphasis on loss and adaptation rather than on maintaining continuity with the influence a loved one had on us while alive. That therapeutic focus only magnifies distress, she explains. Reclaiming parts of the lost relationship is a critical step in reducing emotional pain.

This may feel difficult to do when a loss is still recent, or if a death occurred by suicide, homicide, or by violent accident. The story of a loved one's death may then feel so large and dramatic it overshadows the story of a life. "Whenever I think of my mum the first thing I think of is her dying, and her death, and her being killed in that accident," says British financial journalist and popular money expert Martin Lewis, who was just shy of twelve when his mother died in a horse riding accident. "And that overrides the woman that she was, and the memories that I have. It is far better to remember the wonderful person you lost than to remember you lost a wonderful person."

Charlene also has been trying to shift this perspective after the death of her only sibling, Simon, by suicide eight years ago. Only two years apart in age, Charlene and Simon grew up as close peers. In high school Simon was handsome and popular. In adulthood he was a devoted father and trusted friend. But at age forty-two he chose to take his own life. That last fact carries so much emotional weight in her story of their relationship, Charlene says, that it rushes forth to define Simon's identity whenever she thinks of him today. "The suicide part is so big, and always there, in this huge way," she explains.

To recalibrate this we need to slow down and spend more time in the Before portion of our stories, to consciously step back into selected memories if we have them, or into other people's recollections if we don't. We need to remember who a loved one was to us before they fell ill or died. We are capable of carrying many stories about a relationship. The story of how it ended need not be the dominant one. Folding additional stories of life into our larger stories of loss can be a powerful step toward emotional healing.

Yes, my mother struggled with breast cancer treatment for sixteen months and succumbed to the disease in a brief, frightening, chaotic period of time. She was also someone who could hear a song on the radio and immediately play it on the piano, and who loved the thick Chunky chocolate bars that come wrapped in silver squares. And yes, my father's diagnosis of liver cancer was a grim one that he faced with courage and equanimity. He was also a veteran who was proud of his time served, an avid crossword puzzler, and only a so-so outfielder in the neighborhood softball games that took place every summer in our backyard.

Who they were in dying may have reflected parts of who they were in life, but not all. To abbreviate them in my mind does not do either of them justice. They, and all our loved ones, live in the beginnings of our stories of loss as much as—and often even more than—they live in the middles. That World of the Story, before it was disrupted by illness or death, is where most of them spent most of their time.

So grab that part of your story at both ends and pull on it like taffy, until it's wide enough to hold all the stories of two lives intertwined. It's *your* story of loss. You get to craft it. In its telling, your loved ones can be given a more expansive place to live.

CHAPTER ELEVEN

Story Cracking: Getting from A to Z

M Y FRIEND Christopher's favorite trattoria on West Sixty-eighth Street serves the best meatballs in New York City, according to our highly subjective food panel of two, which is good enough reason to meet there for dinner on a warm September evening. Christopher and I first met more than twenty years ago, when he was a college undergraduate and I was a graduate instructor, and later we became friends and colleagues. During that time, I've watched his career as a business strategist take him from position to position all over the globe. A few years ago he landed in New York, where he co-founded a company and teaches executive development courses at a prestigious university.

By almost any objective standard, Christopher achieved an impressive measure of success by his midforties. Nonetheless, he's found himself reconsidering the choices that led him to this point. Or, rather, the "nonchoices," as he labels them.

Christopher, whom we met in chapter 5, was eight when his father died of heart failure. The year was 1981, the same year that my mother died, when few to no bereavement services were available for grieving families. As a result, Christopher received very little support surrounding the trauma of a sudden loss and of watching paramedics trying to revive his father at home. He and his younger siblings were raised by their mother throughout high school and college. In his twenties, when his friends began pairing off and choosing stable, long-term careers, Christopher was focused on traveling and accumulating life experience. He wasn't laying the kind of groundwork, he now realizes, for what he'd want at forty-five—a life partner, children, and a financial safety net.

He didn't even *know* to want those things back then, he says.

"It's not like I thought about making future plans and then didn't do it. I literally never thought about it," he explains. "It all felt very abstract and nebulous and uncentered at the time. I just didn't have the framework or the inner mechanism to think, 'What do I want to be when I grow up? What kinds of things do I want to do? What kinds of things *are* there to do?' And so, in the absence of knowing what decisions to make, I just did a whole bunch of different stuff."

Christopher's father was an engineer with a methodical, mechanical manner of planning. If he'd survived his second heart attack at age thirty-eight, Christopher feels certain he would have convinced his oldest son to pursue a career in science or engineering. Or at least to choose a marginally practical course of study. Instead, when the university deadline for declaring a major approached, Christopher looked at the courses he'd already taken and picked the major in which he'd accumulated the most credits: French literature. The decision was made "by default," Christopher tells me after we order dinner at the trattoria. That's the way he's made most major decisions, he says.

There's something here I don't quite understand, or maybe a connection I'm missing. The decision-making style Christopher describes sounds like it could be temperamental, the outgrowth of a naturally chill or adventurous spirit, or maybe a long-standing resistance toward limitations or commitments that allows not deciding to become its own form of choice.

"Were you always like this?" I ask. "What I mean is, when you were a kid, did you have the kind of personality that just let things happen?"

Christopher shakes his head in a decisive no. "I guarantee you it's not temperamental," he says. "I actually have a global reputation as a strategic planner, so my core skills are very different." He has no trouble making judicious snap decisions in the workplace, he clarifies. The behaviors he's describing show up only around making long-term plans for himself, which he believes is a function of growing up without his father.

"Everything that does and doesn't exist for me today," he says, "is a direct result of my father dying when I was eight."

Issues of Identity

I DON'T doubt that Christopher's statement is emotionally true, and there may be objective truth to it as well. Witnessing his father's death as a child absolutely could have changed a young boy's assumptions about his future and altered his emerging worldview. Christopher would have been challenged, at eight years old, to develop new and more complex ideas about vulnerability, protection, safety, and predictability than his peers would have been facing at the same age.

When his father died, Christopher also lost his same-sex family role model for becoming a man, a wage-earner, and a father. That also could have affected his identity-forming process. The development of a stable, coherent identity is one of the primary tasks of adolescence. Yet trauma can disrupt that process. When adolescents lose or have already lost a same-sex parent they also lose the relationship they would have relied on to choose which adult qualities and behaviors they want to adopt and which they want to reject. By exploring the different identity alternatives a parent offers, explains psychologist Lara Schultz, teens "begin to define themselves by contrast and continuity."

When the unexpected occurs, a child's personal assumptions about the future are shattered. An imagined pathway to adulthood may need to be revised. Even the most carefully plotted life plan will suffer if the loved one's presence was crucial to its success.

CNN anchor Anderson Cooper, who was ten when his father died of heart failure, has said that his father's death "changed the trajectory of my life. I'm a different person than I feel like I was meant to be."

A profound loss changes us profoundly. How could it not?

Julian, who was in his twenties when both of his parents died, one from cancer and the other from sudden heart failure, says the double loss altered his outlook in ways he never could have imagined. "I was always an optimistic, positive, happy-go-lucky person," he explains. "I was voted 'class optimist' at school. After losing my parents, a big part of my optimism died. It created a new me. Not a bad new me, but a new me in the sense that I ended up relating to the world a little differently."

The deaths of his parents delivered the potent message that the future is neither inevitable nor guaranteed. "I used to always say, 'Oh, *tomorrow*. I'm going to take care of that tomorrow. We'll worry about it tomorrow. See you tomorrow,'" recalls Julian, now fifty-three. "After my parents died, I learned that I have to live in the day. I have to live in the moment. Because sometimes there is no tomorrow."

The decline in Julian's natural optimism coincided with the deaths of his parents, and his memory naturally draws a line of causality between the events. An active mind is always seeking out causal relationships, searching for the shortest, most efficient route between two points, as in:

My optimism died when my parents did.
Because my mother/father/sibling died, I'm afraid to get close to anyone.
Everything that does and doesn't exist for me today is because my father died.

More than statements, these causal relationships we create over time become personal beliefs, which then become truths we accept about ourselves, which then become part of our personal mythologies. And once beliefs about ourselves burrow in that deep, they become part of our identities and are increasingly resistant to change.

The life narratives we create tend to conflate and sometimes misrepresent events. In real life, a movement from cause A to effect Z is rarely that simple or direct. A → Z is often an oversimplified version, and it sells a story short in a few ways.

First, that kind of reductive thinking is more aligned with a child's or a teen's intellect than an adult's. A mature mind knows that loss generates more nuanced and complex outcomes than simple cause-and-effect or binary thinking allows for.

Second, A → Z is a story with a fixed outcome. It offers no entry points or opportunities for change. If your parents' death (A) destroyed your natural optimism (Z), how can you ever regain your optimism if your parents will always be dead?

Third, A → Z is a story compressed. It offers a beginning and an end but no middle. And a story that has a middle that's missing is, at best, only a partial accounting of events.

However, if you take A in one hand and Z in the other and pull them apart, the story cracks open. Often, nestled inside, previously hidden from view, are a string of actions taken and not taken, and a sequence of events that did or should have (but didn't) occur. And just like that, a whole alphabet of events that had been missing from a two-beat causal relationship is revealed.

The Alphabet of Overlooked Events

I REMEMBER very little from ninth-grade algebra, mostly because my best friend Stacey and I spent the majority of each class period passing notes. But for reasons unclear to me still, I paid close attention the week we learned about causal relationships. And I'm glad I did. That's how I learned that a correlation between two values doesn't always mean causality. In other words, Anderson Cooper could have lost his father at age ten and become a CNN anchor at age thirty-four, but that doesn't necessarily mean he became a CNN anchor *because* his dad died when he was ten. That event may have derailed an existing story and set him on a new path, but a whole string of events also occurred between ages ten and thirty-four that probably influenced his professional outcome.

Those intermediary events, or intervening variables, make up the middle of a story. They help explain how two people can suffer a similar loss but have very different outcomes. The variables that emerge or continue to exist after a death in the family are factors that can determine which mourners will suffer most in the aftermath, and which are likely to adapt with minimal distress.

"Let's say one of your parents is an alcoholic and then the other parent dies," says Donna Jackson Nakazawa, author of *Childhood Disrupted*. "That's a big difference between a parent dying and you have a great, amazing other parent who has a lot of self-regulation, and isn't overreacting or underreacting, to help you through."

Intervening variables are also significant because they offer places for intervention as a story is unfolding. In retrospect, when we look back at a past event, they can also offer entry points for change. And therein lies the potential for creating a new outcome for an old story.

This is what I mean:

The causal statement I believed for at least a dozen years was *Because my mother died from breast cancer in her early forties, I'm afraid I'll die from breast cancer, too.* This story was my silent partner, accompanying me on dates, sitting by my side in doctors' examining rooms, waking up with me every morning, accompanying me on work trips. The causal relationship here seemed so obvious, I never thought to question its logic. I mean, *of course* my fear of dying from breast cancer came from watching my mother die from breast cancer. Right? *Hello?*

But when I cracked that story open, I found a long list of variables hiding inside. The new, expanded version looked something like this:

A: My mother died from breast cancer in her early forties.
B: That's when I learned her cancer had been widespread from the start.
C: I also learned the treatments she had in 1981 had been ineffective.

D: Her death was such a shock to me that I experienced it as a trauma.

E: No one talked about her death, and grief support was not available.

F: I had to figure out how to cope with the grief and trauma on my own.

G: Because of my family history I was labeled high risk for breast cancer.

H: No one could say for sure if I'd develop the disease.

I: I was like my mother in so many other ways, I figured I'd be like her in this way, too.

The result?

Z: I'm afraid I'll develop and die from breast cancer.

This cracked-open story now included eight new plot points. Which also meant eight new points of entry, places where I could step back in and effect a change that might, just might, redirect the preexisting course of events and lead to a different outcome.

Here's what happened next.

Because my mother's cancer had been so widespread when she was diagnosed, I went for my first mammogram at age twenty-eight, an appointment I've since been religious about showing up for every year. Fortunately, twenty-first-century medical technology can detect malignancies earlier than the equipment of forty years ago, and treatments are more targeted and more advanced. That makes the ineffective treatments she received for late-stage cancer less of a concern.

When I understood that I'd experienced her death as a trauma, I sought out trauma-informed counseling as an adult. This helped stabilize my trauma responses and eventually helped me talk openly about both her death and her life.

After ten years of not knowing the details of my mother's death, I requested her hospital records, talked with her oncologist, and shared the information with my siblings so we could make decisions based on facts.

And though I'm still considered at high risk for breast cancer, I'm screened annually and stay educated about genetic tests I can take that might show I'm at elevated risk. (I've tested negative so far.)

The result? I'm much calmer now about my chances of developing breast cancer than I was in the years after she died.

Although I was able to address most of the intervening variables in my earlier narrative, such comprehensiveness isn't always necessary. Sometimes by just acknowledging or rectifying one variable you can change a story's emotional outcome. Of course, I can't prevent breast cancer from developing in my body. But by addressing one or more intervening variables, I've been able to reduce my fear that it will.

The Role of the Surviving Parent

THE MOST frequent A → Z belief I encounter draws a direct line between the early loss of a parent or sibling and struggles with intimate relationships as an adult. *Because my mother/father/sibling died when I was young*, the thinking goes, *I'm afraid of being abandoned in my adult relationships.*

On the surface, the logic tracks. If, when you were young, you lost someone you loved, it would make sense that you'd fear it happening again. Psychologists call this having "perceived vulnerability," the abiding fear that if a bad thing happened once, a similar bad thing—specifically the same bad thing—could happen again.

Except study after study after study conducted on bereaved children and adults reveals the same thing: that the most important factor for determining a child's future attachment behavior after a major loss is the kind of relationship the child has with their surviving caretaker. When surviving caregivers were warm, consistent, communicative, and attentive to the child's needs, that child typically shows lower rates of depression and anxiety and more satisfying adult relationships than children whose surviving caregivers were emotionally unavailable, resistant to mourning, preoccupied with their own bereavement, or impaired by mental illness or substance abuse.

A surviving caretaker who doesn't take care of a child, for whatever reason, creates a dual dilemma for that child. "What's wrong with me that one parent died and the other won't parent me?" the child wonders. The intervening variable of consistent aftercare is so important, in fact, that some psychologists believe the care a child receives after a parent dies can have as much long-term impact as the death itself.

When I work with an adult who connects their present-day relationship struggles to early parent loss in the past, one of the first questions I ask is "Who took care of you after your parent died?" The second question is "How were you cared for?" My third question is often "What were your attachment patterns like even before your mother died?" When we crack open the story, we're likely to find an alphabet that includes measures of care and attention that were or weren't received, and patterns that may date back further than we realize. Attachment patterns typically develop in the first eighteen months of life. They can be exacerbated by later trauma but aren't necessarily created by it.

My experience with story cracking, as it happened, didn't erase or invalidate my original fear. The hour I spend in a radiology suite waiting for my scans to be read every spring is still my most nerve-wracking hour of every year. But the new, expanded narrative I created now exists with equal impact alongside my original cause-and-effect equation. Because I watched my mother die from breast cancer in her forties, I have feared dying young from breast cancer. And because my mother died from breast cancer in her forties, I have taken whatever steps I can to write a different story for myself. Both things can be true.

Dominos and ACEs

THE FIRST time I met Juliet was when I buzzed her up to my Manhattan apartment on a Monday evening in 1992. She'd volunteered to participate in a focus group for twentysomething motherless daughters. Juliet joined three other women in my apartment that night, who soon discovered large patches of common ground.

The women ranged in age from twenty-two to twenty-five, all were single, and all were currently living in (though not necessarily from) New York City. Two of their moms had died from cancer, and two by suicide. The word that kept recurring that night was "relief." "I'm relieved to hear you say that," several of the women said. "I'm relieved to learn I'm not the only one."

Juliet was twenty-five when we met that night, and emerging from a long, lonely period of chaos. That was how she'd described the past few years. She'd been fourteen and the much-youngest sibling of six when her mother was diagnosed with breast cancer. Three years later her mother died, leaving seventeen-year-old Juliet at home with her father, an active alcoholic. From age seventeen onward, Juliet explained, she'd pretty much had to raise herself.

That evening she talked about how her mother's death had marked the end of the family's holiday rituals and gatherings. The extreme self-reliance she developed as a matter of survival resulted in a reluctance to ask anyone for help, and contributed to her lack of trust in adult relationships, she said.

"I've never been in a serious relationship with a man," she shared with the group. "I'm twenty-five and I've had a string of one-night stands, starting with my first kiss at fourteen. It's been a series of nonintimate things. It's like I say, 'I'm so fine, I'm taken care of, I don't need your help. Please keep your distance. I'm really in control.' But it's such a sad place to sit, because when I'm really sad and lonely, I want to be the kind of person who can ask for help if they need it. And yet I need you to understand that I'm totally incapable of intimacy. I've always needed to be completely capable and be the parent. Now I feel like I'm chipping my way out of this cave."

As a teenager, Juliet muted her anger and grief with alcohol and drugs, a coping strategy that worked . . . until it didn't work anymore. When we met in 1992, she was one year sober and attending regular twelve-step meetings. "I just feel like I need to parent myself before

I can go on," she told us. "I've had a lot of crap happen and I need to take care of it. But I do feel optimistic."

After that night in my apartment, Juliet and I were out of touch for twenty-seven years, until an elaborate web search and a tentative email inquiry—"Is this the Juliet who . . ." "Yes! It's me!"—led to a FaceTime appointment between my office in Los Angeles and her living room several states away.

I'd spent the afternoon rereading the transcript from our focus group in 1992 and had been struck by how much distance Juliet and I had both traveled since then in terms of geography, time, and lived experience. When she answered my call, there we were: face-to-face (or screen to screen). For the next two hours, two Juliets were there with me: one a confident, animated fifty-two-year-old on my iPhone screen, and the other a soft-focus image of the twenty-five-year-old who'd traveled by subway to a stranger's apartment for a few hours to meet a handful of women who might help her feel less alone.

"One thing I remember from [that night] was that I talked about relationships," Juliet recalls. "I hadn't had steady boyfriends, and I think I even alluded to having one-night stands, moving on, not getting close. It's interesting, twenty-seven years later, to see how I experienced the loss of two parents. One died young and the other was lost to alcoholism. I see now how, together, they both left a mark on my ability to trust. I was approaching this conversation thinking, 'How am I going to speak just to the loss of a mother? How am I going to extract one thread from a tapestry that was just as impacted by the alcoholism and the way people had to act to cope with that?'"

I'm not sure Juliet can separate the two. Or that she should. The death of a loved one occurs both along a continuum of events, and within a context. Sometimes a death is a precipitating event that sets into motion a whole chain of other events, like a row of dominos falling. It can lead, for example, to the dissolution of a family, a geographic move, unexpected financial stress, or substance use or abuse in a surviving family member. On the flip side, the death may be the last domino, the inevitable outcome of a series of prior adversities. A death by suicide, for example, often involves prior mental health struggles, stress or fear in the family, and sometimes even previous attempts. A long-term illness leading to a death may have exacted a steady, heavy toll on a family throughout that time.

"Even before my mother passed away, she was emotionally absent from depression and grief," remembers the author Martha McSweeney Brower, who was twenty when her mother died after a long struggle with ovarian cancer. "The deaths of her four siblings in the previous eight years had shattered her. She'd been a talented, sensitive artist, and now she was not only overcome by sorrow, but she was also overwhelmed by the seven children that she bore in nine years. Her beautiful spirit floated away from us long before her body did. We were a gang of rebellious teenagers during a tumultuous time of social revolution in the sixties, and she died before any of us got to know her as adults. I want to believe that had we been able to ride out those times without her illness, there would have been happy times to eventually share together. But she died with the remnants of teenage anger flying around her like so much trash. Acne and anger, wild hair and incense, fast cars and cigarettes, my brother and his wife shooting heroin. All that was swirling around my mother's death bed."

Adversity has a cumulative effect: Multiple adversities before and after a death mean higher levels of stress for survivors. When such adversities occur before age eighteen, they're also known as Adverse Childhood Experiences, or ACEs.

It's nearly impossible to talk about childhood loss today without discussing the Adverse Childhood Experience Study (ACES) of 1995–97. The ACES, conducted as a joint venture between Kaiser Permanente and the Centers for Disease Control and Prevention, surveyed 17,421 adult health-plan members at Kaiser Permanente in San Diego to look for patterns between exposure to ACEs during childhood and mental and physical problems later in life. The patients filled out extensive questionnaires that asked about ten different types of childhood adversities, in three categories: abuse, neglect, and household challenges. Poverty, race, and exposure to community violence are also widely considered to be ACEs today.

The ten ACEs included in the original study were

- early physical abuse;
- early sexual abuse;
- emotional abuse;
- physical neglect;
- emotional neglect;
- separation from a parent through divorce or death;
- exposure to domestic violence;
- incarceration of a family member;
- mental illness in the home; and
- drug use in the home.

When the results were entered into a database and compared to the patients' medical records, the study's principal researchers, Vincent Felitti and Robert Anda, were amazed by the data that came back. Strong correlations were found between a high number of ACEs during childhood and specific physical and mental ailments in adulthood, including depression, diabetes, autoimmune diseases, and cancer.

In addition, a full two-thirds of the subjects in the study reported that they'd faced at least one adverse experience in childhood. Looked at another way, only one-third of the adults in the study *hadn't* experienced at least one ACE. That's a significant public health finding. The researchers also discovered that ACEs beget ACEs. Having one ACE means you're more likely than not to have two; if you have two, you're more likely than not to have three; and so on.

The number of ACEs in a childhood is important, because the more ACEs a child has experienced, the more chronic, toxic stress that child is likely to have been exposed to. And the more exposure a child has to the hormones of chronic, toxic stress, the more their immune function and brain structure will be affected from an early age.

Chronic, toxic stress changes the architecture of a child's developing brain, alters the expression of genes that control the release of stress hormones, and triggers an overactive inflammatory response that can last for a lifetime and predispose that child to various diseases as an adult, explains Donna Jackson Nakazawa, who has written extensively about ACEs. Nakazawa also comes to the material from personal experience; she was a young girl when her father suddenly died. Her nuclear family struggled in the aftermath and became isolated from their previously close-knit extended family. As she writes in her 2015 book *Childhood Disrupted: How Your Biography Becomes Your Biology, and How You Can Heal,*

I had been exceptionally close to my father and I had looked to him for my sense of being safe, okay, and valued in the world. In every photo of our family, I'm smiling, clasped in his arms. When he died, childhood suddenly ended, overnight. If I am honest with myself, looking back, I cannot recall a single "happy memory" from there on out in my childhood. It was no one's fault. It just was. And I didn't dwell on any of that. In my mind, people who dwelled on their past, and especially on their childhood, were emotionally suspect.

I soldiered on. Life catapulted forward. I created a good life, worked hard as a science journalist to help meaningful causes, married a really good husband, and brought up children I adored—children I worked hard to stay alive for. But other than enjoying the lovely highlights of a hard-won family life, or being with close friends, I was pushing away pain. I felt myself a stranger at life's party. My body never let me forget that inside, pretend as I might, I had been masking a great deal of loss for a very long time. I felt myself to be "not like other people."

For more than a dozen years during her adulthood, Nakazawa struggled with several autoimmune illnesses, including being paralyzed twice by Guillain-Barré syndrome. When she learned about ACEs, the relationship between her childhood adversities and her adult physical health began to make sense.

"My own doctor at Johns Hopkins medical institutions confessed to me that she suspected that, given the chronic stress I'd faced in my childhood, my body and brain had been marinating in toxic inflammatory chemicals my whole life—predisposing me to the diseases I now faced," she wrote.

Nakazawa could have created a simple A → Z relationship between the stress of her father's death when she was young and the impact of that stress on her health as an adult. But cracking open that arrow revealed multiple steps along the way where multiple ACEs during her childhood may have exerted various consequences on both her body and her brain. For example, children who've experienced abuse and neglect show changes to the prefrontal cortex area of the brain, which affects executive functioning, and also to the corpus callosum, which connects the two sides of the brain.

ACEs tend to appear in clusters, like a series of unfortunate events. That was Lily's experience during adolescence. The summer when she was sixteen, her father died of kidney cancer. Lily returned to school two weeks later, where she valiantly tried to act as if nothing had changed. Meanwhile, back at home, nothing was normal at all.

Lily was living alone with her mother, who had been suffering from mental illness and substance abuse for quite a while. "My father's death hit her really, really hard," recalls Lily, now twenty-two. "For months she wouldn't get out of bed. Our house was a wreck. I look back on those first few months after my dad passed away and I'm like, 'How did I get through that?' Other adults were around, my dad's best friend was active in our lives, and my aunt, my dad's sister, lived five minutes away, but in our house, it was just my mom and me. People were worried that she wasn't getting the nutrition she needed to stay alive. I was working at the time, and I had Social Security money from my father, so I was able to feed myself and get through. But it was really rough."

After several months, Lily's mother was admitted to an inpatient psychiatric program and Lily moved in with her aunt. Her new home provided her with the security and continuity she needed to finish high school, but the death of her father, in conjunction with the subsequent months of inconsistent parenting, had exacted a heavy toll. Attending to both a grieving mother and her own day-to-day survival—multiple ACEs—had left Lily without enough bandwidth to address her own emotional needs. She wasn't able to grieve for her father until this past year, she says, when she had the emotional support of a steady boyfriend and the financial stability of a full-time job.

When Lily found connectedness and validation as an adult, she was able to revisit the more painful episodes from her past. This is common among adults who've experienced ACEs as children, Vincent Felitti says. Even years later, just one conversation affirming that this part of your history mattered back then and still matters today can offer emotional and even physical relief. "A mechanism, and moment, for healing is set in place, even for seemingly intractable conditions," Felitti explains.

This is hopeful news for anyone who cracks open a story and finds ACEs inside. Because multiple ACEs by no means doom a story to a gulag of misplaced sorrows. The effects of ACEs on the brain are reversible, no matter how long ago exposure occurred.

What helps to break the cycle?

Mind-body techniques. Meditation. Yoga. Anything that calms the body and slows down the mind. Nakazawa has found mindfulness meditation to be beneficial in relieving some of her symptoms. Writing about her own story has helped as well.

"Creating a coherent narrative is also an important part of healing," she explains. "But resilience isn't so much about just getting a story out. It's the ability to learn from it at some point along the way. You really have to become open and engaged and aware of everything that has happened, how it has affected you, and how it's changed you." As shown by Pennebaker's expressive-writing students, active engagement with a story offers the most direct pathway to healing, and to post-traumatic growth. For that, we need opportunities to express ourselves and, ideally, compassionate listeners.

Let's Get Back to Christopher

DINNER IS finished, the trattoria is starting to wind down for the night, and Christopher and I spill out onto West Sixty-eighth Street. We're still parsing the impact father loss has had on his career choices, and as we walk over to Broadway so I can catch a cab uptown, we agree to continue the conversation by email and by phone. We're not finished with cracking open this story yet. There's much more inside.

Over the next few weeks, as we email and talk by phone, a much fuller picture of Christopher's adolescence and young adulthood starts to emerge. Before long, Christopher's original A → Z statement seems like an artifact from the past. It turns out to have been a very fast summary of a much larger story. A whole bunch of intervening variables are dancing around inside. And once that larger story has been cracked open and we look at the interior with curiosity, both of us start appreciating Christopher's professional trajectory in an entirely new way.

"Growing up I was always kind of the weird kid whose dad died," he tells me in one of our phone discussions. "It's not like people said that, but I just knew I didn't have the same experiences as other kids, who'd come to school in a baseball hat because they'd been to a baseball game. They were having male bonding experiences and could talk about them together, and I had nothing to come back with. But kids adapt, and they make do with what they have.

"It's important to keep in mind that it's not all bad," he continues. "Because a lot of creativity comes out of this. There's a need to adapt, and the fact that there isn't an established 'normal' framework to operate in means you're creating your own even when you're a kid, so that muscle gets primed super early. I'm not talking about artistic creativity. I'm talking about core creativity. It's like you're creating everything for yourself. For me, resourcefulness and creativity and adaptability are just normal, but I know it's not normal for the vast majority of people. The way I think, the way I process information, the way I pull things together. I've been doing this for a long time, on a lot of different levels."

When we started this conversation, Christopher was connecting his global lack of personal planning to his father's death when he was eight. That might still be a valid association to make. But as we talked and emailed more, an alternate narrative started to emerge. This one was richer and more expansive, and connected his father's absence to his enormous resourcefulness and creativity as well. Losing his father when he was eight, and without any male role models who stepped into that void, Christopher lacked the guidance his peers received from their fathers and male mentors. And losing his father when he was eight allowed Christopher to exercise that creativity and resourcefulness that enabled him to invent himself all on his own.

Both things can be true.

Christopher's desire to see as much of the world as possible before turning thirty-eight, in case his father's fate should become his own, set him on a path to have a wide range of experiences, meet a variety of people, and develop skill sets he may never have tapped into if he'd stayed close to home.

"I feel like I've been creating every minute," he says. "I don't want to overstate it like I'm some kind of incredible trailblazer, but that creativity muscle is always sort of on, and it's been on for a very long time. It's not necessarily peaceful or calm, but by virtue of exercising it for so long, many different kinds of experiences happen, and those different experiences give you access to different combinations of new ideas, and it all becomes exponentially more powerful. You wind up with a broader experience base to bring to creative opportunities, and between those two things, it's fundamentally, hugely different than for people who've followed predetermined paths."

The career Christopher created for himself combines all of his

242 : THE AFTERGRIEF

varied interests and experiences, as if he found the elusive string that ties together everything he's done and seen and thought about for the past twenty-five years with a single pull. It's an example of re-combinant innovation, he says, a process by which something exciting and new is created out of components that already exist.

His route to adulthood and professional success may have been more circuitous than the traditional paths taken by his peers, but it's been wholly his own. He can lay claim to every piece. In that regard "it might be even better," he says, and I hear just a touch of wonder in his voice when he says it again: "It might be *better.*"

CHAPTER TWELVE

* * *

Story Mending: Finding Continuity

A N EXTRAORDINARY event occurred on August 15, 2019, when talk-show personality Stephen Colbert sat down in the CNN studio with host Anderson Cooper for an hour-long interview on *Anderson Cooper 360°*. For the first half hour the two men talked about politics, *X-Men*, and truth and authenticity. Then, at the halfway point, the conversation took a sudden turn.

After a commercial break, Cooper opened with this: "You wrote me a letter after my mom died," he said, referencing the death of Gloria Vanderbilt two months earlier. "And in it you said, 'I hope you find peace in your grief.' One of the things I've been thinking a lot about is how we don't really talk about grief and loss. People are not comfortable talking about it."

The conversation that followed was remarkable for two reasons: first, because viewers found themselves watching a frank conversation about the long-term effects of major loss, and such candid, televised conversations are rare; second, because the two people having it were men, and those public conversations are even more scarce.

In addition to losing his mother as an adult, Cooper lost his father, Wyatt Cooper, to sudden heart failure when he was ten years old. Colbert also was ten when his father and two older brothers died in a commercial airline accident. These seismic events during their childhoods, both men agreed, ripped a scar through their personal histories, forever dividing their life stories into segments of Before and After.

To this day, Cooper explained, he marks time in his mind by whether his father was alive or not. That single childhood event, he told Colbert, operates for him "like a new Year Zero. It's like when Pol Pot took over Cambodia," he explained.

"Without a doubt. Without a doubt," Colbert agreed. "Yeah. There is another guy. There's another Steve. There's a Steve Colbert. There's that kid before my father and my brothers died. And it's actually kind of difficult . . . I have fairly vivid memories from right after they died to the present. It's continuous and contiguous, you know, and it's all connected. But there's this big break in the cable of my memory at their death." Everything he remembers from before that time possesses an odd, ghostly quality, he explained.

Such bifurcated life stories frequently appear among survivors of trauma and loss. Life before the loss is perceived to have been one way, and afterward, another. In fact, the perception that one type of self existed before a major loss and a new, different self emerged from the ashes is so common it's considered a universal feature of the trauma narrative. Psychologist Maxine Harris, in her study of adult men and women who experienced early parent loss, referred to it as "the psychological Great Divide, separating the world into a permanent 'before and after.'"

As Kat, who was fourteen when her mother died of heart failure, explains, "It feels like having a B.C. and A.D. in the history of your world. And I kind of got stuck in the thinking that there was life before my mom died with this idyllic childhood, and then after that, life changed, and I'm not the same person anymore."

This happens, in part, because goals or assumptions that were possible at the start of the story were rendered impossible by the trauma. That assumptive world contained its own embedded narrative, with a projected future that even a child can imagine. A major loss derails that story and creates the need for a new personal narrative to emerge, one that may depart from the original so much that it feels as if a different person must occupy the leading role.

A life story is a personal reconstruction of the remembered past, the perceived present, and the anticipated future. The way we tell our life stories reveals how we regard our histories and identities.

Which is a way of saying, the way we tell our life narratives is a pretty accurate reflection of the way we perceive ourselves.

As Stephen Joseph maintains, "The stories we tell ourselves will 'work their way down,' transforming our personalities—first our autobiographical narratives (our life stories), then our personal goals, values, and priorities. Knowing this, we can choose to tell stories that are to our benefit."

Even more than traits, motives, and values, life stories both reflect and establish our identities, explains Dan McAdams, a psychology professor at Northwestern University and the author of *Stories We Live By*. A story, he says, is the best available structure we have for integrating and making sense of a life across time.

That's why a fractured life story—such as one that's divided into Before and After periods—may be ripe for revision: because it can reflect a fractured identity, in which two halves of a life never quite add up to a coherent or satisfying whole.

When the self of the Before is a child or teen, that younger part can become segregated in the past. We're then left carrying two separate selves within us: one who was awash in innocence and one who later understood hard truths. A sense of historical continuity is missing from this story. So is an ability to link past and present in a coherent flow of time.

When a life story is disrupted like this, connecting the person we feel we were with the person we believe we became is a complicated task, says psychologist Robert Neimeyer. "First of all, we may lose compassion for that self we were," he explains. "We may hardly ever talk to her or him or recognize the childlike part of ourselves that is still capable of feeling hurt in those ways. And if we can't take an empathic stance [toward that younger self] that earlier experience becomes kind of off limits, like the other side of the castle. There's no bridge between here and there, and the consequences of that broken narrative continue to be felt but not understood."

For example, Neimeyer says, moments in which we feel radically abandoned, betrayed, alone, frightened, or worthless as adults may remind us of the younger, more vulnerable self we've tried to partition off. Instead of feeling that earlier hurt, we may instead become critical of ourselves. "We try to ignore it, push it down, dis-attend to it," he explains. "We can actually savagely attack ourselves when those vulnerable parts come forward. It's a very uncomfortable, alien state and yet in fact, it's our state. If we had only been more capable of integrating that earlier experience into an evolving narrative of who we are, we would have more self-compassion and probably a better possibility of mirroring and understanding the suffering of others, at any age, who present with similar experiences of abandonment and fear."

Why do trauma survivors so frequently create Before and After life narratives? It's not entirely an individual choice. Every culture provides its members with story paradigms to follow. If so many personal trauma narratives in Western culture depict lives divided into Before and After periods, it's because a lot of us accept that story structure as a framework for thinking about past experience.

"It's a framework we've been given to not only experience who we are and our identities in relationship to a death, but also a framework for how to express those experiences," Stephen Madigan says. In other words, if a fractured life story were soundly rejected by the larger culture, fewer people would be telling their stories that way.

Conceptualizing one's past as segmented may also feel like an emotionally accurate description. A person who walks away from a major loss has witnessed events and had experiences that might have been unimaginable only days before. A loved one's death can destroy illusions of invulnerability, damage the integrity of a family, impair one's sense of agency, and permanently alter existing beliefs that the world is a safe, secure, and predictable place. Loss changes our beliefs about permanence. The faith that what exists now will continue to exist indefinitely can no longer be sustained. Prior states of trust and innocence can never be fully reclaimed.

From there it's often a quick step to a new perception of the self. Once you see yourself as a person to whom a bad thing just happened, you can no longer be the kind of person to whom bad things cannot happen. The way you perceive and respond to this knowledge—through individual lenses of pessimism, optimism, gratitude, altruism, anger, or fear—is eventually converted into action. Your external circumstances may undergo a change as well, including the place of residence, the school or social environment, caretaking behaviors, financial circumstances, and family communications. This is how we wind up with one version of the self before a tragic event and a different version afterward.

Perhaps novelist Haruki Murakami captured it best when he wrote, "And once the storm is over, you won't remember how you made it through, how you managed to survive. You won't even be sure whether the storm is really over. But one thing is certain. When you come out of the storm, you won't be the same person who walked in. That's what this storm's all about."

Western society loves stories of transformation, loves to believe that hardship will inevitably lead to evolution and rebirth. What's the point of weathering the storm if the best-case outcome is only to get wet? Baseline survival is rarely the goal. We want metamorphosis. Expansion. Growth. There's an enormous cultural pressure to plot our personal stories in this direction.

But here's an unexpected twist: We don't need to actually experience a transformation to achieve growth. Sometimes, shaping a story to result in transformation will give us the same result.

Two Kinds of Life Stories

FOR MORE than thirty years, psychologist Dan McAdams has been studying how people shape their life stories to achieve meaning, unity, and purpose. When he spoke one evening at a Northwestern University alumni event in Los Angeles, sixty people gathered in the hosts' living room and quickly became captivated by stories from his research.

A typical narrative of trauma or loss, McAdams told us, follows a predictable pattern. The protagonist starts in a state of comfort and security (the Before period) and is catapulted into a state of hardship (the After) when a tragedy occurs. It's a story of paradise gained and lost.

This is the recipe for what McAdams calls a "Contamination Narrative," a story in which something positive has been spoiled or ruined forever. A hero or heroine might try to valiantly undo the damage, McAdams explains, but their efforts are doomed to fail. What was lost cannot be duplicated or replaced, no matter how earnest nor how skillful a protagonist may be.

In the loss narratives I've encountered over the past twenty-five years, the most common adjective used to describe the Before period is "idyllic." Tellers depict childhoods in which they felt safe, innocent, and loved, only to lose that security after a major loss occurs. I don't doubt that these individuals perceive their childhoods as unmarred by tragedy or dysfunction; I've thought the same about mine. We must remember, however, that stories are artifacts of both individual perception and cultural influence. An author chooses which scenes to link together and how, and what themes are worthy of emphasis. Which means that the author holds the power to change the story's meaning at any time.

When the Before period of a life story is depicted as idyllic, the strong impulse is to make the After narrative track a loss of innocence or a fall from grace. Movement in the narrative tracks the shift from a happy childhood to a distressed one, from a positive emotional state to a negative one. But how often do we stop and consider whether the stories we tell ourselves over and over ring true? Or whether we've created them and hold on to them to reinforce a certain identity or effect?

Forty-six-year-old Abby arrives at my office in Los Angeles one afternoon in March for an interview. We settle into upholstered chairs and face each other as she begins.

Abby was the only child of two professional parents who were prominent community members in a low-key, medium-sized Midwestern city during her preschool years. She can't recall much from this time—most of her story is based on memories her mother has shared—but she describes her early years as peaceful and uncomplicated.

Tragically, when Abby was four, her father died by suicide. Soon after his death, she and her mother moved in with her grandmother, and then they moved again to their own apartment in a major metropolitan area where her mother started a new job. Abby then became the child of a single working mother in an unfamiliar, hectic, yet colorful and stimulating environment—a reversal of her early years in almost every way.

She, too, uses the word "idyllic" to describe her first four years, which were upended by her father's death and a cross-country move. But even in the telling of her story, Abby is aware that her life history is a subjective narrative she has created.

"That idyllic little childhood . . ." she begins, "well, here is where we have to talk about the story I'm placing on it. Because it wasn't idyllic. My father was mentally ill." The narrative that Abby reflexively began to share, the one she'd been carrying inside for so long, blossomed even in the course of its telling into a more nuanced version of events.

Occasionally, a Before period will describe an imperfect or negative state that is improved by a loss event. This can occur when the loved one who died exhibited violent or addictive behavior while living, or engaged in multiple suicide attempts, or suffered from a debilitating illness that persisted over many years and created ongoing stress in the family. Survivors may then fashion stories in which the needle of their story moved from bad to good after a loss, even when other more painful consequences are experienced at the same time.

Forty-six-year-old Sadie, for example, recalls herself as a shy child who was mercilessly bullied in elementary school. Looking back today, she laments never having stood up for herself or pushed back against her aggressors. Her best friend, Lila, was one year older and lived directly across the street. Lila attended a different school and was therefore at a remove from the social scene that Sadie encountered every day. With Lila, Sadie could act naturally and be accepted. In that way, Lila's house and friendship offered Sadie a much-needed refuge from the peer abuse she suffered at school.

Lila was sick on and off throughout their childhoods with an illness Sadie never quite understood. Tragically, she died at the age of thirteen. Sadie remembers what follows as a devastating, confusing time. Along with the unimaginable loss of her best friend and the existential crisis that ensued, Sadie had also lost the place where she felt completely safe as a child. But in the After portion of her story, as she tells it today, Lila's death inspired her to achieve new states of self-actualization and personal growth.

"After [Lila] died I didn't have a refuge anymore," Sadie explains. "I had to make one. I knew it wasn't going to come from outside me. It took me a few years, but I definitely got better at finding my own voice and agency and demanding a little respect. No one else was going to advocate for me. I had to do it myself."

Sadie's Before-and-After story is what Dan McAdams refers to as a "Redemption Narrative," in which a story moves from bad to good, from a state of hardship or suffering to some version of a better world. McAdams has noticed that Redemption Narratives are most common in American adults who are highly generative—meaning those who seek to create a better world for those who will follow. These individuals tend to develop life narratives that emphasize triumph over adversity, featuring a protagonist who faces setbacks and episodes of pain but experiences positive outcomes, often as a direct result of their suffering. Starting with the same set of facts that could produce a Contamination Narrative, these individuals fashion stories of resilience, recovery, and defying the odds. They don't objectively have more positive experiences than their less generative counterparts do. They just *recognize* more redemptive patterns in their lives and create life stories that reflect this.

Redemption themes, I've found, appear most often in the After portion of Before-and-After stories. That's where a survivor's impulse comes through to shape a story of resilience and meaning.

Does the story then portray how they really perceive events? Often, yes. And sometimes, no. Popular culture and mass media in the West condition us to expect the happy ending, and to find the positive spin. When an ending is unnatural or forced, we wind up with what I call "tie-a-bow-around-them stories." Many stories don't have a happy ending. In reality, most life stories are more complicated than a beautifully wrapped narrative box would suggest.

Nevertheless, deliberately shaping a Redemption Narrative has clear benefits to the teller. Numerous studies in the field of post-traumatic growth have shown that individuals who perceive positive outcomes arising from adversity show better long-term psychosocial adjustment. In addition, adults whose life narratives contain more redemption sequences than contamination sequences are more likely to be invested in the well-being of subsequent generations. People who create and repeat Contamination Narratives to depict their life stories, on the other hand, record higher levels of anxiety and depression. The stories we tell ourselves, and the structures we impose upon them, matter: They not only influence our identities, but also affect our mental health.

Finding a balance between acknowledging the gravity of a distressing event and creating a narrative that includes redemption scenes appears key toward achieving hope, sustenance, and positive long-term adjustment after a trauma or loss. That's often what's meant by "integrating" a loss, and this process is essential for those who achieve post-traumatic growth. "They place their life story in a wider context, admitting to both the negative and the positive aspects of their transformation," explains Stephen Joseph. Trauma survivors who can integrate a loss honestly acknowledge both that life is challenging and also that making sense of those challenging experiences can be hard but worthwhile. What happened was tragic, and yet from that tragedy can arise positive growth. Or as my friend Angela succinctly describes it, "Life can suck, and life can also be good." Two truths, side by side.

Not all stories have happy endings, but a story can be reauthored and reconceptualized to reduce suffering in its teller. Otherwise, we run the risk of being lived by our tragic stories, rather than letting our story be extensions of us. That liminal state of letting go of an old story and reconstructing a new one is where change in the self is most possible. We can begin by mending our fractured narratives.

Two Things Can Be True

A BEFORE-AND-AFTER story of loss, upon its creation, separates a life into two story arcs. One covers the Before period that led up to a death, and the second tells the story of all that follows.

It's not unusual for a life story to contain multiple arcs, or "micro-narratives." Nearly all do. Together, the sum creates an overarching "macro-narrative" that spans an entire life. Some of my many micro-narratives, for example, would include the two different stories of losing my mother and losing my father, as well as stories of becoming a writer, raising my daughters, finding and buying a house, learning how to swing dance, overcoming a mouse phobia, and rescuing and raising a rambunctious gray cat. Each of these micro-narratives could be a chapter within a larger book, or a scene within a chapter.

A Before-and-After narrative, however, relies on two separate narratives to tell a single story of loss. Let's revisit the story-arc graphic for an illustration.

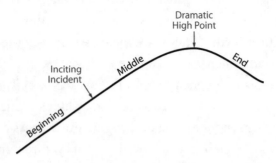

The classic story arc, as described in chapter 9, contains three sections (a Beginning, Middle, and End) and two critical moments (the Inciting Incident and the Dramatic High Point).

In a Before-and-After story, the Before section follows its own discrete arc. When a terminal illness is involved, the Beginning of that story is disrupted by a symptom or diagnosis. The death of a loved one is then positioned as the Dramatic High Point. That's the moment the Before section is leading up to.

When a loss occurs suddenly, the death may be both the Inciting Incident and the Dramatic High Point of the story, with a prior existence that comes to an abrupt end upon news of the loss. In both stories, the whole After section gets crammed into the little part at the end.

A Before portion of a Before-and-After story typically looks like this:

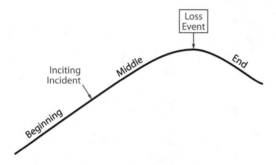

The Story of "Before"

In the book version of a life, however, the end of one chapter will often lead straight into the beginning of the next. The Dramatic High Point of one story becomes the Inciting Incident of another. That's exactly how an After narrative begins.

"The death of my mother basically set me up for the narrative of the rest of my life," says Mary Swander, the current poet laureate of Iowa, "one filled with great joys as well as great struggles."

You might remember that the Dramatic High Point in my original story was my mother's death. The End of that story left us with a scene of the family sitting at the kitchen table the next morning, with my realization that my life had just been split in half. There would forever be the time before my mother died, juxtaposed against the time after. That's very much how it felt to me then. But I was only seventeen in that story. If you were to turn the page, you'd begin a new chapter in that book—one that would pick up later in the summer as I started to adjust to the loss and began making plans for what would come next: my senior year of high school, college in the Midwest, a journalism degree, and my first job. Subsequent chapters would track all of that beginning to happen.

In that way, my mother's death was the Dramatic High Point of one narrative and *also* slid backward on my story arc to become the Inciting Incident of others. That's the typical story of After.

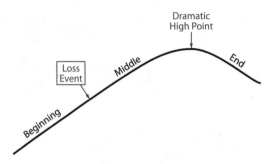

The Story of "After"

As an Inciting Incident, my mother's death set into motion a chain of events that went on to form many other micro-narratives, including one—becoming an author—that eventually led me right here, to writing this book and engaging with you. McAdams would call that a story I've shaped to emphasize redemption.

And now for a different Redemption Narrative, which is also another dominant story in my After:

My mother died when I was seventeen (Inciting Incident), which then caused me to look for a book on early mother loss. I couldn't find one. It didn't exist at the time. Every few years I'd check in bookstores and libraries, still with no luck. Finally, in my late twenties, I decided to write the book myself. And because that book was published, I started a small nonprofit organization with a group of women in New York City to help other motherless women find support. That organization quickly outgrew my living room and needed office space. One of the co-founders knew two men who were looking for additional officemates in a space above an adult theater in Times Square. (True story.) They subleased half of a large room to us, and at the end of the workday, I would often share a cab back downtown with one of the men. We became friendly. About a half year later, we started dating. In 1997 we married, and together we had two children who, for twenty-two years now, have been the brightest lights in my life.

No matter which way I reverse engineer my daughters' existence, I land on my mother's death when I was seventeen. That event was the Dramatic High Point of my original story of mother loss. It also became the Inciting Incident of my daughters' origin story.

I can wish the first story never happened and feel gratitude for the second without either of those sentiments canceling the other out. I can both mourn for the girl of seventeen who lost her innocence on July 12, 1981, and acknowledge that I wouldn't be the person or the mother I am today if that had not happened. Two things can always be true.

The Continuous You: An Experiential Exercise

LET'S NOW turn our attention to mending a fractured identity. To do this exercise, all you'll need is two blank sheets of paper and a writing implement. A laptop works, too.

Start with the first blank sheet of paper. Draw a line straight down the middle. That line represents your loved one's death, the line that you may feel divides your story in two.

On the left side of the page, write "Before" at the top. Then list all of the traits and characteristics you feel describe who you were in this first segment of your story. Were you loved, innocent, safe, secure, protected, content, naïve? Were you stubborn, dependent, bratty, self-absorbed, aloof? Or some combination of what would be considered positive and negative traits? Be as honest as possible. One-word adjectives work best, but feel free to write two or three words if necessary.

When you're finished, write "After" at the top of the right side of the page, on the other side of the dividing line. Then list all of the traits and characteristics you feel describe who you became after the loss occurred. Again, one-word adjectives are ideal. Both short- and long-term characteristics are fine. Did you become more independent, resourceful, assertive, empathetic, compassionate, appreciative, wise? Did you become a person who now felt sad, stressed, scared, lonely, angry, untethered? Try to cover the full spectrum of positive and negative responses to the loss. It's fine if some of the attributes appear on both sides of the page. That often happens. When you're finished, set the lists aside. We'll get back to them later.

Let's return to narrative now, for a final visit.

A majority of loss survivors see the loss as a turning point in their stories. As we've discussed, it can be a moment when so much changes that the self that emerges from the aftermath feels qualitatively different from the self who walked into the storm.

Right now, the loss may seem like the most important event in your life story, especially if it occurred recently. That's completely understandable. Over time, though, how you perceive that loss in the context of your whole life will determine its relative influence.

The general tendency for loss survivors is for that event to define their lives in adverse ways, Robert Neimeyer says. "This predicts the continuation of struggle," he adds. "So to have a death event be highly central in one's definition of one's self and one's life is usually pretty awful."

What Neimeyer and his graduate students have found, however, is that meaning making reduces this negative impact. When survivors can make meaning of a loss, he explains, a death at the center of their stories no longer predicts a poor outcome. The ability to make meaning from a loss even predicts post-traumatic growth. "This validates that we're not passive victims of these events but indeed, what we make of them quite literally can shape who we become," Neimeyer says.

What, exactly, is this meaning making of which Neimeyer speaks?

It doesn't mean imposing an artificial theme or message on our stories, or putting a positive spin on the end. It means making sense of events and finding benefits that grew out of adversity. It means placing the loss in the larger context of an entire life, seeing where it fits in, and drawing meaning from that bigger picture, too. Allowing the macro, not just the micro, to define us.

So, this time, imagine a story arc that represents an autobiographical account of your whole life so far. Start with your birth, and imagine a Dramatic High Point still in the future, as of yet unknown. You'll get there eventually. There's no need to define it yet.

Now position your loved one's death in the middle of this larger story. Don't make it the event everything leads up to, or the triggering event for later growth. Let it be one of many important things that have happened to you in the course of a varied and vibrant life. Like this:

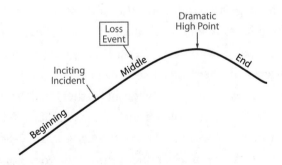

The "Big Picture" Story

How does your story read when you position the loss as one of many experiences you faced along the way to a Dramatic High Point that comes toward the end of your life? Does it have the same power over the story that it did before? Does your younger self's vulnerability remain centralized as a source of ongoing pain, or is it now integrated into the larger story as an episode that inspired resilience and strength?

If you feel strong resistance to this idea, it may mean that your story of loss is very central to your identity. You can then determine whether this is a perception that currently benefits and strengthens you, or if it's something you'd like to change.

Integrating your micro-narrative of loss into the big picture allows you to connect your past to an ongoing present. It also deliberately de-emphasizes the loss so it becomes one of many experiences you've had.

By decentralizing a Before-and-After narrative in this way, you've created a new narrative that can hold both of those segments together in a continuous whole. The loss can still occupy an important place in the middle of this macro-narrative, but it no longer has to sit in the center—or function as the organizing principle of a life.

"In the beginning, a loss is all-consuming and seems like it's your entire world," Terrie Rando says. "But you ultimately want to get to a point where the loss of a loved one is a big chapter in your life story. It may be the biggest chapter, and the most important chapter, but it's not the whole book like it originally seemed. Then the question becomes, How can it become a chapter that's going to inform everything else afterwards, because it's so pivotal?"

As Steve, who was eighteen when his father died from stomach cancer, describes, "In the story of my life, my father's death isn't at the top anymore. Now it's more at, say, the sixty- to sixty-five-percent mark, because it had so much influence on how I developed and allowed me to learn and become who I am."

How do we allow a major loss in the past to inform us, to guide us, even to inspire us, without letting it consume an identity? We decentralize it. We wait and watch and allow for other life experiences to accumulate over the long arc. We actively search for meaning.

Part of this process also means asking, Who am I, then, when the loss is removed as the central reference point in my story?

Let's find out.

Turn to the second sheet of blank paper. At the top, write "Throughout."

Now list all the attributes and characteristics that describe you when you're not on either side of the other page, when that dividing line is removed.

What characteristics make you uniquely you?

Who did you come into the world to be?

Which of your attributes are so constitutionally and fundamentally *you* that they would not have changed, regardless of what life handed you, because they're so baked into your DNA they cannot be taken away?

Perhaps some of them appeared on both sides of your Before and After lists. Maybe they're traits that people have always noticed in you. Or qualities that you've always known about yourself. If you were very young when the death occurred and don't have a sense of yourself before that point, that's okay. You still may be able to intuit your core competencies and rock-bottom strengths.

The self on this page is the continuous you who existed before, after, and during your fractured narrative. It's also the you who's most uniquely suited to heal it. Fundamental, consistent, persistent. The you the loss happened to is, in some very essential ways, the same you that emerged from the storm. This is the self that's capable of stitching past, present, and future together. It's the you who writes your story. And also the you who has the ability to change it at any time.

Nice to meet you, friend.

EPILOGUE

* * *

The Missing Elements of Grief

In the four years it took me to write this book, both the world at large and my world at home went through a series of dramatic changes. I began writing just before the 2016 election. Later that fall, it seemed clear that one portion of the country was having a collective grief response, while another portion of fellow citizens was insisting they "get over it!" Within the next two years, three of my close friends died, and in early 2020 my twenty-three-year marriage came to an end. On the heels of that separation, the Covid-19 pandemic spread across the United States, closely followed by an outpouring of collective pain and suffering due to centuries of systemic racism. To say these current times have been grievous for many would only be underscoring a known point.

At times it was nothing short of surreal to be researching and writing about profound loss while also experiencing and witnessing it every day. The last hundred pages of this book were written from that dual perspective. Like a contractor who possesses the tools and the know-how to rebuild a flattened house yet feels ill-equipped to tackle the task alone, I sat at my dining room table every day under Los Angeles's Safer at Home mandate, surrounded by a mountain of source materials, trying to articulate coherent ideas, wrap my mind around the details of and solutions for massive social pain, and make sense of a divorce, all at the same time. The elements of grief I was writing about—the shock, numbness, helplessness, confusion, disorientation, anger, and fear—were the same ones I was feeling every day. There were moments when I couldn't tell if I was the author or the reader of these pages. Much of the time, I felt like both.

The end of a longtime marriage is not the end of a life—I kept that in perspective—but it was nonetheless the end of something I once believed to be permanent and solid. I've faced enough loss by now to know that what I was feeling, emotionally and physically, as it came to an end was a form of deep grief. There would be no soldiering through it this time, no insistence that "I'm fine" when I clearly wasn't. I was too well versed in the consequences of suppression to let that happen now. I couldn't divert my attention for long, either. The stay-at-home mandate meant there were almost no distractions to be had. The friends who would have filled up my time with activities and support were now accessible only by phone and Internet. Reading the news was the opposite of a reprieve. My younger daughter was doing high school classes online during the day and facetiming with the known universe at night. My older daughter was living across the country, working at her first job.

So, day after day, I sat immersed in my discomfort. I felt all of the painful emotions, ran through the facts in my mind over and over again, tested my stories out on myself, and confided in others. Slowly, I progressed from crying in the middle of every other sentence to getting through a paragraph intact to completing full conversations and even chapters without breaking down.

It was the purest experience of grief I think I've ever had. Raw, honest, and inescapable. And yet despite decades of research and writing about how people adjust to loss, I was still surprised to find that allowing these awful, horrible, no-good feelings to have their way with me was exactly what allowed them, over the months that followed, to start diminishing in intensity. Only through surrender did I regain my power. As the country began adjusting to its new normal, and everyone had to relearn how to live in a world that kept changing all around them, so did I.

At the same time, sitting at my dining room table amidst piles of articles and books and interview transcripts, I couldn't help feeling that my personal problems were small and petty when compared to the giant waves of grief pulsing through society at large. All around me, friends and colleagues were losing loved ones, struggling with the virus, peeling back layers of injustice and rage. It felt indulgent, at the time, to be focused on my own pain in the context of such larger suffering.

And then, in the course of my research, I lucky-stumbled across a video from 2013. It was an edited interview with Francis Weller, the author of *The Wild Edge of Sorrow*. Weller, a psychotherapist and author in Northern California, takes a fierce stand against the "heroic culture" that convinces everyone to muscle their way through sorrow alone rather than leaning on others for support. Grief was never meant to be such a private enterprise. "Grief has always, in our entire story as a species, been a communal process," Weller says in the video. "It's waiting for the village to show up. We need to oscillate between sitting with our own sorrow and feeling it, and then bringing it back out to the community and sharing the pain and finding comfort and acceptance."

That was good advice for 2013. But in 2020, it was harder to implement in the midst of national efforts to reduce human contact. Still, Weller was right. If I have learned anything at all from four years of researching the long arc of grief, it's that growth over the long term is the product of friction, of the movement between two dichotomous poles. In this case, the personal and the public. We must sit with our sorrow, and we must also share it. Then we must sit with it some more, alchemizing meaning and purpose, before we go out into the world and actualize what we've learned about ourselves and others. Growth after loss doesn't come from sitting around and waiting for growth to arrive. It's an active, effortful process of revisiting and reframing our memories, and creating new stories for ourselves moving forward.

Meaning isn't something we stumble upon. It's something we make.

Instead of sitting at my dining room table, waiting for my village to show up, I had to find the village myself. In early April 2020 I was invited to join the online Global COVID-19 Relief Coalition, a task force of professionals, academics, and activists in the fields of death, dying, and bereavement who share our current initiatives and collectively brainstorm guidelines and rituals for these unanticipated times. Like everyone else, I learned how to Zoom like a wizard, and I started co-leading weekly support calls for motherless daughters, including one specifically for women who had just lost their mothers to the virus. Helping others has always been my highest form of recovery, no doubt an expression of the altruism gene I inherited from my mother. So, by healing myself, day by day, I found myself honoring her, too.

We will look back on this pivotal year in history, all of us, multiple times in the years to come. We will inevitably renegotiate and reframe the same sets of facts as the larger narrative expands. This year will look a little bit different each time we revisit it, as a fuller picture of what it has meant to each of us, and to the culture as a whole, comes into sharper focus. Until this past year, I thought of myself as an author and a speaker and a coach, eager to share ideas and help others actualize their goals in a one-sided flow of information and support. Only as I sat in my dining room writing these last hundred pages did I realize how reciprocal this relationship truly is. You all are part of my village. I sat at the table every day as one of you, and also holding each one of you in my mind, inspired by the sum of your courage and your stories. I have written about bereavement and spoken about it for more than two decades, but these past few months were when I truly understood what it means: The only way to get through grief is together.

If trauma forces us to abandon unrealistic or even damaging assumptions about the world, then the loss of those assumptions may be a good thing. I read this line in an article by psychologist Ronnie Janoff-Bulman, and I've thought about it many times these past few months. About what a fitting message it is for these times. And also about how the assumption that we can conquer great pain on our own is a faulty one, and ripe to be abandoned. We'll only get so far on our own. We need others—and the memories of our departed loved ones—to help us acquire the kind of wisdom that suffering can produce. That's what everyone included in this book, in one way or another, has endeavored to say.

I think of all the men and women I've interviewed over almost thirty years, and how many of them have spontaneously spoken about what they've gained from their experiences with early, painful, and often traumatic loss. The same benefits appeared so often in their stories that I came to think of fifteen of them as the Missing Elements of Grief: appreciation, awe, compassion, empathy, faith, grace, gratitude, hope, humility, meaning, perspective, purpose, resilience, wisdom, wonder.

Any of these sound familiar?

These elements can't be pathologized, so they don't receive much attention, but if you've survived a loss you know they're equally as real as any painful emotion. Most of them won't appear soon after a loss. They're features of the Aftergrief, showing up only as we travel the long arc. We recognize their presence over time.

Grief teaches us two kinds of lessons: fast and slow. In the short term we get a quick primer on how fragile life can be, and that human existence is temporary and precious for that reason. We learn that what exists today may no longer exist tomorrow. We are not invulnerable to sorrow or impervious to pain. Safety is an illusion. Today is what we have. These are hard lessons to absorb at any age, and all the more difficult for a child.

But grief conveys gradual messages, too, and some of these are worth waiting for. We discover that deep grief and sadness can be survived. Beyond just surviving, we can leverage this new knowledge to help us thrive. Priorities shift. Gratitude blossoms. And moments of pure joy return.

"Resilience" was a buzzword of the 2010s, much as "dysfunctional" became one in the 1980s. By now the word means different things to different people. After hearing and collecting thousands of stories of major loss, I think "resilience" means something very specific to these survivors. I think it means the ability to carry both the knowledge that terrible, tragic, random things can happen to anyone, at any time, and the belief that if it should happen to you again, you will be able to survive.

Perhaps what "resilience" really represents in the Aftergrief is an unwavering commitment to start each day anew, with hope and faith and wonder, despite not knowing what the day might hold. And to do it with appreciation and gratitude for whatever that day might deliver. If loss teaches us anything enduring, it's that aging is a privilege. And that it's a gift to be alive.

I think almost every day now about something Stephen Colbert said in his August 2019 interview with Anderson Cooper, in the mic-drop moment of the hour. He spoke of the importance of learning to love the thing he most wishes had not happened. That's a statement worth repeating, coming from a man who lost his father and two older brothers suddenly and all together when he was ten. He spoke of *learning to love the thing he most wishes had not happened.*

"I don't want it to have happened," Colbert explained. "I want it to not have happened. But if you are grateful for your life, which I think is a positive thing to do, not everybody is and I'm not always, then you have to be grateful for all of it. You can't pick and choose what you're grateful for."

Every time I rewatch that segment I have to pause the video and let that idea sink in. Learning to love the thing we most wish had not happened. If there's a better definition of gratitude out there, I haven't found it yet.

Popular wisdom tells us we cannot know joy without also knowing sorrow. I'm not convinced that's true. I think it's possible to have a life of suffering without ever getting to feel joy, and also possible to have a joyful life without ever knowing deep suffering. But I do not think it's possible to appreciate human existence in all of its complexity, appreciate it to the point of being brought to tears by the fervency of that appreciation, without having experienced some of its opposite. And I would not want to live in a world without such appreciation. If that means I also have to embrace suffering, I will do so, and I'll be grateful for the opportunity.

The long arc of grief is also, inevitably, the long arc of life. We cannot separate the two. If your loss is still very recent, or if you've just begun your grief journey, this may not yet be evident. In that case, much of what this book offers will make sense only over time. If, right now, you're still trying to get from day to day, you may be wondering if you'll ever feel moments of joy or gratitude again. You may not yet know how your story is capable of changing and expanding and growing. But I can promise you this: The pain you feel today won't go away entirely, but it will turn into something else. It will, over time, become something more bearable. It can become your traveling companion rather than your burden. You'll see.

Until the day that happens, hold out both of your hands. Place your grief in one. In the other, accept the capacity to feel gratitude and awe for what you have witnessed and become. Now bring them together, palm to palm, in front of you. This is what Francis Weller calls "the prayer of life."

When you do this, you can feel the wholeness of your humanity. You will join others in this quest, and by doing so, you will start smoothing the sharp edges of your loss. Your story will begin to soften, expand, and change. Your identity will follow. The tragedy and sorrow of your past will not disappear, but its impact on you will lessen. The hardship and the suffering and the longing for your loved one will always be real. And good things will grow out of it.

These two things will always be true.

Experiences lie ahead for you that you can't yet even imagine. You will feel joy again. At times you may have to fight for its presence for you and others, but that fierceness will serve you well. And I promise you, one day you will look back at the whole, long arc of your grief and you will understand what all of it means. I promise you this. I *promise* you. It will all look so different from there.

Bibliography

*   *   *

INTRODUCTION—GETTING OVER GETTING OVER IT

"A Veil of Tears: One in Seven Americans Lose a Parent or Sibling Before the Age of 20." Comfort Zone Camp, 22 Mar. 2010. pdfslide.net/documents/a-veil-of -tears-one-in-seven-americans-lose-a-parent-tend-to-bear-the-brunt.html. Press release.

Granek, Leeat. "Grief 10 Years Later." *HuffPost*, 11 Sept. 2016, huffingtonpost.com /entry/grief-10-years-later_b_8120688.html.

Granek, Leeat, and Meghan O'Rourke. "What Is Grief Really Like?" *Slate*, 28 Apr. 2011, slate.com/human-interest/2011/04/what-is-grief-really-like.html.

"Grief in the Classroom: Groundbreaking Survey of Educators Shows Overwhelm- ing Interest in Helping Grieving Students and Strong Demand for Training & More Support." American Federation of Teachers and New York Life Founda- tion, 10 Dec. 2012. Press release.

Josselyn, Jamie-Lee, host. "Gabriel Ojeda-Sagué on Where Everything Is In Halves." *Dead Parents Society, episode 3*. Kelly Writers House at the University of Pennsylvania, 14 May 2018. player.fm/series/dead-parents-society/episode-3 -gabriel-ojeda-sague-on-where-everything-is-in-halves.

Kaplow, Julie B., et al. "Psychiatric Symptoms in Bereaved versus Non-Bereaved Youth and Young Adults: A Longitudinal Epidemiological Study." *Journal of the American Academy of Child and Adolescent Psychiatry*, vol. 29, no. 11, Nov. 2010, pp. 1145–54.

Neimeyer, Robert A. *Lessons of Loss: A Guide to Coping.* Center for the Study of Loss and Transition, 2006.

"New survey on childhood grief reveals substantial 'grief gap.'" New York Life Foundation, 15 Nov. 2017. newyorklife.com/newsroom/2017/parental-loss -survey. Press release.

O'Rourke, Meghan. "Good Grief." *The New Yorker*, 25 Jan. 2010, newyorker.com /magazine/2010/02/01/good-grief.

O'Rourke, Meghan, and Leeat Granek. "What Is Grief Actually Like?" *Slate*, 24 Mar. 2011, slate.com/human-interest/2011/03/what-is-grief-actually-like-a -slate-survey.html.

"Supporting the Grieving Student." Aft.org, *American Federation of Teachers*, go.aft .org/bereavement.

"2019 Childhood Bereavement Estimation Model—CBEM." *Judi's House*, judis house.org/cbem.

CHAPTER ONE: THE STORY OF GRIEF

Andrews, Stefan. "Mourning Fashion and Etiquette in the Victorian Era." *The Vintage News*. 16 Sept. 2018. thevintagenews.com/2018-09-16/mourning-fashion/.

Archer, John. *The Nature of Grief: The Evolution and Psychology of Reactions to Loss.* Routledge, 1999.

Aries, Philippe. *The Hour of Our Death: The Classic History of Western Death Over the Last One Thousand Years.* 2nd ed., Vintage Books, 2008.

Blad, Evie. "Educators Often Overlook Student Grief, Experts Say." *Education Week*, 20 Jan. 2015, edweek.org/ew/articles/2015/01/21/educators-often-overlook -student-grief-experts-say.html.

Brewster, Henry. "Grief: A Disrupted Human Relationship." *Human Organization*, vol. 9, no. 1, 1950, pp. 19–22, doi:10.17730/humo.9.1.g718686718498167.

Chevalier, Tracy. "Victorian Mourning Etiquette." *tchevalier.com*, chevalier.com /fallingangels/bckgrnd/mourning/.

Cole, Melissa. "Mourning After: The Victorian Celebration of Dying."

Deutsch, Helene, and Edith Jackson. "Absence of Grief." *The Psychoanalytic Quarterly*, vol. 6, no. 1, 1937, pp. 12–22, doi:10.1080/21674086.1937.11925307.

Freud, Sigmund. "Mourning and Melancholia." *The Standard Edition of the Complete Psychological Works of Sigmund Freud, vol. XIV (1914–1916).* Hogarth Press, 1964.

Granek, Leeat. "Grief as Pathology: The Evolution of Grief Theory in Psychology from Freud to the Present." *History of Psychology*, vol. 13, no. 1, 2010, pp. 46–73, doi:10.1037/a0016991.

"Grief in the Classroom: Groundbreaking Survey of Educators Shows Overwhelming Interest in Helping Grieving Students and Strong Demand for Training & More Support." American Federation of Teachers and New York Life Foundation, 10 Dec. 2012. Press release.

"Halberstadt-Freud, Sophie (1893-1920)." *Encyclopedia.com*, encyclopedia.com /psychology/dictionaries-thesauruses-pictures-and-press-releases/halberstadt -freud-sophie-1893-1920.

Halsey, Ashley. "The Flu Can Kill Tens of Millions of People. In 1918, That's Exactly What It Did." *The Washington Post*, 27 Jan. 2018, washingtonpost.com /news/retropolis/wp/2018/01/27/the-flu-can-kill-tens-of-millions-of-people -in-1918-thats-exactly-what-it-did/.

Halsey, Ashley. "A Killer Flu Was Raging. But in 1918, U.S. Officials Ignored the

Crisis to Fight a War." *The Washington Post*, 3 Feb. 2018, washingtonpost.com /news/retropolis/wp/2018/02/03/a-killer-flu-was-raging-but-in-1918-u-s -officials-ignored-the-crisis-to-fight-a-war/.

Harris, Darcy. "Oppression of the Bereaved: A Critical Analysis of Grief in Western Society." *OMEGA—Journal of Death and Dying*, vol. 60, no. 3, 2010, pp. 241–53, doi:10.2190/om.60.3.c.

Jalland, Patricia. "Bereavement and Mourning Great Britain." *International Encyclopedia of the First World War*, 8 Oct. 2014, http://encyclopedia.1914-1918-online .net/article/bereavement_and_mourning_great_britain.

Koblenz, Jessica. "Growing From Grief." *OMEGA—Journal of Death and Dying*, vol. 73, no. 3, 10 Mar. 2015, pp. 203–30, doi:10.1177/0030222815576123.

Kübler-Ross Elisabeth, and David Kessler. *On Grief & Grieving: Finding the Meaning of Grief through the Five Stages of Loss*. Scribner, 2005.

Lindemann, Erich. "Symptomatology and Management of Acute Grief." *American Journal of Psychiatry*, vol. 101, no. 2, 1944, pp. 141–48, doi:10.1176/ajp.101.2.141.

Lupi, Robert S. "Classics Revisited: Freud's 'Mourning and Melancholia.'" *Journal of the American Psychoanalytic Association*, vol. 46, no. 3, 1998, pp. 867–83, doi:10 .1177/00030651980460030901.

Maciejewski, Paul K., et al. "An Empirical Examination of the Stage Theory of Grief." *JAMA*, vol. 297, no. 7, 21 Feb. 2007, pp. 716–23, doi:10.1001/jama.297 .7.716.

Marsden, Sara J. "The Traditional American Funeral." *US Funerals Online*, us-funerals .com/funeral-articles/traditional-funeral-service.html.

"Mourning After: The Victorian Celebration of Death." Oshawa Community Museum, May 18–November 27, 2016. oshawamuseum.org/pdf/Mourning%20 After%20E%20Book.pdf.

"Oprah Interview with Dr. Elisabeth Kübler-Ross, 'People Are Talking' 1974." *YouTube*, uploaded by Elisabeth Kübler-Ross Foundation, 2 Apr. 2017, youtube .com/watch?v=AlnESKUZFqE.

O'Rourke, Meghan. "Good Grief." *The New Yorker*, 25 Jan. 2010, newyorker.com /magazine/2010/02/01/good-grief.

Parrow, Kyra. "Parkland students like me were told to get over our grief. We didn't get the support to do it." *Vox*, 28 Mar. 2019, vox.com/first-person/2019/3/28 /18282962/suicide-parkland-shooting-marjory-stoneman-douglas.

"The 1918 Flu Pandemic: Why It Matters 100 Years Later." *Public Health Matters Blog*, Centers for Disease Control and Prevention, 19 May 2018, blogs.cdc.gov /publichealthmatters/2018/05/1918-flu/.

Royde-Smith, John Graham, and Dennis E. Showalter. "Killed, Wounded, and Missing." *Encyclopædia Britannica*, britannica.com/event/World-War-I/Killed -wounded-and-missing.

Stroebe, Margaret, et al. "Broken Hearts or Broken Bonds: Love and Death in Historical Perspective." *American Psychologist*, vol. 47, no. 10, 1992, pp. 1205–12, doi:10.1037/0003-066x.47.10.1205.

Stroud, Clover. "Have the British Forgotten How to Grieve?" *The Telegraph*, 20 Feb. 2014, telegraph.co.uk/news/health/10639359/Have-the-British-forgotten-how-to-grieve.html.

Swetz, Frank J. "Mathematical Treasure: Graunt's Early Statistics on Mortality." *Convergence*, Aug. 2019, maa.org/press/periodicals/convergence/mathematical-treasure-graunts-early-statistics-on-mortality.

"US Population from 1900." *Demographia*, demographia.com/db-uspop1900.htm.

Walter, Tony. *On Bereavement: the Culture of Grief.* Open University Press, 1999.

Walter, Tony. "What Is Complicated Grief? A Social Constructionist Perspective." *OMEGA—Journal of Death and Dying*, vol. 52, no. 1, 2006, pp. 71–79, doi:10.2190 /3lx7-cocl-mnwr-jkkq.

Worden, J. William. *Grief Counseling and Grief Therapy: 4th Ed., A Handbook for the Mental Health Practitioner.* Springer, 2008.

Wortman, Camille B., and Roxane Cohen Silver. "The Myths of Coping with Loss." *Journal of Consulting and Clinical Psychology*, vol. 57, no. 3, 1989, pp. 349–57, doi:10.1037//0022-006x.57.3.349.

CHAPTER TWO: GETTING IT TOGETHER

Cacciatore, Joanne. "Appropriate Bereavement Practice after the Death of a Native American Child." *Families in Society: The Journal of Contemporary Social Services*, vol. 90, no. 1, 2009, pp. 46–50, doi:10.1606/1044-3894.3844.

Harris, Darcy. "Oppression of the Bereaved: A Critical Analysis of Grief in Western Society." *OMEGA—Journal of Death and Dying*, vol. 60, no. 3, 2010, pp. 241–53, doi:10.2190/om.60.3.c.

Herzog, Teddy. "Grieving Is a Lost Art." *Teddy Herzog*, 10 Oct. 2014, teddyherzog .com/2014/10/10/grieving-is-a-lost-art.

Krishnan, Vidya. "Coping with bereavement." *The Hindu*, 16 Apr. 2017, thehindu .com/sci-tech/health/coping-with-bereavement/article18062281.ece.

Laungani, Pittu, and Ann Laungani. "Death in a Hindu Family." *Death and Bereavement Across Cultures*, edited by Colin Murray Parkes, et al., Routledge, 2015.

Norton, Michael I., and Francesca Gino. "Rituals Alleviate Grieving for Loved Ones, Lovers, and Lotteries." *Journal of Experimental Psychology: General*, vol. 143, no. 1, 2014, pp. 266–72, doi:10.1037/a0031772.

Parkes, Colin Murray, et al., editors. *Death and Bereavement across Cultures.* Routledge, 2015.

Rosenblatt, Paul. "Grief in Small-Scale Societies." *Death and Bereavement across Cultures*, edited by Colin Murray Parkes, et al., Routledge, 2015.

Rubin, Simon Shimshon. *Working with the Bereaved: Multiple Lenses on Loss and Mourning*. Routledge, 2012.

Silverman, Phyllis R. *Never Too Young to Know: Death in Children's Lives*. Oxford University Press, 2000.

Silverman, Phyllis, Steven Nickman, and J. William Worden. "Detachment Revisited: The Child's Reconstruction of a Dead Parent." *American Journal of Orthopsychiatry*, vol. 62, no. 4, Oct. 1992, pp. 494–503.

Somé, Sobonfu. "Embracing Grief: Surrendering to Your Sorrow Has the Power to Heal the Deepest of Wounds." *Sobonfu.com*, sobonfu.com/articles/writings-by -sobonfu-2/embracing-grief/.

Walter, Tony. "Facing Death without Tradition." *Contemporary Issues in the Sociology of Death, Dying and Disposal*, edited by Glennys Howarth and Peter C. Jupp. Macmillan, 1995.

White, Michael. "Saying Hullo Again: The Incorporation of the Lost Relationship in the Resolution of Grief." *Dulwich Centre Newsletter*, Spring 1988.

Wojcik, Daniel, and Robert Dobler. "What ancient cultures teach us about grief, mourning and continuity of life." *The Conversation*, 1 Nov. 2017, theconversation .com/what-ancient-cultures-teach-us-about-grief-mourning-and-continuity -of-life-86199.

Worden, J. William. *Children and Grief: When a Parent Dies*. Guilford, 1996.

CHAPTER THREE: SOMETHING NEW

@refugeingrief (Megan Devine). "There's a pervasive weirdness in our culture around #grief that's also showing up in reactions to the #covid19 #pandemic. No one needs life-changing loss to become who they're 'meant' to be. Life is call-and-response. The path forward is integration, not betterment." *Twitter*, 22 May 2020, 6:00 P.M., twitter.com/refugeingrief/status/1263952835261104133.

"Bereavement Overload." *Psychology*, Iresearchnet.com, 2 Mar. 2017, psychology .iresearchnet.com/developmental-psychology/death-dying-and-bereavement /bereavement-overload/.

Bowlby, John. "Grief and Mourning in Infancy and Early Childhood." *The Psychoanalytic Study of the Child*, vol. 15, no. 1, 1960, pp. 9–52, doi:10.1080/00797308 .1960.11822566.

Brabant, Sarah. "Old Pain or New Pain: A Social Psychological Approach to Recurrent Grief." *OMEGA—Journal of Death and Dying*, vol. 20, no. 4, 1990, pp. 273–79, doi:10.2190/yaoq-45b2-jtjf-vh3h.

Bylsma, Lauren M., et al. "When and for Whom Does Crying Improve Mood? A Daily Diary Study of 1004 Crying Episodes." *Journal of Research in Personality*, vol. 45, no. 4, 2011, pp. 385–92, doi:10.1016/j.jrp.2011.04.007.

Cavenar, Jesse O., et al. "Anniversary Reactions Masquerading as Manic-Depressive Illness." *American Journal of Psychiatry*, vol. 134, no. 11, 1977, pp. 1273–76, doi:10.1176/ajp.134.11.1273.

Chethik, Neil. *Fatherloss: How Sons of All Ages Come to Terms with the Deaths of Their Dads.* Hyperion, 2001.

Dahl, Melissa. "How Long Does a Typical Crying Binge Last?" *The Cut*, 4 Dec. 2014, thecut.com/2014/12/how-long-does-a-typical-crying-binge-last.html.

Dlin, Barney M. "Psychobiology and Treatment of Anniversary Reactions." *Psychosomatics*, vol. 26, no. 6, 1985, pp. 505–12, doi:10.1016/s0033-3182(85)72831-9.

Ellis, Jackie, et al. "The Long-Term Impact of Early Parental Death: Lessons from a Narrative Study." *Journal of the Royal Society of Medicine*, vol. 106, no. 2, 2013, pp. 57–67, doi:10.1177/0141076812472623.

Hammett, Elliott B., et al. "Atypical Grief: Anniversary Reactions." *Military Medicine*, vol. 144, no. 5, 1979, pp. 320–21, doi:10.1093/milmed/144.5.320.

Harvey, John H., et al. "Trauma Growth and Other Outcomes Attendant to Loss." *Psychological Inquiry*, vol. 15, no. 1, 2004, pp. 26–29.

Kastenbaum, Robert. "Death and Bereavement in Later Life." *Death and Bereavement*, edited by A. H. Kutscher. Charles C. Thomas, 1969, pp. 28–54.

Khan, M. Masud R. "The Concept of Cumulative Trauma." *The Psychoanalytic Study of the Child*, vol. 18, no. 1, 1963, pp. 286–306, doi:10.1080/00797308.1963.11822932.

Klass, Dennis, "Elisabeth Kubler-Ross and the Tradition of the Private Sphere: An Analysis of Symbols." *OMEGA—Journal of Death and Dying*, vol. 12, no. 3, 1982, pp. 241–67.

Kübler-Ross, Elisabeth, and David Kessler. *On Grief & Grieving: Finding the Meaning of Grief through the Five Stages of Loss.* Scribner, 2005.

McCoyd, Judith L. M., and Carolyn Ambler Walter. *Grief and Loss across the Lifespan: A Biopsychosocial Perspective.* Springer, 2016.

Musaph, H. "Anniversary Disease." *Psychotherapy and Psychosomatics*, vol. 22, no. 2-6, 1973, pp. 325–33, doi:10.1159/000286538.

Neimeyer, Robert A., and Jason Holland. "Bereavement Overload." *Encyclopedia of Human Development*, edited by Neil J. Salkind. Sage Publications, 2005.

"No More Tears: Men Really Do Cry Less than Women." *The Telegraph*, 12 Jan. 2015, telegraph.co.uk/men/the-filter/11339610/No-more-tears-men-really-do-cry-less-than-women.html.

Olin, Randi. "A Child's Grief." *Brain, Child Magazine*, 1 Nov. 2014, https://02foa56ef46d93f03c90-22ac5f107621879d5667e0d7ed595bdb.ssl.cf2.rackcdn.com/sites/14962/uploads/24215/Harvard_Child_Bereavement_Study 20180706-20166-3e6sod.pdf.

Pollock, George H. *The Mourning-Liberation Process*, vol. 1. International Universities Press, 1989.

Silverman, Phyllis R. *Never Too Young to Know: Death in Children's Lives.* Oxford University Press, 2000.

Stroebe, Margaret, and Henk Schut. "The Dual Process Model of Coping with Bereavement: Rationale and Description." *Death Studies,* vol. 23, no. 3, 1999, pp. 197–224, doi:10.1080/074811899201046.

Stroebe, Margaret, and Henk Schut. "The Dual Process Model of Coping with Bereavement: A Decade On." *OMEGA—Journal of Death and Dying,* vol. 61, no. 4, 2010, pp. 273–89, doi:10.2190/om.61.4.b.

Van Hemert, Dianne A., et al. "Culture and Crying." *Cross-Cultural Research,* vol. 45, no. 4, 2011, pp. 399–431, doi:10.1177/1069397111404519.

Worden, J. William. *Children and Grief: When a Parent Dies.* Guilford, 1996.

CHAPTER FOUR: OLD GRIEF: RECURRENT AND RESURGENT

Biank, Nancee M., and Allison Werner-Lin. "Growing Up with Grief: Revisiting the Death of a Parent over the Life Course." *OMEGA—Journal of Death and Dying,* vol. 63, no. 3, 2011, pp. 271–90, doi:10.2190/om.63.3.e.

Brabant, Sarah. "Old Pain or New Pain: A Social Psychological Approach to Recurrent Grief." *OMEGA—Journal of Death and Dying,* vol. 20, no. 4, 1990, pp. 273–79, doi:10.2190/yaoq-45b2-jtjf-vh3h.

Fox, Sandra Sutherland. "Children's Anniversary Reactions to the Death of a Family Member." *OMEGA—Journal of Death and Dying,* vol. 15, no. 4, 1985, pp. 291–305, doi:10.2190/2jgc-8g4e-aw3w-4n9q.

Gabriel, Martha A. "Anniversary Reactions: Trauma Revisited." *Clinical Social Work Journal,* vol. 20, no. 2, 1992, pp. 179–92, doi:10.1007/bf00756507.

Gersen, Hannah. "No More Dead Mothers: Reading, Writing, and Grieving." *Literary Hub,* 6 May 2016, lithub.com/no-more-dead-mothers-reading-writing-and-grieving/.

McCoyd, Judith L. M., and Carolyn Ambler Walter. *Grief and Loss across the Lifespan: A Biopsychosocial Perspective.* Springer, 2016.

Mintz, Ira. "The Anniversary Reaction: A Response to the Unconscious Sense of Time." *Journal of the American Psychoanalytic Association,* vol. 19, no. 4, 1971, pp. 720–35, doi:10.1177/000306517101900406.

Neimeyer, Robert A. *Lessons of Loss: A Guide to Coping.* Center for the Study of Loss and Transition, 2006.

Pollock, George H. "Anniversary Reactions, Trauma, and Mourning." *The Psychoanalytic Quarterly,* vol. 39, no. 3, 1970, pp. 347–71, doi:10.1080/21674086.1970.11926533.

Pollock, George H. "Temporal Anniversary Manifestations: Hour, Day, Holiday." *The Psychoanalytic Quarterly,* vol. 40, no. 1, 1971, pp. 123–31, doi:10.1080/21674086.1971.11926554.

Pollock, George H. *The Mourning-Liberation Process*, vol. 1. International Universities Press, 1989.

Rando, Therese A. *Treatment of Complicated Mourning*. Research Press, 1993.

Renvoize, E. B., and J. Jain. "Anniversary Reactions." *British Journal of Psychiatry*, vol. 148, no. 3, 1986, pp. 322–24, doi:10.1192/bjp.148.3.322.

Rosenblatt, Paul. "Grief That Does Not End." *Continuing Bonds: New Understandings of Grief*, edited by Dennis Klass et al. Taylor and Francis, 1996.

CHAPTER FIVE: NEW OLD GRIEF: ONE-TIME TRANSITIONS

Birtchnell, John. "Anniversary Reactions." *British Journal of Psychiatry*, vol. 148, no. 5, 1986, pp. 610–11, doi:10.1192/s0007125000211422.

"The Bonaparte Women: Marie Bonaparte—A Freudian Princess." *History of Royal Women*, 13 July 2019, historyofroyalwomen.com/marie-bonaparte/the-bonaparte-women-marie-bonaparte-a-freudian-princess/.

Hilgard, Josephine R. "Anniversary Reactions in Parents Precipitated by Children." *Psychiatry*, vol. 16, no. 1, 1953, pp. 73–80, doi:10.1080/00332747.1953.11022910.

Hilgard, Josephine R., et al. "Strength of Adult Ego Following Childhood Bereavement." *American Journal of Orthopsychiatry*, vol. 30, no. 4, 1960, pp. 788–98, doi:10.1111/j.1939-0025.1960.tb02094.x.

Livesey, Tony. "Tony Livesey: Life after Mother." *The Independent*, 7 Dec. 2010, independent.co.uk/life-style/health-and-families/features/tony-livesey-life-after-mother-2152961.html.

Pollock, George H. *The Mourning-Liberation Process*, vol. 1. International Universities Press, 1989.

Rando, Therese A. *Treatment of Complicated Mourning*. Research Press, 1993.

CHAPTER SIX: THE RINGS OF GRIEF

@LaurenHerschel (Lauren Herschel). "After what has been a surprisingly okayish Christmas, I had a moment today in SuperStore. Saw a lady who reminded me of my 92yo grandma, who even in the early stages of dementia, completely understood that my mom died. I thought I'd share the Ball in the Box analogy my Dr told me" *Twitter*, 29 Dec. 2017, 6:35 P.M., twitter.com/LaurenHerschel/status/946887540732149760.

Calhoun, Lawrence G., et al. "A Correlational Test of the Relationship between Posttraumatic Growth, Religion, and Cognitive Processing." *Journal of Traumatic Stress*, vol. 13, no. 3, 2000, pp. 521–27, doi:10.1023/a:1007745627077.

Calhoun, Lawrence G., and Richard G. Tedeschi. "The Foundations of Posttraumatic Growth: New Considerations." *Psychological Inquiry*, vol. 15, no. 1, 2004, pp. 93–102, doi:10.1207/s15327965pli1501_03.

Cann, Arnie, et al. "A Short Form of the Posttraumatic Growth Inventory." *Anxiety, Stress & Coping*, vol. 23, no. 2, 2010, pp. 127–37, doi:10.1080/10615800903094273.

Chödrön, Pema. *When Things Fall Apart: Heart Advice for Difficult Times*. Shambhala, 2016.

Edmonds, Sarah, and Karen Hooker. "Perceived Changes in Life Meaning Following Bereavement." *OMEGA—Journal of Death and Dying*, vol. 25, no. 4, 1992, pp. 307–18, doi:10.2190/te7q-5g45-bety-x1tt.

"Grief: It's not something you have to 'get over' (Like Minds Ep.12) BBC Stories," *YouTube*, uploaded by BBC Stories, 1 Mar. 2018, youtube.com/watch ?v=X55TJRj9HUk.

Hogan, Nancy, et al. "Toward an Experiential Theory of Bereavement." *OMEGA— Journal of Death and Dying*, vol. 33, no. 1, 1996, pp. 43–65, doi:10.2190/gu3x -jwvo-ag6g-21fx.

Joseph, Stephen. "The Key to Posttraumatic Growth." *Psychology Today*, 11 Mar. 2013, psychologytoday.com/us/blog/what-doesnt-kill-us/201303/the-key-post traumatic-growth.

Joseph, Stephen. *What Doesn't Kill Us: The New Psychology of Posttraumatic Growth*. Basic Books, 2013.

Rubin, Simon Shimshon. "The Two-Track Model of Bereavement: Overview, Retrospect, and Prospect." *Death Studies*, vol. 23, no. 8, 1999, pp. 681–714, doi:10.1080/074811899200731.

Schwartz, Laura E., et al. "Effect of Time since Loss on Grief, Resilience, and Depression among Bereaved Emerging Adults." *Death Studies*, vol. 42, no. 9, 2018, pp. 537–47, doi:10.1080/07481187.2018.1430082.

Tedeschi, Richard G., and Lawrence G. Calhoun. "Posttraumatic Growth: Conceptual Foundations and Empirical Evidence." *Psychological Inquiry*, vol. 15, no. 1, 2004, pp. 1–18, doi:10.1207/s15327965pli1501_01.

Wolchik, Sharlene A., et al. "Six-Year Longitudinal Predictors of Posttraumatic Growth in Parentally Bereaved Adolescents and Young Adults." *OMEGA—Journal of Death and Dying*, vol. 58, no. 2, 2009, pp. 107–28, doi:10.2190/om.58.2.b.

Wortman, C. "Posttraumatic Growth: Progress and Problems" in (2004) COMMENTARIES on "Posttraumatic Growth: Conceptual Foundations and Empirical Evidence." *Psychological Inquiry*, 15:1, 81–92.

CHAPTER SEVEN: THE POWER OF STORY

Calhoun, Lawrence G., et al. "A Correlational Test of the Relationship between Posttraumatic Growth, Religion, and Cognitive Processing." *Journal of Traumatic Stress*, vol. 13, no. 3, 2000, pp. 521–27, doi:10.1023/a:1007745627077.

Campbell, Keith W., and Amy B. Brunel. "Sitting Here in Limbo: Ego Shock and Posttraumatic Growth." *Psychological Inquiry*, vol. 15, no. 1, 2004, pp. 22–26.

Collins, Rebecca L., et al. "A Better World or a Shattered Vision? Changes in Life Perspectives Following Victimization." *Social Cognition*, vol. 8, no. 3, 1990, pp. 263–85, doi:10.1521/soco.1990.8.3.263.

Frank, Arthur. *Letting Stories Breathe: A Socio-Narratology.* University of Chicago Press, 2010.

Hammack, Phillip L. "Narrative and the Cultural Psychology of Identity." *Personality and Social Psychology Review*, vol. 12, no. 3, 2008, pp. 222–47, doi:10.1177/1088868308316892.

Harvey, John. *Embracing Their Memory: Loss and the Social Psychology of Storytelling.* Allyn & Bacon, 1996.

Harvey, John H., et al. "House of Pain and Hope: Accounts of Loss." *Death Studies*, vol. 16, no. 2, 1992, pp. 99–124, doi:10.1080/07481189208252562.

Hermans, Hubert J. M. "Self-Narrative as Meaning Construction: The Dynamics of Self-Investigation." *Journal of Clinical Psychology*, vol. 55, no. 10, 1999, pp. 1193–1211, doi:10.1002/(sici)1097-4679(199910)55:10<1193::aid-jclp3>3.0.co;2-i.

McAdams, Dan. *Stories We Live By: Personal Myths and the Making of the Self.* William Morrow & Company, 1993.

McAdams, Dan P., et al. "When Bad Things Turn Good and Good Things Turn Bad: Sequences of Redemption and Contamination in Life Narrative and Their Relation to Psychosocial Adaptation in Midlife Adults and in Students." *Personality and Social Psychology Bulletin*, vol. 27, no. 4, 2001, pp. 474–85, doi:10.1177/0146167201274008.

Neimeyer, Robert A. "Fostering Posttraumatic Growth: A Narrative Elaboration." *Psychological Inquiry*, vol. 15, no. 1, 2004, pp. 53–59.

Neimeyer, Robert A. *Meaning Reconstruction & the Experience of Loss.* American Psychological Association, 2001.

Pals, Jennifer L., and Dan P. McAdams. "The Transformed Self: A Narrative Understanding of Posttraumatic Growth." *Psychological Inquiry*, vol. 15, no. 1, 2004, pp. 65–75.

Park, Crystal L. "Making Sense of the Meaning Literature: An Integrative Review of Meaning Making and Its Effects on Adjustment to Stressful Life Events." *Psychological Bulletin*, vol. 136, no. 2, 2010, pp. 257–301, doi:10.1037/a0018301.

Pasupathi, Monisha. "The Social Construction of the Personal Past and Its Implications for Adult Development." *Psychological Bulletin*, vol. 127, no. 5, 2001, pp. 651–72, doi:10.1037/0033-2909.127.5.651.

Roberts, Roxanne. "Suicide is desperate. It is hostile. It is tragic. But mostly, it is a bloody mess." *The Washington Post*, May 18, 1996.

Rose, Ellen. "Hyper Attention and the Rise of the Antinarrative: Reconsidering the

Future of Narrativity." *Narrative Works: Issues, Investigations and Interventions*, vol. 2, no. 2, 2012, pp. 92–102.

Solnit, Rebecca. *The Faraway Nearby*. Penguin Books, 2014.

Valentine, Christine. *Bereavement Narratives: Continuing Bonds in the Twenty-First Century*. Routledge, 2008.

Wortman, Camille B. "Posttraumatic Growth: Progress and Problems." *Psychological Inquiry*, vol. 15, no. 1, 2004, pp. 81–90.

CHAPTER EIGHT: PEOPLE, WE NEED TO TALK (AND WRITE, AND
PAINT, AND PERFORM)

Archer, John. *The Nature of Grief: The Evolution and Psychology of Reactions to Loss*. Routledge, 1999.

Attig, Thomas. "Disenfranchised Grief Revisited: Discounting Hope and Love." *OMEGA—Journal of Death and Dying*, vol. 49, no. 3, 2004, pp. 197–215, doi:10.2190/p4tt-j3bf-kfdr-5jb1.

AZM. "Telling People That Your Parents Are Dead." *Human Parts*, 5 Jan. 2020, humanparts.medium.com/telling-people-that-your-parents-are-dead -56d8d65c1f7a.

Eisenstadt, Marvin, et al. *Parental Loss and Achievement*. International Universities Press, 1989.

Frank, Arthur. *Letting Stories Breathe: A Socio-Narratology*. University of Chicago Press, 2010.

Furman, Robert A. "Death and the Young Child." *The Psychoanalytic Study of the Child*, vol. 19, no. 1, 1964, pp. 321–33, doi:10.1080/00797308.1964.11822872.

Griffin, Susan. *A Chorus of Stones: The Private Life of War*. Anchor Books, 1993.

Harvey, John H., et al. "House of Pain and Hope: Accounts of Loss." *Death Studies*, vol. 16, no. 2, 1992, pp. 99–124, doi:10.1080/07481189208252562.

Joseph, Stephen. *What Doesn't Kill Us: The New Psychology of Posttraumatic Growth*. Basic Books, 2013.

Krulwich, Robert. "Successful Children Who Lost a Parent—Why Are There So Many of Them?" Krulwich Wonders. *NPR*, 16 Oct. 2013, npr.org/sections /krulwich/2013/10/15/234737083/successful-children-who-lost-a-parent-why -are-there-so-many-of-them.

Lichtenthal, Wendy G., and Dean G. Cruess. "Effects of Directed Written Disclosure on Grief and Distress Symptoms among Bereaved Individuals." *Death Studies*, vol. 34, no. 6, 2010, pp. 475–99, doi:10.1080/07481187.2010.483332.

"More than Eight in 10 Men in Prison Suffered Childhood Adversity—New Report." *Phys.org*, 29 Apr. 2019, phys.org/news/2019-04-men-prison-childhood -adversity.html.

Murray, Edward J., and Daniel L. Segal. "Emotional Processing in Vocal and Written Expression of Feelings about Traumatic Experiences." *Journal of Traumatic Stress*, vol. 7, no. 3, 1994, pp. 391–405, doi:10.1002/jts.2490070305.

O'Connor, Mary-Frances, et al. "Emotional Disclosure for Whom? A Study of Vagal Tone in Bereavement." *Biological Psychology*, vol. 68, no. 2, 2005, pp. 135–46, doi:10.1016/j.biopsycho.2004.04.003.

Pasupathi, Monisha. "The Social Construction of the Personal Past and Its Implications for Adult Development." *Psychological Bulletin*, vol. 127, no. 5, 2001, pp. 5651–72, doi:10.1037/0033-2909.127.5.651.

Pennebaker, James W. "Writing About Emotional Experiences as a Therapeutic Process." *Psychological Science*, vol. 8, no. 3, 1997, pp. 162–6, doi:10.1111/j.1467-9280.1997.tb00403.x.

Pennebaker, James W., and Janel D. Seagal. "Forming a Story: The Health Benefits of Narrative." *Journal of Clinical Psychology*, vol. 55, no. 10, 1999, pp. 1243–54, doi:10.1002/(sici)1097-4679(199910)55:10<1243::aid-jclp6>3.0.co;2-n.

Pennebaker, James W., and Joshua M. Smyth. *Opening It Up by Writing It Down: How Expressive Writing Improves Health and Eases Emotional Pain*. 3rd ed., Guilford Press, 2016.

Range, Lillian M., et al. "Does writing about the bereavement lessen grief following sudden, unintentional death?" *Death Studies*, vol. 24, no. 2, 2000, pp. 115–34, doi:10.1080/074811800200603.

Rosen, Helen. "Prohibitions against Mourning in Childhood Sibling Loss." *OMEGA—Journal of Death and Dying*, vol. 15, no. 4, 1985, pp. 307–16, doi:10.2190/dpfa-ura4-ch2k-umq5.

Stroebe, Margaret, et al. "Does Disclosure of Emotions Facilitate Recovery from Bereavement? Evidence from Two Prospective Studies." *Journal of Consulting and Clinical Psychology*, vol. 70, no. 1, 2002, pp. 169–78, doi:10.1037/0022-006x.70.1.169.

Tedeschi, Richard G., and Lawrence G. Calhoun. "Posttraumatic Growth: Conceptual Foundations and Empirical Evidence." *Psychological Inquiry*, vol. 15, no. 1, 2004, pp. 1–18, doi:10.1207/s15327965pli1501_01.

Wortman, Camille B. "Posttraumatic Growth: Progress and Problems." *Psychological Inquiry*, vol. 15, no. 1, 2004, pp. 81–90.

CHAPTER NINE: SIX EXCEPTIONS IN SEARCH OF A NARRATIVE

Aristotle. *The Poetics of Aristotle*, translated by S. H. Butcher. Project Gutenberg, 3 Nov. 2008, gutenberg.org/files/1974/1974-h/1974-h.htm#link2H_4_0009.

Bauer, Patricia J., and Marina Larkina. "The Onset of Childhood Amnesia in Childhood: A Prospective Investigation of the Course and Determinants of Forgetting of Early-Life Events." *Memory*, vol. 22, no. 8, Nov. 2013, pp. 907–24, doi:10.1080/09658211.2013.854806.

Blakley, Theresa, et al. "The Risks and Rewards of Speed: Restorative Retelling Compressed into a Three-Day Retreat." *Death Studies*, vol. 42, no. 1, 2018, pp. 9–15, doi:10.1080/07481187.2017.1370412.

Brown, David W., et al. "Adverse Childhood Experiences and Childhood Autobiographical Memory Disturbance." *Child Abuse & Neglect*, vol. 31, no. 9, 2007, pp. 961–69, doi:10.1016/j.chiabu.2007.02.011.

Callahan, Shawn. "The Link between Memory and Stories." *Anecdote*, 8 Jan. 2015, anecdote.com/2015/01/link-between-memory-and-stories/.

Ellis, Jackie, et al. "The Long-Term Impact of Early Parental Death: Lessons from a Narrative Study." *Journal of the Royal Society of Medicine*, vol. 106, no. 2, 2013, pp. 57–67, doi:10.1177/0141076812472623.

Gammon, Kate. "Birth of Memory: Why Kids Forget What Happened Before Age 7." *Popular Science*, 31 Jan. 2014, popsci.com/blog-network/kinderlab/birth-memory-why-kids-forget-what-happened-age-7/.

Greenhoot, Andrea Follmer, et al. "Stress and Autobiographical Memory Functioning." *Emotion in Memory and Development*, edited by Jody Quas and Robyn Fyvus. Oxford University Press, 2009, pp. 86–118.

Joseph, Stephen. *What Doesn't Kill Us: The New Psychology of Posttraumatic Growth*. Basic Books, 2013.

Lely, Jeannette C. G., et al. "The effectiveness of narrative exposure therapy: a review, meta-analysis and meta-regression analysis. *European Journal of Psychotraumatology*, vol. 10, no. 1, 2019, doi: 10.1080/20008198.2018.1550344.

Levine, Peter A. *Trauma and Memory: Brain and Body in a Search for the Living Past: A Practical Guide for Understanding and Working with Traumatic Memory*. North Atlantic Books, 2015.

Lu, Donna. "The Farewell Explores the Ethics of Lying about a Cancer Diagnosis." *New Scientist*, 29 October 2019, newscientist.com/article/2221673-the-farewell-explores-the-ethics-of-lying-about-a-cancer-diagnosis/.

Nadeau, Janice Winchester. *Families Making Sense of Death*. Sage Publications, 1998.

Neimeyer, Robert A. "Fostering Posttraumatic Growth: A Narrative Elaboration." *Psychological Inquiry*, vol. 15, no. 1, 2004, pp. 53–59.

Parkes, Collin Murray. "Bereavement." *British Journal of Psychiatry*, vol. 146, no. 1, 1985, pp. 11–17, doi:10.1192/bjp.146.1.11.

Pollock, George H. *The Mourning-Liberation Process*, vol. 1. International Universities Press, 1989.

Silverman, Phyllis Rolfe. *Never Too Young to Know: Death in Children's Lives*. Oxford University Press, 2000.

van der Kolk, Bessel. *The Body Keeps the Score: Brain, Mind, and Body in the Healing of Trauma*. Penguin Books, 2014.

Williams, Joah L., and Alyssa A. Rheingold. "Introduction to the Special Section: Creative Applications of Restorative Retelling." *Death Studies*, vol. 42, no. 1, 2018, pp. 1–3, doi:10.1080/07481187.2017.1370415.

Woolley, Jacqueline D. "Thinking about Fantasy: Are Children Fundamentally Different Thinkers and Believers from Adults?" *Child Development*, vol. 68, no. 6, 1997, pp. 991–1011, doi:10.2307/1132282.

Worden, J. William. *Children and Grief: When a Parent Dies*. Guilford Press, 1996.

Wortman, Camille B. "Posttraumatic Growth: Progress and Problems." *Psychological Inquiry*, vol. 15, no. 1, 2004, pp. 81–90.

CHAPTER TEN: REAUTHORING YOUR STORY OF LOSS

Bruner, Jerome. *Acts of Meaning: Four Lectures on Mind and Culture* (The Jerusalem-Harvard Lectures). Harvard University Press, 1990.

Charon, Rita. *Narrative Medicine: Honoring the Stories of Illness*. Oxford University Press, 2006.

Denborough, David. *Retelling the Stories of Our Lives: Everyday Narrative Therapy to Draw Inspiration and Transform Experience*. W. W. Norton & Company, 2014.

Ellis, Jackie, et al. "The Long-Term Impact of Early Parental Death: Lessons from a Narrative Study." *Journal of the Royal Society of Medicine*, vol. 106, no. 2, 2013, pp. 57–67, doi:10.1177/0141076812472623.

Flesner, Jodi. "A Shift in the Conceptual Understanding of Grief: Using Meaning Oriented-Therapies with Bereaved Clients." *Vistas Online*, 2013. pdfs.semantic scholar.org/67ca/bd3461168935dodf1cbd400a651e42372f94.pdf.

Frank, Arthur. *Letting Stories Breathe: A Socio-Narratology*. University of Chicago Press, 2010.

Frankl, Viktor E. *Man's Search for Meaning*. Beacon Press, 2006.

Gornick, Vivian. *The Situation and the Story: The Art of Personal Narrative*. Farrar, Straus and Giroux, 2002.

Haupt, Jennifer. "Death, Memory, and Other Superpowers." *The Rumpus*, 8 Aug. 2017, therumpus.net/2017/08/death-memory-and-other-superpowers/.

Hedtke, Lorraine, and John Winslade. *The Crafting of Grief: Constructing Aesthetic Responses to Loss*. Routledge, 2017.

Huxley, Aldous. *Texts and Pretexts: An Anthology with Commentaries*. Forgotten Books, 2017.

Joseph, Stephen. *What Doesn't Kill Us: The New Psychology of Posttraumatic Growth*. Basic Books, 2013.

Silverman, Phyllis, and Nickman, Steven. "Children's Construction of Their Dead

Parents." *Continuing Bonds: New Understanding of Grief,* edited by Dennis Klass, et al. Taylor & Francis, 1996.

Werner-Lin, Allison, and Daniel S. Gardner. "Family Illness Narratives of Inherited Cancer Risk: Continuity and Transformation." *Families, Systems, & Health,* vol. 27, no. 3, 2009, pp. 201–12, doi:10.1037/a0016983.

CHAPTER ELEVEN: STORY CRACKING: GETTING FROM A TO Z

"Adverse Childhood Experiences (ACEs)." cdc.gov, Centers for Disease Control and Prevention, 3 Apr. 2020, cdc.gov/violenceprevention/acestudy/.

Bruner, Charles. "ACE, Place, Race, and Poverty." *Academic Pediatrics,* vol. 17, no. 7S, 2017, pp. S123–29, doi:10.1016/j.acap.2017.05.009.

Felitti, Vincent J. "The relation between adverse childhood experiences and adult health: turning gold into lead." *The Permanente Journal,* vol. 6, no. 1, 2002, pp. 44–47, doi:10.13109/zptm.2002.48.4.359.

McCoyd, Judith L. M., and Carolyn Ambler Walter. *Grief and Loss across the Lifespan: A Biopsychosocial Perspective.* Springer, 2016.

Nakazawa, Donna Jackson. *Childhood Disrupted: How Your Biography Becomes Your Biology, and How You Can Heal.* Atria Books, 2015.

Parkes, Collin Murray. "Bereavement." *British Journal of Psychiatry,* vol. 146, no. 1, 1985, pp. 11–17, doi:10.1192/bjp.146.1.11.

Schultz, Lara E. "The Influence of Maternal Loss on Young Women's Experience of Identity Development in Emerging Adulthood." *Death Studies,* vol. 31, no. 1, 2007, pp. 17–43, doi:10.1080/07481180600925401.

CHAPTER TWELVE: STORY MENDING: CREATING A CONTINUOUS YOU

@LaurenHerschel (Lauren Herschel). "After what has been a surprisingly okayish Christmas, I had a moment today in SuperStore. Saw a lady who reminded me of my 92yo grandma, who even in the early stages of dementia, completely understood that my mom died. I thought I'd share the Ball in the Box analogy my Dr told me." *Twitter,* 29 Dec. 2017, 6:35 P.M., twitter.com/LaurenHerschel/status/946887540732149760.

"Anderson Cooper 360 Degrees." CNN, 15 Aug. 2019. Transcript. transcripts.cnn.com/TRANSCRIPTS/1908/15/acd.01.html.

Calhoun, Lawrence G., et al. "A Correlational Test of the Relationship between Posttraumatic Growth, Religion, and Cognitive Processing." *Journal of Traumatic Stress,* vol. 13, no. 3, 2000, pp. 521–27, doi:10.1023/a:1007745627077.

Campbell, Keith W., et al. "Sitting Here in Limbo: Ego Shock and Posttraumatic Growth." *Psychological Inquiry,* vol. 15, no. 1, 2004, pp. 22–26.

Gabriel, Martha A. "Anniversary Reactions: Trauma Revisited." *Clinical Social Work Journal*, vol. 20, no. 2, 1992, pp. 179–92, doi:10.1007/bf00756507.

Hammack, Phillip L. "Narrative and the Cultural Psychology of Identity." *Personality and Social Psychology Review*, vol. 12, no. 3, 2008, pp. 222–47, doi:10.1177/1088868308316892.

Harris, Maxine. *The Loss That Is Forever: The Lifelong Impact of the Early Death of a Mother or Father.* Penguin Books, 1995.

Harvey, John H., et al. "House of Pain and Hope: Accounts of Loss." *Death Studies*, vol. 16, no. 2, 1992, pp. 99–124, doi:10.1080/07481189208252562.

Joseph, Stephen. *What Doesn't Kill Us: The New Psychology of Posttraumatic Growth.* Basic Books, 2013.

McAdams, Dan P. "The Redemptive Self: Generativity and the Stories Americans Live By." *Research in Human Development*, vol. 3, no. 2-3, 2006, pp. 81–100, doi:10.1080/15427609.2006.9683363.

McAdams, Dan. P. *The Redemptive Self: Stories Americans Live By.* Oxford University Press, 2013.

McAdams, Dan P., et. al. "When Bad Things Turn Good and Good Things Turn Bad: Sequences of Redemption and Contamination in Life Narrative and Their Relation to Psychosocial Adaptation in Midlife Adults and in Students." *Personality and Social Psychology Bulletin*, vol. 27, no. 4, April 2001, 474–85, doi:10.1177/0146167201274008.

McMillen, J. Curtis. "Posttraumatic Growth: What's It All About." *Psychological Inquiry*, vol. 15, no. 1, 2004, pp. 48–51.

Romanoff, Bronn D. "Research as Therapy: The Power of Narrative to Effect Change." *Meaning Reconstruction & the Experience of Loss*, edited by Robert A. Neimeyer. American Psychological Association, 2001.

Tedeschi, Richard G., and Lawrence G. Calhoun. "Posttraumatic Growth: Conceptual Foundations and Empirical Evidence." *Psychological Inquiry*, vol. 15, no. 1, 2004, pp. 1–18, doi:10.1207/s15327965pli1501_01.

EPILOGUE: THE MISSING ELEMENTS OF GRIEF

"Anderson Cooper 360 Degrees." CNN, 15 Aug. 2019. Transcript. transcripts.cnn.com/TRANSCRIPTS/1908/15/acd.01.html.

Edmonds, Sarah, and Karen Hooker. "Perceived Changes in Life Meaning Following Bereavement." *OMEGA—Journal of Death and Dying*, vol. 25, no. 4, 1992, pp. 307–18, doi:10.2190/te7q-5g45-bety-x1tt.

Lichtenthal, Wendy G., and Dean G. Cruess. "Effects of Directed Written Disclosure on Grief and Distress Symptoms among Bereaved Individuals." *Death Studies*, vol. 34, no. 6, 2010, pp. 475–99, doi:10.1080/07481187.2010.483332.

McAdams, Dan P., et. al. "When Bad Things Turn Good and Good Things

Turn Bad: Sequences of Redemption and Contamination in Life Narrative and Their Relation to Psychosocial Adaptation in Midlife Adults and in Students." *Personality and Social Psychology Bulletin*, vol 27, no. 4, 2001, pp. 474–85, doi:10.1177/0146167201274008.

Tedeschi, Richard G., and Lawrence G. Calhoun. "Posttraumatic Growth: Conceptual Foundations and Empirical Evidence." *Psychological Inquiry*, vol. 15, no. 1, 2004, pp. 1–18, doi:10.1207/s15327965pli1501_01.

Weller, Francis. "Francis Weller on Grief (2013)," *YouTube*, uploaded by Minnesota Men's Conference, 29 Jan. 2014, youtube.com/watch?v=EaI-4c92Mqo.

* * *

Acknowledgments

FROM CONCEPTION to completed manuscript this book took four years, and many people were instrumental in helping it along. It takes a small city to write a book like this, and I'm fortunate to have been living in a densely populated one.

Elizabeth Kaplan, my agent, and Marnie Cochran at Penguin Random House—you are the A+ team of A+ teams. This book would never have come into being or made it out into the world without you. You both have my unerring admiration and my devotion, always.

To the brilliant minds in this field, past and present, whose work served as both foundation and inspiration to me every day, thank you for leading the way: Tom Attig, David Denborough, Leeat Granek, John Harvey, Lorraine Hedtke, Stephen Madigan, Bob Neimeyer, Terrie Rando, Ted Rynearson, Bill Worden, and the late Phyllis Silverman and Michael White.

My earliest mentors are never far from my side: Carl Klaus, my graduate advisor and the most learned person I know; Mary Swander, my most influential professor and nearly lifelong friend; and the late Liz Perle, my first editor and a devoted champion of this work, to whom this book is dedicated, with admiration and love.

Melissa Vincel, coordinator of all things Motherless Daughters, tends to the needs and hearts of thousands of women a year with compassion and grace. Melissa, I don't know how you do all that you do, but I couldn't do my part without you.

My very dear colleague, Claire Bidwell Smith, who co-founded Motherless Daughters Retreats, is a bright light in this field. I value our friendship immensely. Allison Gilbert, you are a powerhouse, a marketing genius, and a loyal friend. I look forward to many more crazy ideas to come. Sarah Saffian and Elissa Berman, I couldn't have asked for smarter or more compassionate partners in this work. You change lives. And to the hundreds of women who've attended Motherless Daughters retreats, workshops, online courses, and support groups, thank you for sharing your stories and your big, generous hearts with us all.

A very special shout-out to the eighteen original interviewees of Motherless Daughters who agreed to be reinterviewed nearly three decades later and provided invaluable insight into how stories of loss change over time. I loved meeting up with you again after all these years, every one of you.

To Vito Zingarelli, Amy Wheeler, and everyone at Hedgebrook women's writing retreat, endless gratitude to you for offering me space, time, and radical hospitality. To Melissa McFarlane and Parker Bennett, thank you for your marketing finesse. We have so much more to accomplish together. Big thanks also to Amy Margolis at the Iowa Summer Writing Festival for running the tightest and most seaworthy ship around; to Brauna Brickman and Skip Walsh for providing sanctuary; to Angela Nelson Schellenberg, mother trekker extraordinaire, for consistent encouragement and inspiration; to Cara Belvin of EmpowerHER, Denna Babul of The Fatherless Daughters Project, Brennan Wood at the Dougy Center, Darcy Krause of the Uplift Center for Grieving Children, Rebecca Soffer of Modern Loss, and Cynthia Whipple of The Conversation for all the brilliant and essential work you do; to Ryan McManus for thirty years of friendship—good thing I taught rhetoric!; to all of the women in Northwestern's C100 for your leadership and vision; to everyone at Re-Imagine (especially Brad, Jeannie, and Dara) for your innovation and inclusion; to Daed Laroche for under-the-gun editorial assistance; and to Jo-Ann Lautman, founder of Our House, for being a trailblazer and role model for more than twenty-five years.

Big, big love and admiration to all the friends and colleagues in the bereavement and literary worlds who offered their support, solidarity, and encouragement over the past four years: Bruce Bauman, Kelly Carlin, Nana-Ama Danquah, Megan Devine, Kathy Eldon, Liz Gilbert, Shelley Gilbert, Kate Gleeson, Mandy Gosling, Michael Hebb, Tim Hillegonds, Monica Holloway, Mollie Marti, Nancy Mc-Glasson, Jacob Moore, Kimberly Paul, John Price, Cheryl Strayed, and Natasha Gregson Wagner.

Eternal thanks to the posse that lifted me up during the final six months: Brian Aldredge, Katherine Alteneder, Janae Bakken, Amrei Blaesing, Cindy Chupack, Jim Crowley, Jennifer DeNicola, Gail Eisenberg, Elizabeth George, Jonathan Greenberg, Susie and Larry Laffer, Electra Manwiller, Karen Moyer, Jennifer New, Lori Precious, Belen Ricoy and Ziv Cohen, Sally Riggs, Irene Rubaum-Keller, Nicolle Sanchez, Stacey Siegel, Amanda Uhry, the Kakiat and Ramapo Girls' Group, and the Shahar family—Haim, Elisabetta, Matteo, and Luca. Best quaranteam ever.

My dear, dear, one-of-a-kind friend Sky Kunerth passed away during the writing of this book, a loss that can't ever be undone. Her daughter Ashlyn and husband Mark are always close in my heart, as are the Malibu Skysters: Noreen Austin, Teri Carcano, Kathie Ferbas, and Lily Foster. And to the memories of Darryle Pollack and Ned Stuckey-French, outstanding humans who knew what true friendship means. You will be forever missed.

Hannah Kozak, huge thanks to you, Momi, for the photographs, kombuchas, finches, Billy Joel songs, Pops Laroni encounters, and some totally goiked adapulators.

Verne Varona, you showed up at the very end, completely by surprise, with laughter and awe and 42,639 emails to help give this book the *reallyfast* push it needed to cross the finish line. It wouldn't be the same without you, Chet.

Perennial love and appreciation to my now and always family—Michele Edelman, Amy Jupiter, Glenn Edelman, Allyson Edelman,

Arlene and Glenn Englander, Noa and Dror Avisar, Ruth Eliahou, and Rachel Eliahou. Whether you're my family of origin or my family of choice, you're all family of my heart.

Finally, I bow my head in gratitude to Uzi, who lived with this book in its various iterations for nearly four years, and to Maya and Eden, who have inspired me, every moment, for the past twenty-two. The long arc of loss led me straight to you. You are, and always will be, my greatest and forever loves.

*   *   *

ABOUT THE AUTHOR

HOPE EDELMAN is the author of eight nonfiction books, including the #1 *New York Times* bestseller *Motherless Daughters, Motherless Mothers* and the memoir *The Possibility of Everything*. Her original essays have appeared in many anthologies, including *The Bitch in the House, Behind the Bedroom Door,* and *Goodbye to All That*. Her work has received a *New York Times* notable book of the year designation and a Pushcart Prize for creative nonfiction. The recipient of the 2020 Community Educator Award from the Association for Death Education and Counseling, she is a certified Martha Beck Life Coach, and facilitates Motherless Daughters retreats and workshops all over the world. She lives and works in Los Angeles and Iowa City.

hopeedelman.com
theaftergrief.com